Ingo Maurer intim. Design or What?

Die Neue Sammlung – The Design Museum
Koenig Books, London

Pendulum
2019

Das PENDULUM hat Ingo Maurer für Die Neue
Sammlung – The Design Museum in der Rotunde
der Pinakothek der Moderne in München realisiert.
Es spiegelt das Licht der Tages- und Jahreszeiten.
Die Kombination aus der harmonischen Form
des Eies und der beruhigenden Pendel-Bewegung
sind für ihn Ausgangspunkte, um eine neue
Raumerfahrung zu ermöglichen. Das PENDULUM,
das von Mai 2019 bis Februar 2020 zu sehen ist,
misst 290 × 170 cm, wiegt 125 kg und wird manuell
angestoßen.
Die Neue Sammlung startet mit dieser Installation
das erste Projekt in der Rotunde, die ab 2019
alternierend von den vier Museen in der Pinakothek
der Moderne mit einem ortsspezifischen Werk
bespielt wird.

Ingo Maurer realized the PENDULUM for Die Neue Sammlung –
The Design Museum in the Rotunda at Pinakothek der Moderne
in Munich. It reflects the daylight and thus the way light changes
with the seasons. The combination of harmonious egg shape
and calming pendulum movement laid, he felt, the basis for a
new type of spatial experience. The PENDULUM is on show
from May 2019 to February 2020 and measures 290 × 170 cm,
weighs 125 kg, and is set in motion by hand.
With it, Die Neue Sammlung has launched the first project
in the Rotunda – from 2019 onwards a site-specific work will
be created alternately for the four museums of the Pinakothek
der Moderne.

Angelika Nollert
Die Sichtbarkeit des Lichts / The Visibility of Light

Ohne die Sonne ist kein Leben möglich. Die Schöpfungsriten der Menschheit sind untrennbar mit diesem licht- und wärmespendenden Stern verbunden. Licht ist ein Symbol des Göttlichen.

Licht schenkt Sichtbarkeit, Licht erleuchtet, Licht bringt Erkenntnis.

Von epochaler Bedeutung war die neuzeitliche Erfindung der elektrisch betriebenen Glühlampe. Die Industrialisierung führte auch zu massenproduzierten Konsumgütern, die in Warenhäusern und im eigenen Heim dank der Glühlampe in neuem Licht erstrahlen konnten. Das elektrische Licht und seine Beleuchtung haben die Menschen mit einer neuen Wahrnehmungsqualität ausgestattet.

Der Lichtgestalter Ingo Maurer hat sich in seinem Werk immer wieder mit der Glühlampe und ihrer Bedeutung auseinandergesetzt. Seine zahlreichen Lichtobjekte in Form von Glühbirnen und seine Leuchten, die sich im Namen auf Thomas Alva Edison beziehen, können – auch in der Zeit neuer Lichttechnologien – als Hommage an diesen revolutionären Beginn des Leuchtendesigns gelesen werden.

Der 1932 auf der Insel Reichenau im Bodensee geborene Ingo Maurer begann seine Laufbahn als Gebrauchsgrafiker. Er hatte nach einer Ausbildung zum Schriftsetzer und Typografen ein Grafikstudium in München begonnen. 1960 ging

Life is not possible without the sun. Humankind's creation rites are inextricably linked with this light and warmth-generating star. Light is a symbol of the divine. Light confers visibility, light illuminates, light brings knowledge.

Something of epochal significance was the invention of the modern electric light bulb. One of the results of industrialization was mass-produced consumer goods which were now, thanks to the electric bulb, able to bask in a new light, both in department stores and in people's own homes. Electric light and the illumination it provided have afforded man a new quality of perception.

In his work, light designer Ingo Maurer has repeatedly looked at the electric light bulb and its significance. Even in these days of new lighting technologies, his numerous lighting objects in the shape of light bulbs and his lights with names that reference Thomas Alva Edison can be interpreted as a homage to those revolutionary beginnings of lighting design.

Born on the Island of Reichenau, Lake Constance in 1932, -Maurer began his career as a commercial artist. After training as a typesetter and typographer, he started studying Graphic Design in Munich. In 1960, he moved to the United States, where he worked as a freelance designer in New York. He then returned to Munich in 1963 for personal reasons and opened his own company, "Design M." in 1966, with the aim of establishing himself as a lighting designer.

er in die USA, wo er als freier Designer in New York tätig wurde. 1963 erfolgte aus familiären Gründen die Rückkehr nach München, und 1966 gründete er seine Firma Design M, um sich als Lichtgestalter zu etablieren.

Seit über 50 Jahren widmet sich Ingo Maurer seiner Profession, dabei definiert er seit Beginn seine Firma als verantwortlich für Entwurf, Produktion, Vertrieb und Marketing, um so alle Unternehmensbereiche in eigener effizienter Regie abzudecken. Hierzu gehören auch seine Showrooms in München und New York. Ingo Maurer sieht seine Mitarbeiter*innen als Team, mit dem er auch gemeinsam entwirft und das er entsprechend als Co-Autoren der Produkte benennt. Heute besteht seine Firma aus über 50 festen und freien Mitarbeiter*innen.

Im Gründungsjahr seiner Firma entstand seine erste Leuchte BULB, ein radikaler Entwurf in Gestalt einer großen gläsernen Glühbirne, die die Glühbirne als Lichtquelle ins Zentrum stellt. 1984 schuf er mit dem Niedervolt-Lichtsystem YAYAHO eines der ersten Seilsysteme für Halogenreflektoren. Seine EL.E.DEE aus dem Jahre 2001 gilt als erste LED-Tischleuchte. Seit dem Jahrtausendwechsel entstanden LED-Tische und LED-Bänke oder auch LED-Tapeten und LED-Decken, in denen Ingo Maurer Lichtquellen unabhängig von Leuchten definiert. 2006 entwarf Ingo Maurer

Maurer has been engaged in his profession for more than 50 years now. Since the very outset he has explained that his company is responsible for designing, production, sales and marketing, in order to have all areas of his company in his own hands and functioning efficiently. This also includes his showrooms in Munich and New York. Maurer sees his staff as a team, one in which he too is involved in the design process and is accordingly able to call himself the co-author of the relevant products. Today his company consists of over 50 salaried and freelance staffers.

The year when the company was established also saw the genesis of his first luminaire BULB, a radical design in the shape of a large glass light bulb which focuses on the light bulb as a source of light. In 1984, with his low-voltage lighting system YAYAHO he produced one of the first cable systems for halogen reflectors. His EL.E.DEE, which dates from 2001, is considered one of the first LED table lamps. Since the turn of the millennium, Maurer has developed not only LED tables and LED benches but also LED wallpaper and LED ceilings, in which he defines light sources independent of luminaires. In 2006, in FLYING FUTURE Maurer designed a lighting object with OLED modules and in 2008 he joined forces with Osram to come up with EARLY FUTURE, the world's OLED luminaire ready to go into serial production.

Alongside luminaires and lighting objects, and increasingly as of the 1980s, Maurer also devises lighting concepts for the public and private spheres.

mit FLYING FUTURE ein Lichtobjekt mit OLED-Modulen und 2008 entwickelten Ingo Maurer und Osram mit EARLY FUTURE die weltweit erste serienreife OLED-Leuchte. Neben Leuchten und Lichtobjekten entwickelt Ingo Maurer, zunehmend ab den 1980er-Jahren, auch Lichtkonzepte für den privaten und den öffentlichen Raum.

　　Immer ist Ingo Maurer an den neuesten Technologien für Licht und ihren Möglichkeiten interessiert. Dabei reagiert er nicht lediglich auf technische Entwicklungen, sondern er selbst arbeitet an Lösungen und sucht hierfür innovative Gestaltungen. Der Pionier des Lichtdesigns setzt sich dabei immer auch kritisch mit diesen technischen Veränderungen auseinander. Denn die Qualität des Lichtes und ihr Einfluss auf den Menschen sind für ihn besonders wichtig und von gesellschaftlicher Relevanz.

　　Ingo Maurer geht mit seinen Entwürfen spielerisch um. Er schafft ungewöhnliche und originelle Leuchten, die jenseits tradierter Auffassungen liegen. Damit hat er sich eine unverkennbare Handschrift geschaffen. Mit viel Poesie, mit großem Zauber, aber auch mit Ironie, Humor und großer Leichtigkeit interpretiert Ingo Maurer souverän Lampen und Leuchten. Ein Movens von Ingo Maurer ist, mit seinen Leuchten Emotionen zu schaffen und Freude zu schenken. „Erfolgreich sind wir, wenn wir ein Gefühl in den Menschen auslösen" ist ein bekannter Satz von ihm.

　　Ingo Maurer zählt schon lange zu den weltweit bedeutendsten und innovativsten Charakteren des Lichtdesigns. Seine durch seine spezifische Haltung geprägten Objekte haben ihn international bekannt gemacht und ihm zahlreiche internationale und renommierte Preise eingebracht.

　　Maurer is always interested in the latest lighting technologies and the possibilities they afford. In this context he not only reacts to technical developments but also works on solutions himself, searching for innovative designs that will serve his purposes.

　　This pioneer of lighting design always adopts a critical approach to any technical changes. Indeed, for him, the quality of light and its effect on people are particularly important, as well as of social relevance.

　　Maurer adopts a playful approach to his designs, creating unusual and original luminaires which go beyond traditional approaches to the subject. And in so doing he has created his own unmistakable style. He demonstrates great assurance in his interpretations of lamps and luminaires, handling them with a great gift for the poetic and the magical, as well as manifesting irony, humor and great lightness in his execution.

　　One of Maurer's driving forces is the desire to elicit emotions and to give pleasure with his luminaires. "We are successful when we evoke some kind of feeling in people," is one of his well-known sayings.

　　Maurer has long been one of the world's most important and innovative personalities in lighting design. Characterized by his own particular approach, the items he creates have made him famous the world over and brought him numerous international and renowned prizes.

　　Many of his designs have become icons; after all, his luminaires are not only well-designed lighting objects, they also possess specific

Viele seiner Entwürfe sind zu Ikonen geworden, denn seine Leuchten sind nicht nur in Form gebrachte Lampen, sondern sie weisen mit spezifischen Eigenschaften über sich selbst hinaus.

Ingo Maurer ist fasziniert von der Immaterialität des Lichtes und setzt Wasser oder Metalle wie Aluminium, Kupfer oder Gold ein, um Licht einzufangen und zu reflektieren. Hierzu zählen seine raumfüllenden Lichtobjekte GOLDEN RIBBON oder seine Leuchten THE HUMBLIES, die durch ihre Metallfolien mit Blattgold Licht zum Strahlen bringen. Ein weiteres Beispiel sind seine Wasserobjekte wie EARTH-BOUND – UNBOUND, ein großes Wasserbassin mit sich ständig bewegenden und schwebenden transparenten Elementen, die durch Licht erst erkennbar werden.

In diesen Kontext gehört ebenfalls das PENDULUM aus hochglanzpoliertem Aluminium, das Ingo Maurer auf Einladung der Neuen Sammlung für die Rotunde der Pinakothek der Moderne realisiert hat. Das gleichsam über dem Boden schwebende PENDULUM im Zentrum der Rotunde wird regelmäßig in eine leichte Bewegung gebracht und schwingt dann langsam wieder aus. In seinen Maßen von rund 3 Metern Höhe und 2 Metern Durchmesser spiegelt es in Bewegung und im Stillstand das sich im Tagesverlauf und in den Jahreszeiten stets verändernde Licht, den Raum mit seiner charakteristischen Architektur sowie die dort anwesenden Besucher*innen und wird damit auch ein Symbol für Zeit.

Diese Beispiele verweisen ebenfalls auf ein weiteres zentrales Motiv im Schaffen Ingo Maurers, die Kinetik, die optische Variabilität erlaubt. Pendel – seien es pendelnde Leuchten oder schwingende metallene Ellipsoide – sind für Ingo Maurer

characteristics that allow them to transcend their actual functions.

Maurer is fascinated by the immateriality of light and uses water or metals such as aluminum, copper and gold to catch and reflect it.

Examples of this include his space-consuming lighting object GOLDEN RIBBON and his THE HUMBLIES which, with their gold-leaf metal foil, cause light to actually gleam.

Another example is his water objects such as EARTHBOUND – UNBOUND, a large water basin with transparent elements which float, are constantly in motion and only become recognizable through the effect of light.

An item that should also be mentioned in this context is the PENDULUM made of high-gloss aluminum realized by Maurer at the invitation of Die Neue Sammlung for the Rotunda in the Pinakothek der Moderne. Appearing to hover above the ground, the PENDULUM in the middle of the Rotunda is regularly set in gentle motion, before slowly coming to rest again. With its dimensions of some 3 meters in height and 2 meters in diameter, whether in motion or at rest, the pendulum reflects both the light that changes constantly over the course of the day and the seasons meaning that the room with its characteristic architecture and its visitors, also becoming a symbol of time.

The above examples also highlight yet another of the principal motifs in Maurer's oeuvre – the kinetics that allow for visual variability. Pendulums – be they pendant luminaires or swinging metal ellipsoids– represent an important element of Maurer's work, an opportunity to use simple means to make light mobile. On top of this, for Maurer

ein wichtiges Thema in seinem Werk, um mit einfachen Mitteln Licht mobil machen zu können. Darüber hinaus gehört für Ingo Maurer die Beobachtung eines Pendels zu den kinetischen Erlebnissen, die sich durch ihre ruhige und regelmäßige Bewegung auf das Wohlbefinden auswirken.

Ist in Hängeleuchten die Möglichkeit einer Bewegung ohnehin vielfach inhärent, steigert Ingo Maurer dieses Motiv in assoziativem Maße. Da gibt es Leuchten, die sich gleich in Bewegung zu setzen scheinen, wie LUCELLINO oder BIRDS BIRDS BIRDS mit Flügeln, wie FLATTERBY mit Schmetterlingen, mit Vogelbeinen bei BIBIBIBI oder in der Schlangenform bei ZUFALL. Oder sie wirken wie eine Momentaufnahme im Prozess höchster Dynamik, so wie bei PORCA MISERIA!, einer Leuchte, die gleichsam in Explosion begriffen ist. Andere Leuchten wie ZETTEL'Z sind interaktiv angelegt und reagieren auf Luftzug. Wieder andere Leuchten sind in ständiger Bewegung wie FLYING FLAMES in Nachahmung einer analogen Kerzenflamme.

Ein weiteres Thema innerhalb dieser Gruppe kinetischer Objekte sind Ingo Maurers Zitate künstlerischer Werke. Seine Leuchte OH MAN, IT'S A RAY! ist ein mit Glühbirnen versehenes, ebenfalls mobiles Zitat des Ready-Made-Mobiles *Obstruction* aus Kleiderbügeln des Surrealisten Man Ray. Auch eine seiner jüngsten Leuchten OOP'S zitiert die spiralförmige *Lampshade* von Man Ray. Mit REMEMBER YVES verleiht Ingo Maurer dem in einer Schwarz-Weiß-Fotografie festgehaltenen Sprung Yves Kleins aus dem Fenster eine dritte Dimension. Ingo Maurer hat die Figur des Künstlers in dessen berühmtem Blau als ein aus der

observing a pendulum represents the kind of kinetic experience whose steady and regular movement impacts on our sense of well-being.

Although the possibility of movement is anyway pretty well intrinsic in suspended luminaires, Maurer enhances this aspect in an associative way. And then there are the kinds of lights which seem to be on the point of setting themselves in motion, as with LUCELLINO or BIRDS BIRDS BIRDS with wings, FLATTERBY with butterflies, BIBIBIBI with birds' legs or in the shape of snakes, as with "Zufall T". Or they look like a snapshot during a situation of the utmost dynamics, as with "Porca Miseria", a light which appears to be engaged in exploding.

Other luminaires, such as ZETTEL'Z are constructed interactively and react to the motion of air. Others are in constant motion, such as FLYING FLAMES, which imitates an analogue candle's flame.

Another topic relevant to this group of mobile objects is Maurer's habit of citing works of art. His luminaire OH MAN, IT'S A RAY! quotes "Obstruction", Surrealist Man Ray's coat-hanger ready-made, but provides it with a light bulb; Maurer's piece is also mobile. One of his most recent luminaires, OOP'S also quotes Man Ray, the latter's spiral "Lampshade", to be more precise. With REMEMBER YVES Maurer lends a third dimension to a black and white photograph taken by Ray of Yves Klein jumping out of a window. Maurer reproduces the figure of the artist, in his famous blue, as a figure jumping out of the wall, with its shadow producing a duplicated version of it.

Wand springendes Objekt nachgebildet, das durch seinen Schattenwurf eine Dopplung erfährt. Das Blau, für Yves Klein das „sichtbar werdende Unsichtbare", wird hier zum Äquivalent von Licht und Schatten.

Diese Symbiose von Licht und Schatten ist ein weiteres wichtiges Sujet für Ingo Maurer. Für ihn ist es dabei wichtig, auch den Schatten zu gestalten, im Sinne, dass der Schatten nicht allein als natürliche Folge von Licht erscheint, sondern autonomen Wert erhält. In den gegenläufig rotierenden Scheiben von ECLIPSE ELLIPSE ist der Schlagschatten ein integraler Bestandteil der gesamten Form. Das Phänomen, dass Schatten das zweidimensionale Echo auf dreidimensionale Formen sind, übersetzt Ingo Maurer in die Arbeiten LOOKSOFLAT, bei der die Leuchte selbst zur Fläche ihres Schattens wird, und LÜSTER, wo ein Lüster wie die Zeichnung eines Schattens auf einer Glasfläche abgebildet erscheint.

Leuchten und Leuchtobjekte in eingeschaltetem wie in ausgeschaltetem Modus sowie die in ihnen gespiegelten notwendigen Gegensätze von Tag und Nacht, von Licht und Schatten, Ruhe und Bewegung, Ganzheit und Fragment stellen bei Ingo Maurer wie das chinesische Yin und Yang eine perfekte Balance für den Menschen dar. Und so ist die Eigenschaft des Ganzheitlichen das übergeordnete Charakteristikum seiner Werke. Ingo Maurer denkt ganzheitlich, er glaubt an „unser All-Sein".

In diesem Sinne ist Ingo Maurer zutiefst humanistisch und zutiefst philanthropisch. Das Licht als Symbol für Existenz und Energie bringt Ingo Maurer durch seine Leuchten zu den Menschen, in den Alltag. In seinen Gestaltungen erschafft Licht Sichtbarkeit und wird Licht sichtbar.

Here this blue, for Klein the "invisible becoming visible", becomes the equivalent of light and shade.

This symbiosis of light and shade is another important subject for Maurer. With his lights, it is important for him to design the shade, as well, in the sense that shade is not only the natural consequence of light, it also has value in itself. In ECLIPSE ELLIPSE, the shadow cast by its discs, which rotate in opposite directions, is an integral part of the luminaire's overall shape. The phenomenon that shadows are the two-dimensional echo of three-dimensional shapes is interpreted by Maurer in the works LOOKSOFLAT in which the luminaire itself becomes the surface of its shadow and LÜSTER where a chandelier appears to be pictured on a glass surface like a drawing of a shadow.

For Maurer, not only luminaires and lighting objects, both in switched-on and in switched-off modes, but also the necessary antitheses they represent between day and night, light and shade, repose and movement, entirety and fragment, amounts, as with the Chinese yin and yang, to a perfect balance for humankind. Accordingly, the quality of the holistic is the overarching characteristic of his work. Maurer thinks holistically, he believes in the fact of "our being everything".

In this sense, Maurer is both deeply humanist and deeply philanthropic. With his luminaires, Maurer brings light as a symbol of existence and energy to human beings, into their everyday lives. In his designs light creates visibility, light becomes something visible.

Der vorliegende Katalog bildet in chronologischer Folge Leuchten und Licht-objekte ab. Dieser Bildteil wird ergänzt durch eine Bildstrecke von der ortsspe-zifischen Installation PENDULUM in der Rotunde der Pinakothek der Moderne sowie von Bildern seiner Lichtkonzepte für den öffentlichen Raum. Der Katalog präsentiert im Sinne des Ausstellungstitels „Ingo Maurer intim. Design or what?" die transdisziplinäre Qualität von Ingo Maurers Werken mit ihren Grenzbereichen zu Kunst und Architektur sowie den persönlichen Blick auf sein Schaffen. In diesem Kontext sind die Abbildungen seiner Serviettenzeichnungen zu lesen, seine skizzierten ersten Ideen für neue Entwürfe, sowie das Gespräch mit seinem Team.

Ein großer Dank gilt der Kuratorin Xenia Riemann-Tyroller für ihre verantwor-tungsvolle Realisierung von Ausstellung und Katalog. Die Ausstellung wurde in enger Zusammenarbeit mit Hagen Sczech und Gabriele Kümmerlin erarbeitet, mit denen Ingo Maurer das Konzept entwickelt hat. Für ihre kuratorische Assis-tenz danken wir Rosa Carole Rodeck. Sehr herzlich danken wir Claude Maurer für all ihre Unterstützung. Auch danken wir allen Mitarbeiter*innen der Firma Ingo Maurer und der Neuen Sammlung, die an der Realisierung beteiligt waren.

Für ihre Textbeiträge danken wir sehr herzlich den von Ingo Maurer eingela-denen externen Autor*innen Barbara Bloemink, Michele De Lucchi, Bernhard Dessecker, Kim Hastreiter, Nasir Kassamali sowie Tom Vack. Es handelt sich hierbei um Persönlichkeiten, die Ingo Maurer und sein Werk seit langem kenntnis-reich begleitet haben und ihn daher in besonderem Maße würdigen können.

The catalogue under consideration illustrates luminaires and lighting objects in chronological order. This pictorial section is com-plemented by a photo spread of the location-specific installation PENDULUM in the Rotunda at Pinakothek der Moderne and by pic-tures of its concept for the public sphere. The catalogue presents, in line with the exhibition's title "Ingo Maurer intim. Design or what?" (Ingo Maurer close up. Design or what?) Maurer's transdisciplinary quality, with border zones located between art and architecture and a personal view of his oeuvre. The serviette drawings should be seen in this context, initial ideas for new designs, along with discus-sions with his team.

Our great thanks go to curator Xenia Riemann-Tyroller for her careful realization of the exhibition and catalog. The exhibition was devised in close collaboration with Hagen Sczech and Gabriele Kümmerlin, with whom Ingo Maurer developed the concept. We would like to thank Rosa Carole Rodeck for her curatorial assis-tance. We are most grateful to Claude Maurer for all her support. And we likewise thank all the staff at the Ingo Maurer company and Neue Sammlung, who helped realize the show.

We are most grateful to the outside authors Ingo Maurer invited to contribute essays, namely to Barbara Bloemink, Michele De Lucchi, Bernhard Dessecker, Kim Hastreiter, Nasir Kassamali, and Tom Vack. They are all outstanding minds who have for many years been supporting and following Ingo Maurer and his oeuvre and who can therefore best assess and appreciate his work. We are also most

Wir danken ebenfalls David Engelhorn, Sebastian Hepting, Gabriele Kümmerlin, Marisa Mariscal, Axel Schmid und Sebastian Utermühlen aus dem Team Ingo Maurer, die in ihrem Gespräch mit Xenia Riemann-Tyroller und Rose Carole Rodeck einen nahen Blick auf Ingo Maurer gewähren.

Es freut uns, dass diese Publikation erneut im Verlag Koenig Books erscheinen kann. Wir danken Petra Lüer vom Grafikbüro wigel für die grafische Gestaltung der vorliegenden Publikation.
Sehr herzlich möchten wir uns bei PIN. Freunde der Pinakothek für ihre große Unterstützung bedanken, ohne die eine Installation wie das PENDULUM in dieser Form nicht möglich wäre.

Der größte Dank gebührt Ingo Maurer. Wir freuen uns und fühlen uns geehrt, dass Ingo Maurer neben unserer Einladung zur Realisierung des PENDULUMS für die Rotunde, auch unserer Einladung für eine Ausstellung über sein Werk und sein Wirken zugestimmt hat. Von Herzen sagen wir Dank für seine Konzeption, seine Gedanken und Ideen zu Ausstellung und Katalog sowie vor allem auch für die guten und intensiven gemeinsamen Gespräche. Wir sind sehr traurig, dass Ingo Maurer kurz vor Eröffnung seiner Ausstellung verstorben ist.

Wir verneigen uns vor seiner Persönlichkeit, deren Wesen von Offenheit und Großzügigkeit, Klugheit und Wissen, unermüdlicher Energie und Disziplin geprägt war.

Ingo Maurer selbst ist eine Lichtgestalt.

grateful to David Engelhorn, Sebastian Hepting, Gabriele Kümmerlin, Marisa Mariscal, Axel Schmid, and Sebastian Utermühlen from Team Ingo Maurer, who in conversation with Xenia Riemann-Tyroller and Rose Carole Rodeck offered many an insight into Ingo Maurer.

We are delighted that this publication is again coming out with Verlag Koenig Books. We would like to thank Petra Lüer at Grafikbüro wigel for her graphic design for the present publication.

We would like to most cordially thank PIN. Freunde der Pinakothek for their generous support without which an installation such as the PENDULUM would simply not have been possible in this form.

Our great thanks goes to Ingo Maurer himself. We are most happy and feel honored that Ingo Maurer not only took up our invitation to realize the PENDULUM for the Rotunda but also agreed to our invitation to organize an exhibition on his oeuvre and impact. We are truly grateful for his concept, his thoughts and ideas, for both the show and the catalog, and above all for the good and intense conversations we had. We are very sad that Ingo Maurer died shortly before the opening of his exhibition.

We bow down before his outlook, his combination of openness and generosity, his wisdom and knowledge, his unflagging energy and discipline.

Ingo Maurer is himself a bright light in the design firmament.

ANGELIKA NOLLERT
(GEB. 1966, DUISBURG)
ist seit 2014 Direktorin der Neuen Sammlung – The Design Museum in München. Sie war u. a. Kuratorin des Portikus in Frankfurt am Main (1997–2000), Projektleiterin der Documentva 11 (2001/2002) und Projektleiterin des Bereichs Bildende Kunst beim Siemens Arts Program (2002–2007). Von 2007 bis 2014 war sie Direktorin des Neuen Museums für Kunst und Design in Nürnberg.

ANGELIKA NOLLERT
(BORN 1966, DUISBURG)
has been the director of Die Neue Sammlung – The Design Museum in Munich since 2014. Among other roles, she was curator of Portikus in Frankfurt (1997–2000), project manager at Documenta 11 (2001/2002) and project manager for the Fine Arts section of the Siemens Arts Program (2002–2007). From 2007 to 2014 she was director of the Neues Museum für Kunst und Design in Nuremberg.

Barbara Bloemink
Licht sehen – Magie erschaffen / Provoking Magic: Seeing Light

Licht lässt unsere Welt sichtbar werden.

Über Hunderttausende von Jahren mussten Menschen ihr Leben nach dem Sonnenlicht ausrichten, da es ihre einzige Lichtquelle war. In der griechischen Antike glaubte man, Prometheus hätte den Göttern getrotzt und das Feuer vom Himmel gestohlen, um es der Menschheit zu schenken, damit sie erstmals das Dunkel erhellen konnte. Ab diesem Zeitpunkt verwendeten die Griechen für Licht das gleiche Wort wie für Wahrheit.

Trotz der vielen Tausend Jahre, die seit dem Beginn der Zivilisation vergangen sind, wissen wir immer noch nicht genau, was „Licht" eigentlich ist. Seit dem frühen Zwanzigsten Jahrhundert machen wir uns das Licht zunutze – seinerzeit betrachtete man es als magisches Phänomen – und es ermöglicht uns nach Belieben, in der Dunkelheit zu sehen. Physiker, Astronomen, Kosmologen und andere Wissenschaftler streiten seit Langem darüber, ob Licht aus Partikeln oder Wellen besteht, sie haben Licht gemessen und viele seiner komplexen Eigenschaften erforscht und können es dennoch bis heute nicht genau erklären.

Neue Technologien der Lichterfassung und -nutzung verändern sich in einem immer rasanter werdenden Tempo. Das Vorhandensein des Lichts ist so allgegen-

Light makes our world visible.

For hundreds of thousands of years, humans had to organize their lives around the hours of sunlight because it was the only time when there was sufficient light to see. The Ancient Greeks believed Prometheus defied the gods by stealing fire from the heavens and giving it to humanity. This gave humans the first opportunity to add light to the darkness. They thereafter used the same word for light as for truth.

Despite the thousands of years that have passed since the rise of civilization, we still do not know what "light" is. Since the early twentieth century, humans have harnessed light – something that was considered magic in its time – providing us with a way to see in the darkness whenever we choose. Over the years, physicists, astronomers, cosmologists, and other scientists have debated whether light ultimately consists of particles or waves, they have measured light and researched many of its other complex features, but ultimately we still do not fully understand it.

New technologies to capture light and use it are changing at an ever more rapid pace. However, its existence in our lives is so pervasive that today it is generally taken for granted. Like the computer and the cellphone, it is hard for most of us to imagine living without interior lighting. As a result, we hardly notice light anymore, simply assuming its existence, allowing us to actively live and work as we choose, twenty-four hours a day.

By contrast, every aspect of Ingo Maurer's work consciously contradicts the virtually invisible, bland, colorless sameness of how

wärtig, dass wir es im Allgemeinen als selbstverständlich erachten. Ein Leben ohne Innenbeleuchtung scheint genauso unvorstellbar wie eines ohne Computer und Handy. Insofern nehmen wir das Licht kaum noch wahr, sehen seine Existenz als gegeben an, die es uns erlaubt, so zu leben und zu arbeiten, wie es uns beliebt, vierundzwanzig Stunden am Tag.

Das Werk Ingo Maurers widerspricht hingegen in allen seinen Aspekten der quasi unsichtbaren, faden, farblosen Gleichförmigkeit des Lichts, zu der es sich in unserem technologischen Zeitalter entwickelt hat. Stattdessen beflügeln seine Leuchten mit ihren unendlichen Variationen von Schönheit, Humor und Form unsere Fantasie. Alle Entwürfe von Maurer sind funktionierende Kunstwerke, die die ausgedehnte oder wiederholte Betrachtung und Verwendung belohnen. Zugleich erinnern sie uns an das ewige Mysterium und Wunder des Lichts. So schreibt Maurer selbst über Licht:

„Ich glaube, Licht ist so geheimnisvoll, weil es sich so unglaublich schnell und auf so unterschiedliche Weise bewegen kann und man nie wirklich weiß, woher es kommt. Das mag ich sehr gerne."

Maurer hat eine starke Affinität zu japanischer Ästhetik, er führt daher häufig

light has evolved in our technological era. Instead, his lighting actively provokes our imaginations with infinite variations of beauty, humor, and form. All of Maurer's creations are functioning works of art that, every time they are seen or used, reward repeated and extended viewing. At the same time, they remind us of the continuing mystery and miracle of light. As Maurer notes of light itself:

"I think it is mysterious because light travels so incredibly fast in so many different ways that you never really know where it comes from. I like that very much."

Maurer often makes lights that exude ultimate minimalism, building on his love of Japanese aesthetics, reducing lighting to its simplest, most beautiful elements. In RUKUKU, for example, the basic principle of the light is balance, as a simple light bulb is balanced on a simple line of steel by a stunningly simple, white oval form that sits on top of the opposite side. A series of lights in variations of scale, the THE HUMBLIES stand like Japanese lanterns, made of very thin black metal structures. Inside small lights, hanging between fitted sheets of gold, rust, or white that look like rice paper, create soft glowing illumination.

Humor has always been one characteristic of Maurer's lighting. His ideas often come from mundane, found objects that he picks up during his travels. In some of his earlier work this has included adding white goose feathers to light bulbs, having resin nude figures float within lit water containers or gold figures climbing up a ceiling light, hiding animals in bright golden mesh cages, or creating a cluster

Beleuchtung auf ihre einfachsten und schönsten Elemente zurück und schafft so Leuchten von ultimativem Minimalismus. So ist RUKUKU beispielsweise im wahrsten Sinne des Wortes ein Balanceakt. Auf einer schlichten Geraden aus Stahl wird eine einfache Glühlampe auf der einen Seite durch eine erstaunlich simple, weiße und ovale Form auf der anderen Seite austariert. Für THE HUMBLIES hat Maurer eine Serie von unterschiedlich dimensionierten Lichtobjekten aus filigranen schwarzen Metallkonstruktionen wie japanische Laternen arrangiert. In ihnen befinden sich kleine LEDs, die zwischen feinen vergoldeten, rostfarbenen und weißen reispapierähnlichen Blättern hängen und ein weiches Licht verströmen.

Ein charakteristisches Merkmal von Maurers Leuchten ist immer der Humor. Seine Ideen sind häufig von banalen alltäglichen und auf seinen Reisen gefundenen Objekten inspiriert. So hat er bei einigen seiner früheren Entwürfe zum Beispiel Glühbirnen mit weißen Gänsefedern versehen, er ließ Aktfiguren aus Kunstharz in beleuchteten Wasserbehältnissen treiben oder goldene Figuren eine Deckenleuchte erklimmen, er hat Tiere in leuchtend goldenen Gitterboxen versteckt oder ein hängendes Arrangement aus den zerbrochenen Teilen lächelnder chinesischer Puppenköpfe aus Porzellan geschaffen. Zu den neuen, ausgesprochen geistreichen und witzigen Leuchtenentwürfen Maurers zählen COMIC EXPLOSION mit den Superhelden des Comics, oder auch verschiedene Varianten der LUZY-Serie mit Gummihandschuhen in Yves-Klein-Blau (der Name LUZY TAKE FIVE heißt so viel „wie sich fünf Minuten Zeit für sich selbst nehmen"). In der TOTO-Serie vergnügt sich Maurer mit Variationen von Micky-Maus-Ohren über die Absurditäten des

of hanging broken parts of smiling, porcelain Chinese dolls' heads. Maurer's brilliantly humorous new lighting ranges from his COMIC EXPLOSION themed around comic-strip super heroes to his Yves-Klein-blue rubber gloves used as support for the variations of his LUZY series (including LUZY TAKE FIVE, an idiom for taking five minutes to relax). Maurer pokes fun at the absurdity of life in variations of Mickey Mouse ears on the light bulbs in the Toto series, and the surreal pair of lamps, VERAMENTE AL DENTE, in which a stainless-steel tower of stacked cutlery holds up four stacked dishes from which soft light shines. The top, fifth plate is laden with trompe l'œil, tomato sauce-covered pasta, from which, magically, a spoon has grasped a long, string of pasta that it holds, floating, in midair. Sometimes the humor is subtler, as in BIG BULB WHITE, where myriad iridescent butterflies and two dragonflies circle around a large hanging bulb, attracted to the light. In the massive BROKEN EGG chandelier, bright light is visible, shining through the large cracks that circle the oval that hangs from the ceiling. The cracks create an ominous sense of imminent disaster, as if the dangling, precarious form will crack open and fall to the ground any minute.

It is impossible to come across an Ingo Maurer light and not have an emotional reaction – whether a gasp at its beauty or ingenuity, or a burst of laughter at its absurdity. That, of course, is Maurer's intention:

"A thing shouldn't stand there like a lump of concrete, like a monument for eternity. We are successful when we manage to strike a chord or feeling in people."

Lebens und bei VERAMENTE AL DENTE, einem surrealen Leuchtenpaar, ruhen vier gestapelte Teller, aus denen ein weiches Licht hervortritt, auf einem Arrangement aus hochkant aufgetürmten Edelstahlbestecken. Der obere fünfte Teller ist mit einer Portion Trompe-l'œil-Pasta-mit-Tomatensauce versehen, über der, wie von Zauberhand geführt, ein Löffel mit herunterhängenden Nudeln schwebt. Manchmal nimmt der Humor auch etwas subtilere Formen an, so zum Beispiel bei BIG BULB WHITE. Hier kreisen unzählige schillernde Schmetterlinge und zwei Libellen um eine große hängende Glühlampe, die vom Licht offenkundig wie magisch angezogen sind. Bei der imposanten Leuchte BROKEN EGG scheint helles Licht durch die klaffenden Risse der ovalen Form, die von der Decke hängt. Es scheint fast, als würde ein drohendes Unheil kurz bevorstehen und die fragile Form jeden Moment auseinanderbrechen und zu Boden stürzen.

Es ist wohl unmöglich, einer Lampe von Ingo Maurer ohne emotionale Reaktion zu begegnen – ob es ein Ausruf des Erstaunens angesichts ihrer Schönheit oder Raffiniertheit ist oder ein lautes Lachen angesichts ihrer Absurdität. Aber genau das ist natürlich Ingo Maurers Intention:

„Ein Objekt sollte nicht wie ein Betonklotz in der Gegend stehen, wie ein Monument für alle Ewigkeit. Wenn wir es schaffen, ein Gefühl im Betrachter auszulösen, ist uns etwas gelungen."

Gelegentlich entwirft Maurer auch Arbeiten, die die Definition des Lichts selbst erweitern, und zwar sowohl durch groß angelegte Lichtinstallationen im Außenbereich als auch durch kleinere für Innenräume. So hat er ein Lichtkonzept für die

On occasion, Maurer creates works that expand the definition of light itself, through both large-scale exterior and smaller interior lighting installations. He has created lighting installations for the Westfriedhof subway station in Munich and a spectacular lighting entrance for the Kruisherenhotel in Maastricht in the Netherlands, as well as for the interior of the Atomium in Brussels, Belgium. Several of his interior installations play on images from art and human history. With the monumental chandelier, OH MAN, IT'S A RAY!, Maurer offers an homage to the Dada artist Man Ray. In 1920 Man Ray created a well-known "readymade" that he titled *Obstruction*, out of sixty-three wooden coat-hangers. In his version, Maurer added light bulbs to the lower wood slats and printed his ironic title on each.

The artist turned his minimal, technological MY NEW FLAME light (that can also be used individually or hung in a group as a chandelier,) into an installation with a new significance. By placing them in front of a large-scale blue-tinted photograph of Impressionist painter Edouard Manet's infamous painting, *Olympia*, the small "candle-lights" appear to be lighting the nude woman for an evening tryst. Manet painted a prostitute, offering her body to potential customers in 1865, and it caused a major scandal when it was exhibited at the Paris Salon of that year. The placement of the small vertical lights before the image in the painting, therefore, gives its title a new, humorous and sexual interpretation. T.T. MOON, a vertical chandelier, is made of metal strips and various red and black circular and rectangular geometric shapes that are attached like docked spaceships.

U-Bahn-Station Westfriedhof in München entwickelt oder auch einen spektakulären lichterfüllten Eingang für das Kruisherenhotel in Maastricht in den Niederlanden sowie für den Innenbereich des Atomiums in Brüssel, Belgien. Einige seiner Installationen für Innenräume spielen mit Bildern aus der Kunst- und Menschheitsgeschichte. Seine raumgreifende Deckenleuchte OH MAN, IT'S A RAY! ist beispielsweise eine Hommage an den DADA-Künstler Man Ray. Man Ray hatte 1920 aus dreiundsechzig Holzkleiderbügeln das bekannte *Readymade* mit dem Titel *Obstruction* geschaffen. Maurer hat bei seiner Version die unteren Holzlatten jeweils mit Leuchtmitteln und seinem ironischen Titel versehen.

Seine minimalistische und technologische Leuchte MY NEW FLAME hat Maurer in eine Installation mit neuer Bedeutung verwandelt (sie kann einzeln verwendet oder als Gruppe zu einem Hängeleuchter arrangiert werden). Indem sie vor einer großformatigen, blau getönten Fotografie des berühmt-berüchtigten Gemäldes *Olympia* von Edouard Manet positioniert wurden, entsteht der Eindruck, als würden die kleinen „Kerzenlichter" die nackte Frau bei einem nächtlichen Schäferstündchen bescheinen. Manet hatte 1865 eine Prostituierte gemalt, die ihren Körper potenziellen Kunden anbot. Entsprechend löste das Bild einen großen Skandal aus, als es in jenem Jahr auf dem Pariser Salon ausgestellt wurde. Die kleinen vertikalen Lichter vor dem Bild sind insofern eine neue und humorvolle Interpretation mit einem durchaus sexuellen Unterton.

T.T. MOON, eine Deckenleuchte, besteht aus Metallstreifen und verschiedenen roten und schwarzen, runden und rechteckigen geometrischen Formen, die wie

A strip of small lights glows at each docking station. Behind this hyper-elegant light, a huge contrasting photographic wall by Tom Vack shows a devastated city above which futuristic armed soldiers float, firing weapons. Perhaps the installation is a warning by the artist to protect our planet, as Maurer has worked for years on using increasingly sustainable technology for his work.

Maurer has been at the forefront of new technology for forty years, always in the service of his works as functioning, visual pleasures, and with an awareness of environmental sustainability. In 1984, he introduced a creative low-voltage halogen light system of double cables for a beautiful series of lights (YAYAHO). In the 1990s Maurer created a number of works using LED lights. As early as 2006 he began work on OLEDs (organic light-emitting diodes). Made of sheets of organic material, they are thinner and more efficient than LED lights. Today, a series of his lights use OLED, including the beautiful WHISPER WIND table lamp, its "leaves" emitting soft, bright light, bending gracefully forward on wire branches. His DOUBLE FUTURE lights are made up of circular OLED discs in octagon frames that can either hang from the ceiling or stand on a table. All are visually beautiful and technologically advanced.

Starting out in Munich in 1966 with only five staff members, today there are more than fifty people on Maurer's team. As Maurer acknowledges,

"I work with wonderful people and I couldn't do anything without them. It is like a great family…. Work begins with an

Raumschiffe an diese angedockt zu sein scheinen. Jede dieser Andockstellen ist mit einem Streifen kleiner LED versehen. Auf einem Foto von Tom Vack ist hinter dieser überaus eleganten Leuchte auf einer Fotowand eine zerstörte Stadt zu sehen, über der futuristisch ausgerüstete Soldaten schweben und ihre Waffen abfeuern. Vielleicht möchte Maurer diese Installation als Aufruf für den Schutz unserer Erde verstanden wissen.

Viele Jahre schon beschäftigt er sich in seiner Arbeit mit nachhaltigen Technologien. Seit vierzig Jahren ist er Pionier in Sachen neuer Technologien, die er immer in den Dienst seiner Arbeit gestellt hat, um funktionale und visuell ansprechende und vor allem ökologisch nachhaltige Lichtlösungen zu entwickeln.

1984 entwickelte er mit YAYAHO ein innovatives System, bei dem Niedervolt-Halogenlampen flexibel auf zwei parallel gespannten Metallseilen befestigt werden. 1990 folgte eine Reihe von Projekten, für die er LED einsetzte. Außerdem hat Maurer bereits 2006 mit OLED, organischen Leuchtdioden, zu arbeiten begonnen. Sie beruhen auf einer organischen Dünnschichttechnik, die dünner und effizienter ist als bei LED. Eine Reihe seiner Leuchten sind heute mit OLED ausgestattet, darunter auch die beeindruckende Tischleuchte WHISPER WIND, deren „Blätter" ein weiches, helles Licht verströmen und sich dabei anmutig an ihren verästelten Drähten nach vorne neigen. Oder auch die DOUBLE FUTURE-Leuchten aus runden OLED-Modulen in achteckigen Rahmen, die entweder an die Decke gehängt oder auf den Tisch gestellt werden können. Sie alle sind visuell ausgesprochen ansprechend und technologisch fortschrittlich.

idea I have or a mood I want to create. I then go to people who I think can realize that idea and tell them what I have in mind.... perhaps through a sketch on paper or a napkin. We discuss it so that they become really involved and show me how they might solve the problem...Then I let them go.... I am open to the designers fighting for their ideas. The fun is the dialog of working together to find the right solution. There are these moments when this happens, when we all shout, 'We've got it!' that are so wonderful. There is an enormous sense of intimacy among all of us – sharing the success together."

In our world of increasing human isolation, technology, and sameness, Ingo Maurer's lighting celebrates the individual, funny, emotional, thoughtful, and creative aspects of what makes us human. We may not know exactly what light is, but Maurer is a magician who uniquely conjures enchantment, laughter, and fascination from light; and uses its properties to produce illusions that fool our eyes through his sleight of hand and imagination. In all of his works, Ingo Maurer magically provokes us to notice the light in our lives.

Maurer hat 1966 mit nur fünf Mitarbeitern angefangen, heute sind es mehr als 50 Mitarbeiter*innen. Er fasst das so in Worte:

„Ich arbeite mit wunderbaren Menschen und würde ohne sie gar nichts zustande bringen. Wir sind wie eine große Familie … Am Anfang steht eine Idee oder ich möchte eine spezielle Stimmung kreieren. Dann gehe ich damit zu den Leuten, von denen ich glaube, dass sie diese Idee umsetzen können, und erkläre ihnen, was mir vorschwebt … vielleicht mithilfe einer Zeichnung auf einer Serviette. Wir reden eine Weile darüber, bis sie im Thema drin sind und mir sagen können, wie man das Problem am besten lösen könnte … Dann lasse ich sie gehen … Ich finde es gut, den Designer für seine Ideen kämpfen zu lassen. Der Spaß ist das Gespräch, in dem nach der richtigen Lösung gesucht wird. Es gibt diese Momente, wenn es plötzlich gelingt, und wir alle schreien: ‚Wir haben es geschafft!‘, das ist wunderbar. Es gibt eine große Vertrautheit unter uns und wir genießen den gemeinsamen Erfolg."

In einer Welt der zunehmenden menschlichen Isolation, der Technologie und Gleichförmigkeit, zelebrieren Ingo Maurers Leuchten die einzigartigen, lustigen, emotionalen, gedankenvollen und kreativen Aspekte unseres Menschseins. Wir wissen vielleicht nicht genau, was Licht ist, aber Maurer vermag es auf unnachahmliche Weise, aus Licht Begeisterung, Lachen und Faszination zu zaubern, und nutzt diese Fähigkeit, um unsere Augen mit seinen Tricks und seiner Fantasie im wahrsten Sinne des Wortes hinter das Licht zu führen. Und nicht zuletzt werden wir durch seine Leuchten plötzlich auf das Licht in unserem Leben aufmerksam.

BARBARA J. BLOEMINK
(GEB. 1953)
ist freie Kuratorin für zeitgenössische Kunst und Design und Museumsberaterin. Sie war u. a. Curatorial Director des Cooper Hewitt, Smithsonian Design Museum und Managing Director des Guggenheim & Guggenheim Hermitage Museum in Las Vegas. Des Weiteren ist sie im Verwaltungsrat der Designmesse DesignMiami/Basel und Autorin zahlreicher Publikationen.

BARBARA J. BLOEMINK
(BORN 1953)
is a freelance curator for contemporary art and design and a museum consultant. Her roles have included Curatorial Director of the Cooper Hewitt, Smithsonian Design Museum and Managing Director of the Guggenheim & Guggenheim Hermitage Museum in Las Vegas. She is also a member of the administrative board of the design fair DesignMiami/Basel and the author of numerous publications.

Exponate / Exhibits
1966–2019

Die folgenden Leuchten und Lichtobjekte orientieren sich an den Exponaten der Ausstellung „Ingo Maurer intim. Design or what?". Sie sind chronologisch von 1966 bis 2019 geordnet und zeigen einen umfassenden Einblick in das facettenreiche Gesamtwerk Ingo Maurers. Die Leuchten sind seine Entwürfe, Teamentwicklungen und Kooperationen mit externen Gestaltern. Einzigartige Formensprache, außergewöhnliche Namensgebung und inszenierte Fotografie sind bei ihm untrennbar miteinander verbunden.

The following luminaires and light objects all relate to the exhibition "Ingo Maurer intim. Design or what?". They are arranged chronologically from 1966 to 2019 and offer a comprehensive overview of Ingo Maurer's multi-faceted oeuvre. The luminaires are the result of either his designs, team projects, or collaborations with outside designers. For him, the unique formal idiom, the extraordinary names, and the staged photographs are all inextricably part of the approach.

Bulb
1966

Ingo Maurer
Chrom, Glas, Metall
Chrome, glass, metal

Giant Bulb Clear
1966

Ingo Maurer
Chrom, Glas, Metall
Chrome, glass, metal

Pollux
1967

Ingo Maurer
Chrom, Metall
Chrome, metal

Spirale
1967

Ingo Maurer
Chrom, Metall,
Opalinglas
Chrome, metal,
opal glass

Head Light
1968

Ingo Maurer
Kunststoff,
Metall verchromt,
lackiert
Plastic,
metal chromed,
painted

Scherenlampe
1968

Dorothee Becker,
Ingo Maurer
Chrom, Metall
Chrome, metal

Big M
1970

Ingo Maurer
Chrom, Metall, Glas
Chrome, metal, glass

Light Structure LED
1970/2013

Peter Hamburger,
Ingo Maurer
Glas, Kunststoff
Glass, plastic

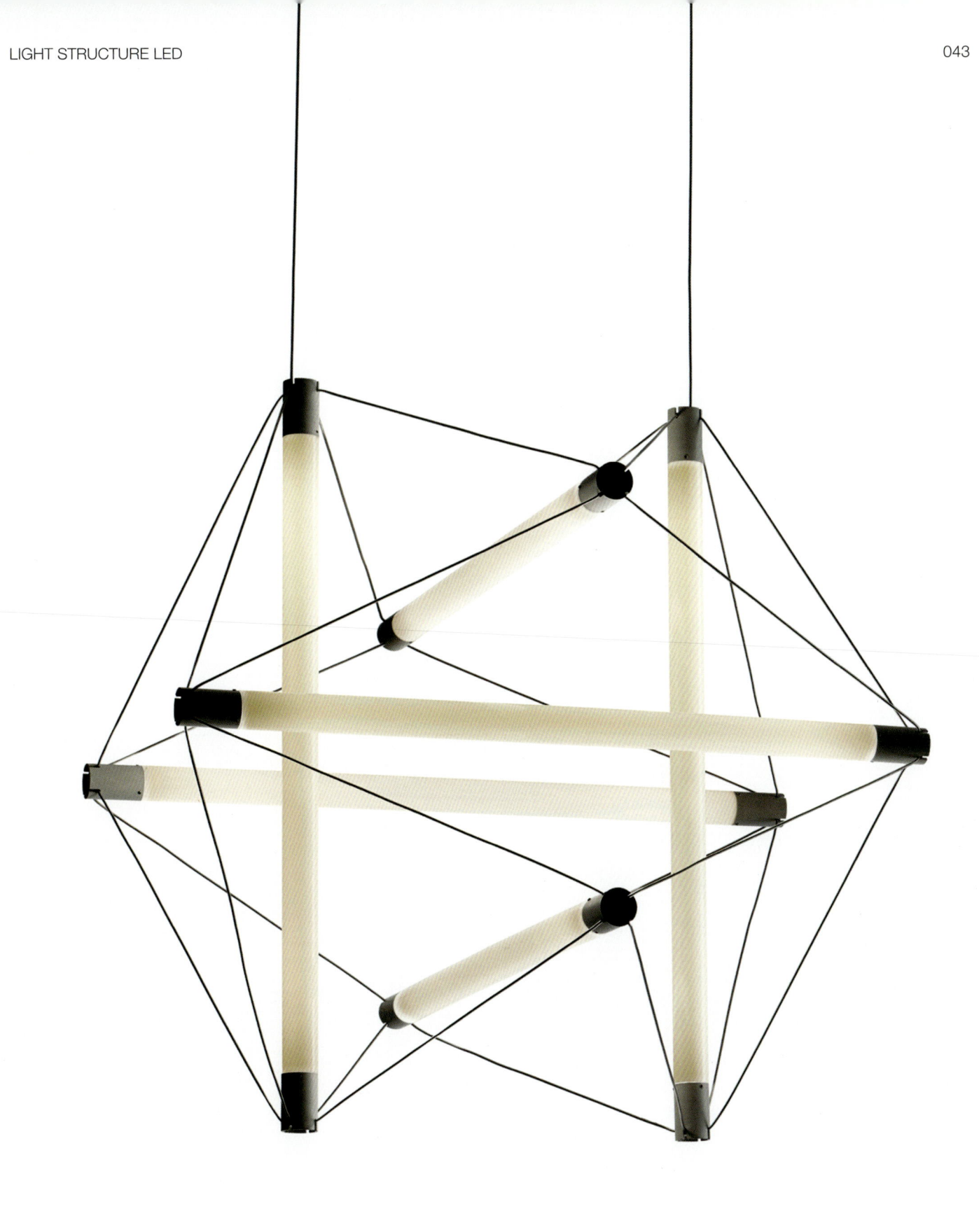

Schreibtischlampe
1972

Ingo Maurer
Hochglanzpoliertes
Chrom, Glas
Highly polished
chrome, glass

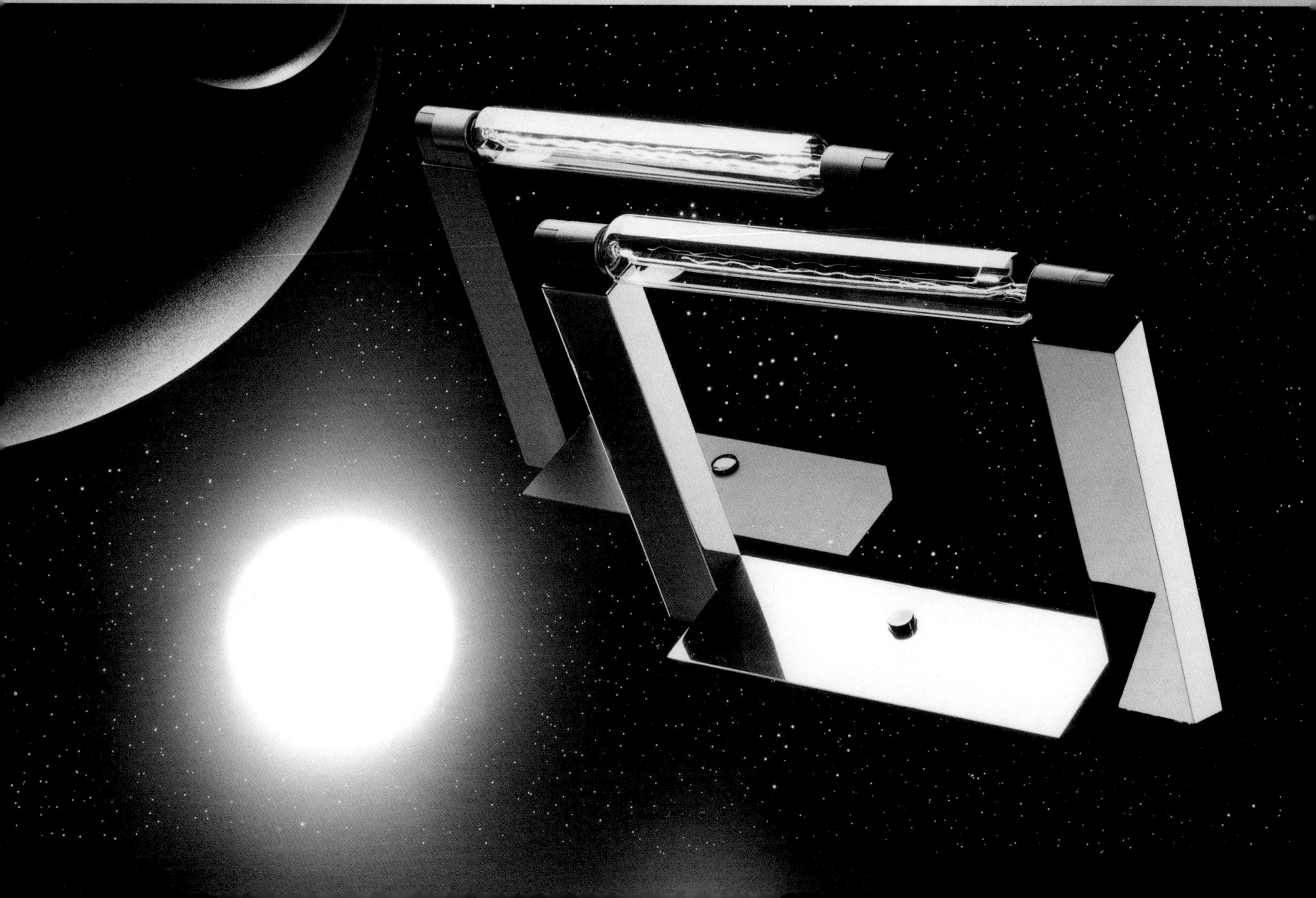

Thomas Alva Edison
1979

Ingo Maurer
Chrom, Glas
Chrome, glass

Lampampe
1980

Japanpapier,
Metall
Japanese paper,
metal

Floatation
1980

Japanpapier,
Metall
Japanese paper,
metal

Bibibibi
1982

Ingo Maurer
Porzellan, Metall,
Kunststoff
Porcelain, metal,
plastic

Ilios
1983

Ingo Maurer,
Franz Ringelhahn
Metall, Glas,
Kunststoff
Metal, glass,
plastic

YaYaHo
1984

Ingo Maurer + Team
Glas, Porzellan,
Metall, Kunststoff
Glass, porcelain,
metal, plastic

Fukushú
1984

Ingo Maurer
Metall, Kunststoff
Metal, plastic

Iló-Ilú
1986

Ingo Maurer + Team
Kunststoff, Glas
Plastic, glass

Tijuca
1986

Ingo Maurer + Team
Metall, Kunststoff
Metal, plastic

Don Quixote
1989

Ingo Maurer + Team
Stahl, Aluminium,
Kunststoff
Steel, aluminum,
plastic

One From The Heart
1989

Ingo Maurer
Metall, Spiegel,
Kunststoff
Metal, mirror, plastic

Golden Ribbon
1990

Ingo Maurer
Aluminium, Blattgold
Aluminum, gold leaf

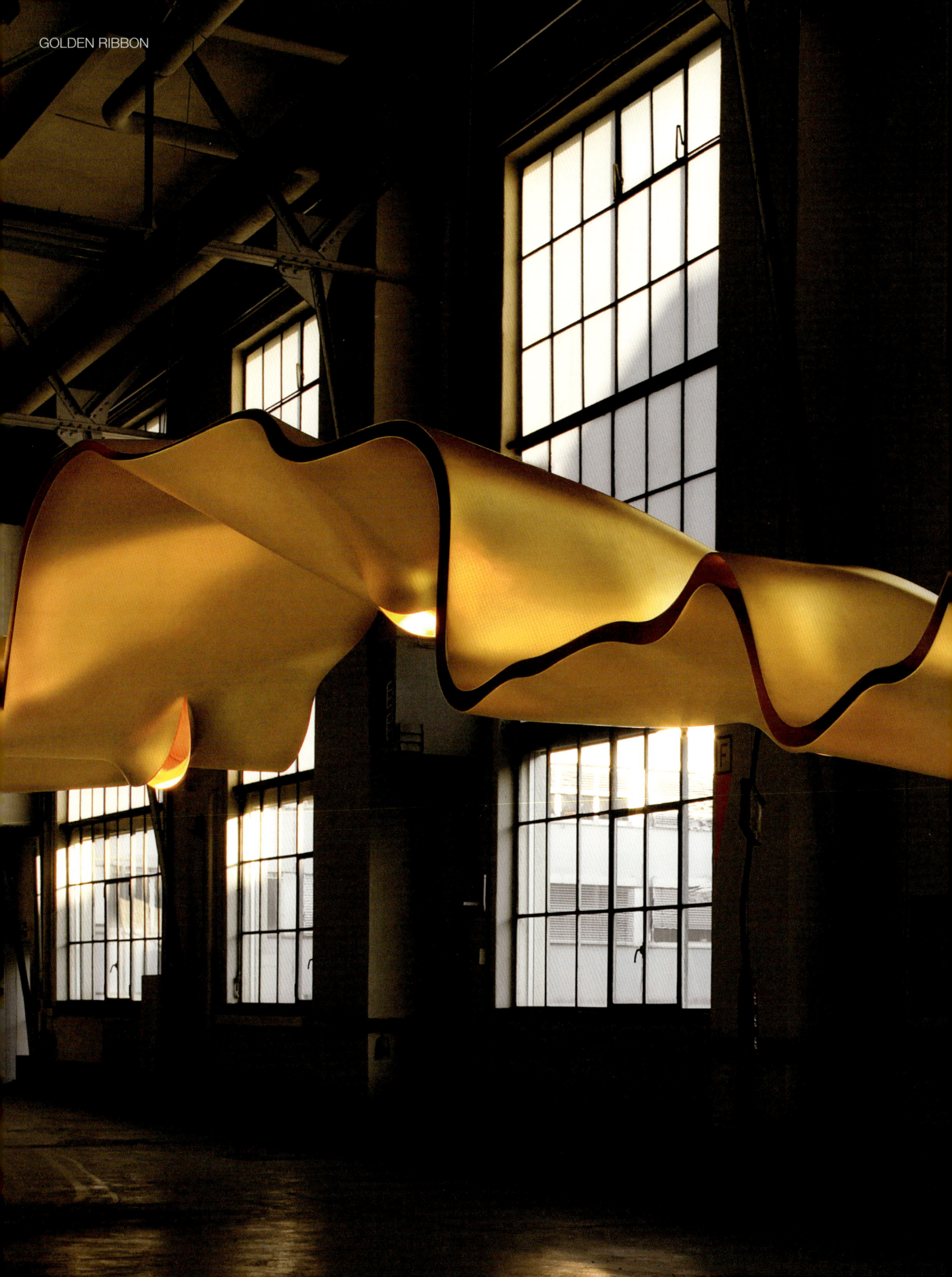

Lucellino T
1992

Ingo Maurer
Messing, Glas,
Kunststoff, Gänsefedern
Brass, glass, plastic,
goose feathers

Lucellino Wall
1992

Ingo Maurer
Messing, Glas,
Kunststoff, Gänsefedern
Brass, glass, plastic, goose feathers

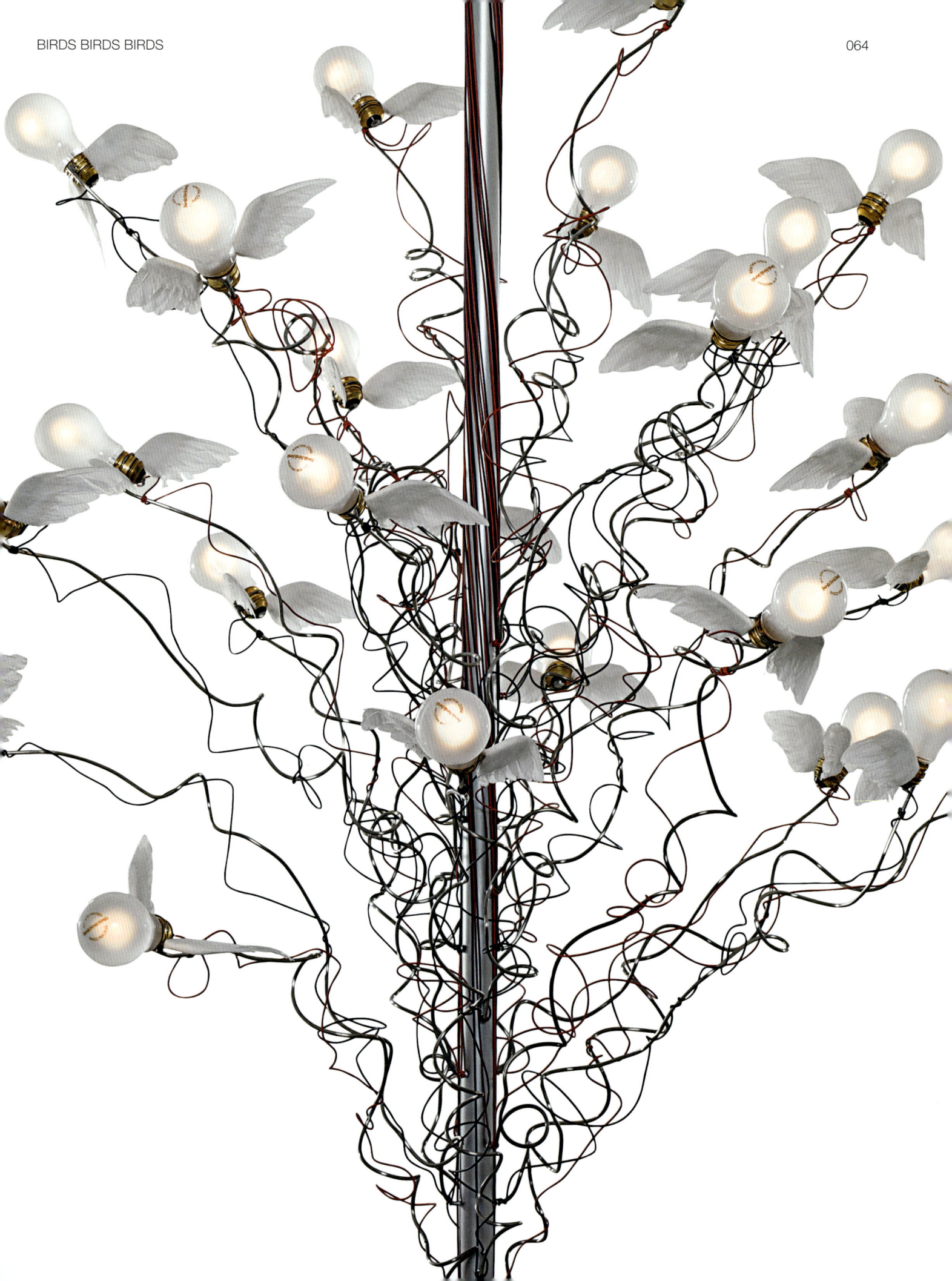

Birds Birds Birds
1992

Ingo Maurer
Niedervolt-Glühlampen,
Metall, Glas,
Gänsefedern
Low-voltage bulbs,
metal, glass,
goose feathers

Hot Achille
1994/2019

Ingo Maurer + Team
Edelstahl, Aluminium,
Kunststoff
Stainless steel,
aluminum, plastic

<u>Porca Miseria!</u>
1994

Ingo Maurer
Porzellan, Besteck,
Metall
Porcelain, silverware,
metal

L'Eclat Joyeux
1994/2005

Ingo Maurer + Team
Porzellan, Metall
Porcelaine, metal

Pierre ou Paul
1996

Ingo Maurer + Team
Aluminium, Edelstahl
Aluminum, stainless steel

Bernhard Dessecker
Die Poesie der Technologie / The Poetry of Technology

Für Ingo Maurer waren das Unbekannte, die Technik und das Potenzial, das dahinter steckt, immer etwas Positives, immer Inspirationsquelle und Herausforderung. Nie Selbstzweck. Er hat damit immer Neues kreiert und den Weg bereitet für viele andere.

Ein paar Monate vor seinem 50. Geburtstag sprach ich im August 1981 mit Ingo während der Frankfurter Herbstmesse. Er erzählte sehr begeistert davon, dass er in der zweiten Hälfte seines Lebens eine neue Tiefe, Qualität und auch technische Raffinesse in seine Entwürfe einbringen wolle. Dafür hatte er sich entschlossen, mit Designern und Ingenieuren zusammenzuarbeiten. So entstand die „Designerei". Ich war damals noch Student der Innenarchitektur, aber schon fasziniert von seiner Arbeit sowie von Licht und seinen unendlichen Möglichkeiten. Während ich noch in meinem ersten Job nach dem Studium bei Studio Morsa in New York arbeitete, fragte er mich, ob ich nach meiner Rückkehr in seinem Team mitarbeiten wolle. Ich war neugierig und sagte begeistert zu.

Das Abenteuer begann für mich im April 1984. Ingo war immer ein Pionier, und die neuen Grenzen, die auszuloten waren, schienen unendlich. Das Niedervoltsystem YAYAHO war die erste große technische Herausforderung für ihn und uns,

For Ingo Maurer, the unknown, technology and the potential it harbors, has always been something positive, always a source of inspiration and a challenge. Never was it an end in itself. He always used it to create something new, and in doing so paved the way for many others.

A few months before his 50th birthday, I spoke to Ingo in August 1981 at the Frankfurt Autumn Fair. He spoke with enthusiasm about how he wanted to bring a new depth, quality and also technical sophistication to his designs in the second half of his life. With this aim in mind, he decided to collaborate with designers and engineers. The result was the "Designerei". At the time, I was still a student of interior design, but was already fascinated by his work and by light and its endless possibilities. While I was still in my first job after my degree at Studio Morsa in New York, he asked me if I wanted to join his team when I returned home. I was curious and immediately agreed.

The adventure for me began in April 1984. Ingo was always a pioneer, and the new limits to be explored appeared endless. The YAYAHO low-voltage system was the first major technical challenge for both him and us, then still a small team of just four people. From today's perspective, everything seems so clear and simple, but at the time it was all new. There was virtually nothing to use except halogen lamps from car headlights, very expensive halogen cold-light reflector lamps for slide projectors, and bulky sockets.

das damals noch sehr kleine Team von vier Mitarbeitern. Aus heutiger Sicht sieht das alles so simpel und klar aus, aber damals war alles neu. Es gab fast nichts außer Halogenlampen aus Autoscheinwerfern, sehr teure Diaprojektor-Halogen-Kaltlichtspiegellampen und die sperrigen Fassungen dafür.

YAYAHO wurde ein Welterfolg und damit ging es erst richtig los. Ohne zu übertreiben: Es änderte die Welt der Beleuchtung, die Leuchtmittelindustrie und natürlich das Leben von Ingo und die Dynamik seiner Firma Design M, wie sie damals noch genannt wurde.

Ingo hatte seit 1982 sein Team, das ihm Technologien näherbrachte, verständlich machte und die Ideen umsetzte. Aber ist es nicht so, dass in den wenigsten Fällen etwas von nur einem Individuum erschaffen wird? Das ist ja eines der wichtigsten Alleinstellungsmerkmale des Menschen: die Fähigkeit zum Teamwork!

Ingo ist jedoch ganz klar derjenige, der meistens die Grundidee vorgibt, das Risiko trägt und die entsprechenden Entscheidungen treffen muss. Bis zum Tod seiner zweiten Frau Jenny Lau im Herbst 2014 tat er das immer in Abstimmung mit ihr.

Die nächste große Herausforderung in technologischer Hinsicht war das Niedervolt Trafodimmer System. Als der Elektroniker Hermann Kovacs Ingo Maurer wegen einer Zusammenarbeit ansprach, die etwas ganz anderes zum Gegenstand hatte, nahm das Gespräch plötzlich eine neue Richtung: Idee war ein Trafo für 12 V und Dimmen durch die Berührung jedes möglichen Strom leitenden Bestandteils der Leuchte. Bald kam Hermann mit einem rudimentären Prototyp und viel Enthusiasmus zurück. Was darauf folgte, waren Jahre der Entwicklung, tolle

YAYAHO became a global success and that's when things really took off. With no exaggeration, it changed the world of lighting, the lighting industry, and of course Ingo's life and the dynamism of his company Design M, as it was still called back then.

Ingo had assembled his team, which helped him with technologies, explaining them to him and implementing his ideas, back in 1982. Isn't it always the way, though, that only in the fewest of cases is something achieved by just one individual? This is indeed one of mankind's most important characteristics – the ability for teamwork!

Nevertheless, it goes without saying that Ingo is the person who generally comes up with the basic idea, who bears the risk, and who makes decisions accordingly. Up until the death of his second wife Jenny Lau in fall 2014, he always did so in consultation with her.

The next major challenge in terms of technology was the low-voltage transformer dimmer system. When the electrician Hermann Kovacs approached Ingo Maurer about a collaboration for something else entirely, the conversation suddenly took a different turn, and the pair got talking about a transformer for 12 V and dimming the potential conducting components of the light through touch. Hermann soon returned with a rudimentary prototype and bags of enthusiasm. What followed was years of development, great products, but also huge problems. Today it goes without saying that you can turn lights on and off and dim them through touch. Now, in the age of smartphones, you might even catch yourself accidentally attempting to

Produkte, aber auch riesige Probleme. Heute ist es so selbstverständlich, dass man Schalten und Dimmen kann, indem man etwas berührt. Heute, im Zeitalter von Smartphones, ertappt man sich vielleicht sogar dabei, ein analoges Bild anzufassen, um es zu vergrößern oder zu bearbeiten. Aber ich schreibe hier von 1986 und den folgenden Jahren. Auch durch Rückschläge und Probleme ließ sich Ingo als hoffnungsvoller Optimist nie davon abbringen, neue technische Errungenschaften zu erforschen. Tatsächlich ist es so, dass er das Potenzial für die gestalterischen und lichttechnischen Aspekte viel früher erkannte als die allermeisten Designer. In den späten 1980er-Jahren folgte eine ganze Reihe von Produkten aus der Familie der FINGERSPITZENLICHTMAGIE. Es waren oft technische Gratwanderungen, die leider nicht immer so funktionierten, wie wir es uns und der Kunde es sich wünschten. Das führte zu einer Reihe von elektronischen Weiterentwicklungen und Verbesserungen im Bereich der Niedervolt-Trafo-Sensor-Technik. Am Ende übernahm eine weit größere Firma die Technologie und zahlte Lizenzgebühren.

Und dann – Gottseidank möchte man rufen – gab es 1996 den Ausflug in die Welt der Holografie, der Dank der Zusammenarbeit zwischen dem kongenialen Hologrammspezialisten Eckhard Knuth und Ingo Maurer zu so wundervoll magischen und poetischen Lichtobjekten und Leuchten wie WO BIST DU, EDISON …? und HOLONZKI führte, die immer noch Teil der Ingo-Maurer-Kollektion sind und auf Messen und Ausstellungen Menschen jeden Alters immer zum Staunen und Lächeln bringen.

enlarge or edit an analog image. But I'm talking about 1986 and the years after that. Even through setbacks and problems Ingo, ever the hopeful optimist, never let himself be swayed from researching new technological achievements. In fact, he recognized the potential for the design-related and lighting-technology aspects far earlier than most of the designers. In the late 1980s there followed a whole series of products in the FINGERSPITZENLICHTMAGIE family. These often involved technical balancing acts that unfortunately didn't always work the way we and the customer wanted – nevertheless, this led to a series of further electronic developments and improvements in the area of low-voltage transformer sensor technology. Ultimately, a far larger company took over the technology and paid license fees.

And then – thank goodness, one might say – in 1996 came the foray into the world of holography which, thanks to the collaboration between the amiable hologram specialist Eckhard Knuth and Ingo Maurer, produced such wonderfully magical and poetic light objects and luminaires. These include WO BIST DU, EDISON …? and HOLONZKI, which are still part of the Ingo Maurer collection and have people of all ages smiling in amazement at trade shows and exhibitions.

LED
When LED technology first appeared on the horizon and initially very expensive but also very different modules came about, once again it was Ingo Maurer who made this futuristic aesthetic visible and used the necessary plates as design elements. Hence in 1997

LED

Als am Horizont die LED-Technologie erschien und erste, sehr teure, aber auch sehr andersartige Module auftauchten, war es wieder Ingo Maurer, der diese futuristische Ästhetik sichtbar machte und die notwendigen Platinen als gestalterische Elemente verwendete. So entstand 1997 BELLISSIMA BRUTTA, mehr ein Statement zu LED als eine „Lampe". Sehr humorvoll, schräg und für viele Menschen eine Provokation – im besten Fall. Viele Menschen verstanden damals überhaupt noch nicht, was LED überhaupt ist, geschweige denn das Potenzial, das mit dieser Technologie verbunden war.

Durch seine früheren Arbeiten war Ingo Maurer bekannt für seine Offenheit gegenüber neuen Abenteuern, sein Ausloten und Überwinden von Grenzen. Deshalb kontaktierten viele Firmen die Firma Ingo Maurer oder sprachen ihn oder seine Mitarbeiter*innen an und boten eine Kooperation an, kamen mit vorher nie gesehenen Mustern vorbei und inspirierten so Ingo und sein Team. Denn sie wussten, dass die Ergebnisse in Form von Lichtobjekten und neuartigen Leuchten immer viel Publicity und Aufmerksamkeit bei der Presse, der Fachwelt und den aufgeschlossenen Kunden bedeuten. Darüber wird später noch in Bezug auf OLED zu reden sein.

Es war eine aufregende, faszinierende und interessante Zeit. *New frontiers* aller Orten, scheinbar unendliche gestalterische Möglichkeiten breiteten sich vor dem geistigen Auge Ingos aus. Ich für meinen Teil konnte manchmal nicht mithalten und war fasziniert von seiner Vorstellungskraft und der Energie, die in ihm deutlich spürbar überzukochen drohte.

came BELLISSIMA BRUTTA, more a statement on LED than a lamp as such. Very humorous, sharply angled, and for many people a provocation – in the best case. Back then, many people simply didn't understand what LED even was, let alone the potential associated with this technology.

From his earlier works, Ingo Maurer was known for his openness towards new adventures, his exploration and his pushing of boundaries. It was for this reason that many companies contacted Ingo Maurer, approached him or one of his employees about a collaboration, or came along with never-before-seen samples to inspire Ingo and his team. After all, they knew that the results in the form of light objects and new kinds of lamps always meant a great deal of publicity and attention in the press, industry circles, and receptive customers. There will be more to say on this later in relation to OLED.

It was an exciting, fascinating and interesting time. New frontiers in all areas and apparently endless design possibilities stretched out before Ingo's hungry eyes. For my part, I was sometimes unable to keep up and was fascinated by his vision and the energy that very noticeably threatened to boil over.

But let's stay with LED technology for now. After the first statement of BELLISSIMA BRUTTA, further works followed that took the theme of LED and plates into new dimensions. Provocations like the chandelier YOOHOODOO in 1999, in which Ingo quoted the words from the Gabriel García Márquez novel "Love in the Time of Cholera": "El mundo está dividido entre los que cagan bien y

Aber bleiben wir bei der LED-Technologie. Nach dem ersten Statement der BELLISSIMA BRUTTA folgten weitere Arbeiten, die das Thema LED und Platinen in neue Dimensionen erweiterte. Provokationen wie der Lüster YOOHOODOO im Jahr 1999, in dem Ingo die Worte aus dem Roman „Liebe in Zeiten der Cholera" von Gabriel García Márquez zitierte: „El mundo está dividido entre los que cagan bien y los que cagan mal". Aber auch eine Arbeits- und Tischleuchte mit dem programmatischen Namen EL.E.DEE, reduziert auf das bare Minimum und mit integrierter Dimmfunktion, kam 2001 in damals limitierter Auflage auf den Markt. Die Edition war bald vergriffen. Inzwischen gibt es eine aktualisierte, neue Version in Serie.

Es begann das Spiel mit der LED-Technologie. Platinen in verschiedenen Formen und Farben, mit Glühlampenmotiv (immer noch Ingos Lieblingslichtquelle) und freien Formen von LED, die sämtliche bisherigen Dimensionen sprengten und ganze Räume einnahmen. WIZ WIZARD zum Beispiel war ein 2005 präsentiertes System, das aus einer zwischen zwei Wänden gespannten flexiblen Leiterbahn bestand, an der alle möglichen Elemente, Kombinationen von LED- und Halogen-lichtelementen angebracht werden konnten. Der Clou war ein in das System integriertes LED-Panel, auf dem man per SMS-Nachricht Botschaften aufleuchten lassen konnte. Es entstanden grandiose Einzelstücke und Installationen. Um nur ein paar zu nennen: die ironisch-subversive Anspielung auf die Seidentapete im großbürgerlichen Heim (ROSE, ROSE ON THE WALL ...), der fliegende LED-Teppich 1001 LIGHTS, entstanden als eine Projektleuchte für einen offenen Geist (mit dickem

los que cagan mal". But there was also a desk and table lamp with a name that said it all, EL.E.DEE, which was reduced to a bare minimum and boasted the integrated dimming function, launching on the market as a limited edition in 2001. The edition soon sold out completely. Now there is a new, updated version in series production.

Thus, we began to "play" with LED technology. Plates in various forms and colors with bulb motifs (always Ingo's favorite light source) and free forms of LED that blew apart all the dimensions that had preceded them and occupied entire rooms. WIZ WIZARD, for example, was a system we presented in 2005, which consisted of a flexible conductor path stretched between two walls, to which all possible elements, combinations of LED and halogen light elements, could be attached. The kicker here lay in the LED panel that was in-tegrated into the system, on which users could have SMS messages displayed in lights. Superb individual pieces and installations were created. To name but a few: the ironically subversive play on the silk wall coverings in stately homes (ROSE, ROSE ON THE WALL...), the flying LED carpet 1001 LIGHTS that developed as a project luminaire for an open-minded soul (with a healthy bank account) or LICHT.ENSTEIN, a lamp that combined LED plates and the bulb motif as a lampshade with halogen.

These and many other creations are testament to a creative freedom, unbridled fantasy, humor, courage, farsightedness and non-conformism.

Bankkonto) oder LICHT.ENSTEIN, eine Leuchte, in der LED-Platinen mit Glühlampen-motiv als Lampenschirm mit Halogen kombiniert wurden.

Diese und viele andere Kreationen zeugen von gestalterischer Freiheit, unbändi-ger Fantasie, Humor, Mut, Weitsicht und Nonkonformismus.

Ein Bestseller in der Kollektion ist seit der Präsentation 2013 die Platinenlampe FLYING FLAMES, ein Spiel mit LED-Technologie und dem digitalisierten Kerzenlicht, das in Zusammenarbeit mit und auf einer Idee von Moritz Waldemeyer basierend entstanden ist. – Apropos Leichtigkeit: Extrem faszinierend war die einzigartige Technologie von POWER GLASS, bei der eine transparente Schicht die Leitung des Stroms übernimmt. LED sitzen ohne sichtbare Leiter miteinander verbunden auf klarem Glas und leuchten. Was für eine wundervolle Technik! STARDUST war der erste Prototyp, der 2001 mit dieser Technologie auf der Euroluce in Mailand gezeigt wurde. In Kollaboration mit der Firma Glas Platz hat Ingo Maurer eine Reihe atemberaubender Möbel sowie einen Lüster entworfen und auch größere Projekte an verschiedenen Plätzen der Welt realisiert.

Und dann war da noch das LED-WALLPAPER. Eine leuchtende Tapete, die in Zusammenarbeit mit dem Entwickler und Ingenieur Hans Layer zustande kam. Hier waren die beiden ihrer Zeit klar voraus. Obwohl wir im Team ein serienreifes Produkt entwickelten, scheiterte es dann an dem Vertrieb des vielseitig nutzbaren und faszinierenden Wandbelags. Es wurden einige Projekte damit realisiert, aber die Zusammenarbeit mit einem marktführenden Tapetenhersteller blieb trotz großer Anstrengungen beider Seiten ohne den gewünschten Erfolg.

A bestseller in the collection since its presentation in 2013 has been the plate lamp FLYING FLAMES, a play on LED technology and the digitized candlelight that developed in cooperation with and based on an idea by Moritz Waldemeyer.

On the subject of lightness: A particularly fascinating develop-ment was the unique technology of POWER GLASS, in which a transparent layer conducts the electricity. LEDs sit alongside one another on clear glass, emitting light with no visible conductor. What magnificent technology! STARDUST was the first prototype to be exhibited with this technology, launching at Euroluce in Milan in 2001. In cooperation with the company Glas Platz, Ingo Maurer also designed a series of breathtaking furniture and a chandelier, as well as larger projects in different sites around the world.

And then there was also the LED WALLPAPER, a wall covering that incorporated illumination, developed in cooperation with the developer and engineer Hans Layer. Here, the pair were clearly ahead of their time. Although we were developing a series-ready product within the team, sales of this versatile and fascinating wall covering failed. It was used in a few projects, but the collaboration with a market-leading wallpaper manufacturer did not achieve the desired successes, despite great efforts on both sides.

After the total victory of LED over bulbs, the unpopular energy-saving lamps, fluorescent tubes and halogen lamps, qualities like fantasy, freedom of design, non-conformism and the focus on light quality in the lighting and illumination market regrettably became

Nach dem totalen Siegeszug der LED über die Glühlampe, die ungeliebte Energiesparlampe, die Leuchtstoffröhre und auch über die Halogenlampe sind Eigenschaften wie Fantasie, gestalterische Freiheit, Nonkonformismus und der Schwerpunkt Lichtqualität im Leuchten- und Beleuchtungsmarkt im Zuge der Kommerzialisierung der LED bedauerlicherweise größtenteils verloren gegangen. Wie schon im Kielwasser der YAYAHO unendlich viele und auch unsägliche, nach-äffende Entwürfe und banale Kopien entstanden, so hat sich auch in der Welt der LED eine klare, zurechtgestutzte Designsprache breitgemacht, der nur ein paar mutige und innovative Designer bzw. Produzenten entfliehen, die die technischen Möglichkeiten auf eine höhere Ebene bringen. Die Qualität der Beleuchtung hat sich im Allgemeinen nicht wirklich verbessert. Aber die Halbleiterindustrie hat sehr hart daran gearbeitet, das Lichtspektrum und die Effizienz der LED zu verbessern. Das Image und die technischen Merkmale der LED sind nun deutlich besser. In den Anfängen der Nutzung für Beleuchtung wurde die LED wegen ihrer Kälte – zu Recht oder zu Unrecht, das hängt auch von der geografischen Position ab – viel gescholten und von den meisten abgelehnt. Heute geht an LED-Licht kein Weg mehr vorbei.

OLED

Im Jahr 2005 sprach mich mein Freund Christian Gärtner an. Ein guter Bekannter von ihm arbeitete bei dem Chemiekonzern Merck an einer neuartigen Lichtquelle, genannt OLED (Organic Light-Emitting Diode). Ob Ingo sich vorstellen könne, damit

lost to a great extent during the course of the commercialization of LEDs. As previously in the wake of the YAYAHO, endless and even unspeakable imitation designs and banal copies emerged, hence in the world of LED too, a clear, veritably curtailed design language spread, which only a few brave and innovative designers/producers moved away from, taking the technical possibilities to new heights. In general, the quality of lighting did not really improve. Nevertheless, the semiconductor industry worked very hard on improving the light spectrum and the efficiency of LEDs. The image and the technical characteristics of the LED have now notably improved. When it first came into use for lighting purposes, the coldness of the LED meant that – rightly or wrongly and partly depending on the geographic position – it was much maligned and rejected by many. These days, lighting without LEDs is unthinkable.

OLED

In 2005 I was approached by my friend Christian Gärtner. Someone he knew at the chemical company Merck was working on a new light source, dubbed OLED (organic light-emitting diode). He wondered whether or not Ingo could imagine himself designing something with this that would generate attention and positive publicity internationally. He showed me a yellow-lit piece of glass the size of a slide, and I knew Ingo well enough to say "yes" immediately. This thin, glowing glass square was technically fascinating and unbelievably inspiring in aesthetic terms. This happens when

etwas zu entwerfen, was Aufmerksamkeit und international positive Publicity kreieren würde? Er zeigte mir ein gelb leuchtendes Stück Glas der Größe eines Dias. Ich kannte Ingo gut genug, um sofort „Ja" zu sagen. Dieses dünne, leuchtende, gläserne Quadrat war technisch faszinierend und ästhetisch unglaublich reizvoll. Das passiert, wenn Ingenieure so in ihre Arbeit vertieft sind, dass sie sich nicht um die Gestaltung scheren, sondern nur entsprechend der technischen Zwänge entwickeln. Bald darauf fuhren Ingo und ich nach Darmstadt und besuchten mit Christian das OLED-Labor von Merck. Wir fanden Reinräume, Hightech vom Feinsten und eine Gruppe von unglaublich engagierten Ingenieuren vor, die voller Stolz ihre Entwicklung präsentierten und extrem aufgeschlossen waren für Ideen, die ihr „Baby" in einen neuen Kontext setzen und der Welt zeigen würden, was OLED alles kann. Der Zeitrahmen war sehr knapp, denn die nächste Gelegenheit war nur vier Monate entfernt.

Das Ergebnis dieser einmalig guten Zusammenarbeit war FLYING FUTURE. Der Name war Programm und ich kann mit Bestimmtheit und auch Stolz sagen, dass es später kein OLED-Lichtobjekt gab, das diese Lässigkeit, Leichtigkeit und Faszination zu gleichen Teilen in sich vereinte. Es zelebrierte nicht die technische Komplexität des Materials, sondern tat im Gegenteil so, als wäre es das Einfachste der Welt, ein paar hauchdünne Glasmodule zusammenzufügen zu einem fliegenden Lichtteppich und damit eine Weltneuheit zu präsentieren.

In Wirklichkeit war alles mit heißer Nadel gestrickt, sehr kompliziert und hochsensibel, aber das wussten nur die Ingenieure von Merck und wir vom Team.

engineers are so engrossed in their work that they pay less heed to the design and rather develop technology according to possibility. Soon after Ingo and I travelled to Darmstadt to visit Merck's OLED laboratory with Christian. There, we found cleanrooms, technology of the highest order, and a group of unbelievably committed engineers, who presented their developments with great pride and were clearly tremendously open to ideas for placing their "baby" in a new context and showing the world what OLED could do. The timeframes were very tight, however, because the next opportunity was just four months away.

The result of this uniquely wonderful collaboration was FLYING FUTURE. The name says it all, and I am able to say with great certainty and pride that no other subsequent OLED light object combined informality, lightness and fascination to the same extent. Rather than celebrate the technical complexity of the materials, it did the opposite, as if it was the easiest thing in the world to merge a few paper-thin glass modules to create a flying light carpet and thus present a global innovation.

In reality, it was all very complicated and highly sensitive, and the work had been done under pressure, but only the engineers at Merck and we in our team were aware of this. I believe even Ingo himself was not entirely aware of everything that was going on behind the scenes, or that during the last few weeks before the presentation the Merck engineers were working around the clock on the highly sensitive modules in order to be able to deliver

Ich glaube, selbst Ingo war sich nicht ganz bewusst, was da alles hinter den Kulissen ablief und dass bei Merck in den letzten Wochen vor der Präsentation 24 Stunden am Tag an den hochempfindlichen Modulen gearbeitet wurde, um die gewünschte Menge liefern zu können. Der Ausschuss war enorm hoch. In der Zwischenzeit entwickelten wir in München mit Dummies die gestalterischen und technischen Rahmenbedingungen für die „Fliegende Zukunft".

Die Präsentation war ein voller Erfolg. Merck gab sein Know-how danach an Osram weiter, und im Verlauf der nächsten Jahre arbeiteten wir gemeinsam mit der OLED-Abteilung von Osram und anderen Firmen an einigen weiteren Lichtobjekten.

Erwähnen möchte ich hier noch das erste Serienprodukt einer OLED-Leuchte, wenn auch nur in einer Edition von 25 Stück aufgelegt: Es handelt sich um die Arbeits- und Tischleuchte mit dem Namen EARLY FUTURE, die 2008 präsentiert wurde. Sie bestand aus 10 OLED-Modulen, die individuell drehbar waren und in zwei Reihen von fünf Leuchtelementen angeordnet waren. Als Ingo Maurer zu einem OLED-Kongress nach Boston eingeladen wurde, schickte er mich mit EARLY FUTURE dorthin. Ich muss heute noch schmunzeln, wenn ich an die Gesichter der Ingenieure aus aller Welt denke, die wie kleine Kinder um den Weihnachtsbaum um diese Leuchte standen und sie bestaunten, als hätten sie noch nie eine OLED gesehen.

2014 hat Ingo Maurer wieder ein wegweisendes OLED-Objekt (WHISPER WIND) gezeigt, diesmal in Zusammenarbeit mit der Firma Konica Minolta. Hierbei wurden flexible OLED, eine weitere technische Herausforderung, verwendet. Im kommerziellen Sektor hat die OLED als Lichtquelle jedoch bisher (noch) nicht die Dynamik

the quantity required. The reject rate was extremely high. In the meantime, in Munich we were working with dummies to develop the design and technical framework conditions for FLYING FUTURE.

The presentation was a resounding success. Merck then passed on its expertise to Osram, and over the course of the next few years we worked together with the OLED department at Osram and other companies on our own further light objects. Here, I would just like to mention the first series OLED light product, albeit one that was produced only in limited editions of 25. It was a desk and table lamp with the name EARLY FUTURE and was presented in 2008.

It consists of 10 OLED modules that could be turned individually and were arranged in two rows of five light elements. When Ingo Maurer was invited to an OLED conference in Boston, he told me to go instead and to take EARLY FUTURE with me. Even today, I can't help but chuckle when I remember all the faces of the engineers from all over the world, who stood before these lights like children around a Christmas tree and marveled as if they had never seen an OLED.

In 2014 Ingo Maurer exhibited a pioneering OLED object once again (WHISPER WIND), this time in cooperation with Konica-Minolta. This involved the use of flexible OLEDs, a further technical development. Within the commercial sector, however, OLEDs had previously not (yet) been able to achieve the dynamism of the LED. In the area of LEDs too, there were ever new, interesting developments that Ingo Maurer made use of. Hence, for example, a transparent and

der LED erreichen können. Auch im Bereich LED gibt es immer wieder neue, interessante Entwicklungen, die sich Ingo Maurer zu Nutze macht. So zum Beispiel eine transparente und flexible Folie, bestückt mit einer Vielzahl von LED, die in ein Lichtobjekt mit dem poetischen Namen „Tautropfen" mündete – quasi schwebendes Licht.

Und diese Leichtigkeit ist es, die die Arbeit von Ingo Maurer ausmacht: Er brachte immer schon selbst hartgesottene Kunden, die sonst keine Miene verziehen, zum Schmunzeln oder Lachen. Und ich denke da nicht nur an den Umgang mit Technologie, sondern auch an frühe Messestände, zum Beispiel auf der Frankfurter Messe mit seinem „quietschenden Obst" (*Tutti Frutti*) oder an die Präsentation der Leuchte BIBIBIBI mit Hühnergegackere vom Band im Hintergrund.

Er nimmt sich nicht zu ernst, wollte und will immer Spaß haben beim Entwerfen, beim Entwickeln und auch beim Verkaufen. Dieses Vergnügen soll auch den Mitmenschen zuteilwerden, egal, ob sie die Leuchten nur ansehen oder auch besitzen und benutzen.

Gutes Licht macht glücklich, Ingo Maurers Kreationen machen glücklicher!

flexible film bedecked with an array of LEDs eventually became a light object with the poetic name DEW DROPS. Here, the light virtually floated.

And it's this lightness that defines the work by Ingo Maurer: Time and again, he'd have even seasoned purchasers who otherwise remained straight-faced grinning or laughing out loud. And here I'm not referring only to how he dealt with technology, but also to his early trade show stands, for example at the Frankfurt Fair with "squeaky fruit" (*Tutti frutti*), or at the presentation of the BIBIBIBI lamp with the clucking of hens from the band in the background.

Ingo Maurer never takes himself too seriously; he wanted and will always want to have fun with the design and development process and even the selling. This enjoyment is something he aims to spread to those around him, regardless of whether they are just looking at lamps or also owning and using them.

Good lighting makes you happy, Ingo Maurer's creations make you happier!

BERNHARD DESSECKER
(GEB. 1961, MÜNCHEN)
arbeitet als Innenarchitekt und Designer. Er ist seit den frühen 1980er-Jahren beruflich und privat eng mit Ingo Maurer verbunden. Seit 2014 lebt und arbeitet er in Deutschland und den USA.

BERNHARD DESSECKER
(BORN 1961, MUNICH)
works as an interior architect and designer. He has maintained close professional and personal links with Ingo Maurer since the early 1980s. Since 2014 he has lived and worked in Germany and the USA.

Xenia Riemann-Tyroller
BangBoom! Produktnamen bei Ingo Maurer / BangBoom! The Names of Ingo Maurer's Products

Ingo Maurers „Lampen" – er bevorzugt selbst das Wort Lampe für seine Leuchten[1] – und Installationen haben nicht irgendwelche Namen. Sie sind Beschreibungen, die den Charakter der Leuchten und Installationen wiedergeben, die auf die Entstehungsgeschichte oder das Material Bezug nehmen, die wie die besonderen und außergewöhnlichen Entwürfe ebenso besonders und außergewöhnlich sind. Namen, die eine gewisse Zuneigung zum eigenen Entwurf, die Humor und Esprit spiegeln. Sie sind inspiriert von Filmen, Musik, Geräuschen, Menschen oder Märchen. Es sind Namen, die mit ihrem Namensinhaber eine unzertrennliche Symbiose eingehen. Sie sind erfunden, zusammengesetzt, lautmalerisch, künstlich und aus verschiedenen Sprachen gewonnen. Ingo Maurer hat ein Faible für fremde Sprachen, aber er meinte nur lapidar dazu, „Mehrsprachigkeit wäre einfach notwendig, da er seine Entwürfe international anbiete."[2]

Da Maurer seine Leuchten selber herstellt, liegt auch die Produktbenennung in seiner Hand. Hier ein paar Beispiele von Namensgeschichten, die überliefert sind:

Die BULB (1966) spricht auf Englisch aus, was die Leuchte ist: eine Glühbirne. Maurer zitiert mit seiner ersten Leuchte das Leuchtmittel, das für Licht steht. Die Kraft dieser Metapher setzte erstmals Peter Behrens zu Beginn des 20. Jahrhunderts

Ingo Maurer's "lamps" (Maurer himself prefers the word lamp for his luminaires[1]) and installations are not just given any old names. They are descriptions that reveal the character of the luminaires and installations, that reference their genesis, or the materials used, and which, like the special and extraordinary designs, are likewise special and extraordinary. The names reflect a certain affinity with the design, humor and esprit. They are inspired by movies, music, sounds, people, and fairytales. They are names that enter into an inseparable symbiosis with the relevant object. They are invented, compiled, onomatopoetic, artificial, and derived from several languages. Ingo Maurer has a soft spot for foreign languages, but in that context all he had to say was that multilingualism was just a necessity because his designs were marketed globally.[2]

Given that Ingo Maurer produces his luminaires himself, it is up to him to name his products. Here are just a few examples of the story behind the name: BULB (1966) says it all. The luminaire is precisely that. With his very first luminaire Ingo Maurer referenced the illuminant that stands for light. Peter Behrens first used the power of these metaphors in the early 20th century for a new image for the company AEG, (fig. 1) thereby modernizing the perception of light in line with the new era of electrification, and replacing the almost bare torch allegory that had been standard until then. 50 years later, Maurer had just got back from several years in the USA, where he had encountered American Pop Art, liberated the bulb from its proportions and its servile character, and put it on a pedestal.

als neues Bild für die AEG ein (Abb. 1) und modernisierte damit die Wahrnehmung des neuen Zeitalters der Elektrifizierung – er löste damit die bis dahin übliche, fast unbekleidete Frauengestalt mit Fackel als Allegorie des Lichts ab. Ein halbes Jahrhundert später, Maurer war während seines mehrjährigen Aufenthalts in den USA der amerikanischen Pop Art begegnet, befreit er die Glühbirne von ihren Proportionen und ihrem dienenden Charakter und stellt sie auf den Sockel.

BIBIBIBI (1982) wurde inspiriert von einem übrig gebliebenen Kunststoffpaar roter Storchenbeine, die Maurer einem Supermarkt entwendete, nachdem er sie als Einzelteile nicht kaufen konnte. Die Vogel-Leuchte mit dem Federkopf macht zwar kein tierisches Geräusch, dafür das laute Wiedergeben des Namens.[3] Ähnlich verhält es sich mit der MOZZKITO (1996) oder auch mit dem aus der Comic-Sprache entliehenen ÖFF ÖFF (1996).

Seine Herz-Leuchte ONE FROM THE HEART (1989) ist inspiriert vom gleich-namigen Musicalfilm Francis Ford Coppolas von 1982, in dem sich ein Liebespaar trennt und findet, begleitet von blinkender und bunter Neon-Reklame der Enter-tainment-Stadt Las Vegas.[4] Dieser strahlende Ort ist ebenfalls für eine spätere Leuchte Namensgeber: LIVING VEGAS (2007), bestehend aus den Neonröhren für

BIBIBIBI (1982) was inspired by a leftover pair of red plastic stork legs which Maurer, not having been able to buy them separately, stole from a supermarket. Though the bird-shaped luminaire with a feather head does not make an animal noise, the loud rendition of its name certainly does.[3] The situation is similar in the case of MOZZKITO (1996), and ÖFF ÖFF (1996), which is derived from the language used in comics.

His heart-shaped luminaire ONE FROM THE HEART (1989) was inspired by Francis Ford Coppola's 1982 musical film, in which a pair of lovers break up and get back together, accompanied by the bright, flashing neon advertising of the capital of entertainment, Las Vegas.[4] This dazzling place also provides the name for a later luminaire: LIVING VEGAS (2007), comprising the neon tubes for American license plates, which Maurer had stocked himself up with by the boxload in New York.

To a symmetrical ceiling luminaire made of aluminum discs and which from the side looks like the footprint of the Temple of Hatshepsut in Luxor, Ingo Maurer added a note that read "The name of an Egyptian girl I know."[5] The luminaire and girl are both called OH MEI MA WEISS (2005).

It was on Haiti in 1980 that Maurer came up with the idea for the YAYAHO (1984) light system, the first low-voltage halogen system of its kind, which features taut wire cables from which delicate, tech-noid-looking tiny lamps are suspended. He had seen open electrici-ty cables there, onto which wired lightbulbs had been soldered.

1
Peter Behrens
Werbegrafik / Advertising brochure, 1907
AEG, Berlin
Foto / Photo: Tilmann Buddensieg (Hg.): Industriekultur.
Peter Behrens und die AEG, 1907–1914. Berlin 1979, S. D 221.

2
Hartmut Voigt
Varolux automatic, 1986
VEB Meßgerätewerk „Erich Wienert",
Magdeburg
Foto / Photo: Die Neue Sammlung
(Alexander Laurenzo)

3
Achille Castiglioni, Pier Giacomo
Castiglioni
Snoopy, 1967
Flos, Bovezzo
Foto / Photo: Die Neue Sammlung
(Alexander Laurenzo)

amerikanische *license plates* (KFZ-Kennzeichen), die Maurer auf Vorrat karton-
weise in New York aufgekauft hatte.

Über die symmetrisch aus Aluminiumscheiben aufgebaute Deckenleuchte,
die von der Seite aussieht wie der Grundriss des Hatschepsut-Tempels in Luxor,
notierte Ingo Maurer „The name of an Egyptian girl I know."[5] Leuchte und Mädchen
heißen beide OH MEI MA WEISS (2005).

Die Idee für das Lichtsystem YAYAHO (1984), das erste Niedervolt-Halogen-
System seiner Art, mit seinen gespannten Drahtseilen und davon abgehängten,
grazilen und technoid wirkenden Lämpchen, hatte Maurer 1980 auf Haiti. Er sah
dort offen verlaufende Stromkabel, an denen ungefasste Glühbirnen angelötet
waren. YAYAHO klingt weniger kreolisch als asiatisch, wurde jedoch von einem
„Ja, ja, so" abgeleitet, das er auf die Frage, wie das System nun heißen solle,
so dahingesagt hatte.[6]

Die leuchtende Porzellanexplosion PORCA MISERIA! (1994) war ursprünglich
nach dem Film *Zabriskie Point* (1970) benannt, einer Hommage an die Hippie-
Bewegung von Michelangelo Antonioni. Das Filmende zeigt mehrere Explosions-
sequenzen u. a. einer avantgardistischen Villa, einer idyllischen Strandszene
oder eines Kleiderschrankes. In *slow motion* erstarren die Einzelteile zu eigen-
ständigen Skulpturen. Zur Leuchtenmesse Euroluce 1994 wurde der Lüster
erstmals vorgestellt. Ein italienischer Gast ließ sich beim Anblick der auseinander-
fliegenden Geschirrscherben zum Ausruf verleiten: „Porca Miseria! Che fantastico,
Ingo! Tu sei pazzo, geniale!"[7]. Die Leuchte wurde umbenannt.

YAYAHO sounds more Asian than Creole, but was derived from the
words "Ja, ja, so" he had spoken when asked what the system was
going to be called.[6]

The luminous porcelain explosion PORCA MISERIA! (1994) was
originally named after Michelangelo Antonioni's movie *Zabriskie
Point* (1970), a homage to the hippie movement. At the end of the
movie, there are several explosion sequences, including one of an
avant-garde villa, an idyllic beach scene, and a wardrobe. In slow
motion the individual parts solidify as sculptures in their own right.
The chandelier was first presented at the 1994 Euroluce fair. At the
sight of the broken pieces of crockery an Italian guest exclaimed:
"Porca Miseria! Che fantastico, Ingo! Tu sei pazzo, geniale!"[7]. The
luminaire was renamed.

"To a certain extent the name can be compared to wrapping
paper: additional attention, a fortunate find, poetic flavoring. It opens
the door to communication".[8] Ingo Maurer creates names highly
intuitively and through them communicates the special nature of his
company. And the question arises whether with his word creations
Maurer is unique and with them has ushered in a new era of product
names.

Name researchers, who only became interested in product
names as a subject in the 1970s, discern a trend towards proper
names for products as of 1945. Geographic names of cities, rivers,
and islands were extremely widespread. Female given names were,
and indeed still are, even more common. We associate harmony and

„Der Name ist in gewisser Weise mit Geschenkpapier zu vergleichen: eine zusätzliche Aufmerksamkeit, ein glücklicher Fund, ein poetischer Beigeschmack. Er ist die Eintrittskarte für die Kommunikation."[8] Ingo Maurer kreiert sehr intuitiv Namen und kommuniziert mit ihnen die Besonderheit seiner Firma. Und es stellt sich die Frage, ob Maurer mit seinen Wortkreationen einzigartig ist oder damit eine neue Ära von Produktnamen eingeläutet hat.

Die Namensforscher, die sich erst in den 1970er-Jahren wissenschaftlich für Warennamen zu interessieren beginnen, sehen nach 1945 in beiden deutschen Staaten weiterhin den Trend zu Eigennamen für Produkte. Starke Verbreitung hatten geografische Namen von Städten, Flüssen und Inseln. Noch stärker vertreten waren (und sind) weibliche Vornamen. Mit ihnen verbindet man Wohlklang und Attraktivität. Die Endung auf -a wurde werbepsychologisch als günstig betrachtet.[9]

Bei westdeutschen Leuchtenherstellern, die für den Wohnbereich produzierten, stehen Städtenamen für Weltläufigkeit und Exklusivität, die dem Kunden einen Hauch von Internationalität ins Wohnzimmer trugen. Der rheinische Hersteller Peill + Putzler benannte Leuchten von Aloys Ferdinand Gangkofner nach italienischen Städten (*Venezia*).[10] Eine Hommage an das geteilte Berlin war die Serie von Wilhelm Braun-Feldweg, u. a. benannt mit den Leuchten *Avus*, *Kreuzberg* oder *Tegel*, die er für das Doria-Werk in Fürth 1962 entworfen hat.[11] Daneben wurden Namen aus der antiken Mythologie – etwa *Hera* oder *Helios* – oder der altägyptischen Religion wie *Osiris* bemüht.[12]

attractiveness with them. In advertising psychology, a name ending in an 'a' is considered favorable.[9]

In the case of West German luminaire manufacturers, whose products were intended for living areas, the names of cities stand for cosmopolitan attitudes and exclusivity, which added an international touch to customers' living rooms. The Rhineland manufacturer Peill + Putzler named luminaires by Aloys Ferdinand Gangkofner after Italian cities (*Venezia*).[10] The series by Wilhelm Braun-Feldweg was a homage to divided Berlin and included luminaires by the name of *Avus*, *Kreuzberg* and *Tegel*, which he designed for the Doria works in Fürth in 1962.[11] Names from classical mythology – for example *Hera* and *Helios* – or from Ancient Egyptian religion, such as *Osiris* were trotted out.[12]

Following a decades-long tradition, in then East Germany the state luminaire manufacturers gave their products sober names in which an abridged version of the manufacturer's name and a model number formed part of the name, or they chose indicative abbreviations of the function: The ceiling luminaire *RLZ* was made by the state-owned company VEB Raumleuchten Zeulenroda, while a table and piano luminaire by VEB Metalldrücker Halle went by the name of *TK 501* (around 1965). Later designs were given made-up names, such as the *Varolux automatic* table luminaire (1986) by VEB Meß-gerätewerk "Erich Wienert" in Magdeburg. (fig. 2)

Companies operating internationally also used the designer's initials; in this context the ceiling luminaire *PH 5* by Poul Henningsen

In der DDR vergaben die verstaatlichten Leuchtenhersteller nüchternere Warennamen in der Tradition der vorherigen Jahrzehnte, in der der Name des Herstellers in abgekürzter Form zusammen mit einer Modellnummer Bestandteil des Namens ist, oder sie wählten indikative Abkürzungen der Funktion: Die Deckenleuchte *RLZ* stammte von dem VEB Raumleuchten Zeulenroda, eine Tisch- und Klavierleuchte des VEB Metalldrücker Halle hatte den Namen *TK 501* (um 1965). Die jüngeren Entwürfe erhielten erfundene Namen wie die Tischleuchte *Varolux automatic* (1986) des VEB Meßgerätewerk „Erich Wienert" in Magdeburg. (Abb. 2)

International wurde auch mit den Initialen des Entwerfers gearbeitet, denkt man an die Deckenleuchte *PH 5* von Poul Henningsen für den dänischen Hersteller Louis Poulsen (1957). Ingo Maurers erste Serienleuchten (1967–1973) hatten die Abkürzung ML (Maurer Leuchten) und eine laufende Nummer, Name des Entwerfers und Herstellers fielen hier zusammen.[13]

Blickt man nach Italien, fallen die Leuchtennamen der Gebrüder Castiglioni besonders auf. Eine aus vier Stäben bestehende Stehleuchte für Girardi e Barzaghi heißt *Luminator* (1955). Mit der verkleinernden, vielleicht auch verniedlichenden Endung *-ino* wurde von denselben Entwerfern eine Tischleuchte bedacht, die aus einer vierfach gebogenen Röhre besteht: *Tubino* (1950) für Arredoluce. Bis heute produziert wird deren Tischleuchte *Snoopy* (1967) für Flos, benannt nach dem schlauen Beagle-Hund aus der Comicserie *Peanuts*. (Abb. 3) Der Leuchtenschirm spielt auf den wohlgeformten Hundekopf an, der auf einem schrägstehenden

for the Danish manufacturer Louis Poulsen (1957) springs to mind. Ingo Maurer's first series-production luminaires (1967–1973) also bore the abbreviation ML (Maurer Leuchten) and a serial number, the name of the designer and the manufacturer coincided here.[13]

With regard to Italy, the names of luminaires by the Castiglioni brothers are particularly striking. An upright luminaire for Girardi e Barzaghi comprising four rods is called *Luminator* (1955). The same designers gave a table luminaire comprising a tube bent fourfold the diminutive, perhaps cute ending 'ino': "*Tubino*" (1950) for Arredoluce. Their table luminaire "*Snoopy*" (1967) for Flos, named after the beagle in the *Peanuts* comic series, is still being produced today. (fig. 3) Resting on a slanting marble pedestal, the lampshade alludes to the dog's prominent snout. Ingo Maurer became familiar with the Castiglionis' designs at trade fairs in the 1960s.[14]

"The historical invention of naming is almost linear, from the manufacturer's name and descriptive names to those that are made up. In future, the latter will be the rule rather than the exception to it."[15] This trend is evident in the case of Maurer, too. His conservative use of proper names did not last long and he swiftly went on to discover an unconventional and playful openness towards word creations such as NO FUSS (1969) or GAUKELEIA (1976).

The temporal context also plays a role in these names. Against the backdrop of the political and social change and upheaval that occurred as of the late 1960s, design conventions also began to be questioned, for example by the Italian Anti-Design movement and

Marmorsockel sitzt. Ingo Maurer hatte Castiglionis Entwürfe auf den Messen in den 1960er-Jahren kennengelernt.[14]

„Die historische Erfindung der Namensgebung verläuft fast linear vom Herstellernamen über beschreibende bis hin zu frei erfundenen Namen. Letztere werden in Zukunft eher die Regel als die Ausnahme bilden."[15] Diese Entwicklung lässt sich bei Maurer ablesen. Er hält sich nicht lange bei der konservativen Anwendung von Eigennamen auf und entdeckt eine unkonventionelle und spielerische Offenheit für neue Wortkreationen wie NO FUSS (1969) oder GAUKELEIA (1976).

Für diese neuen Namen spielt auch der zeitliche Kontext eine Rolle. Vor dem Hintergrund politischer und gesellschaftlicher Veränderungen, die sich seit Ende der 1960er-Jahre vollzogen, wurden Konventionen in der Gestaltung hinterfragt, wie es die italienische Anti-Design-Bewegung oder die amerikanischen Vertreter der Postmoderne taten. Die neuen radikalen Positionen finden sich gleichfalls in der Symbiose von Form und Name wie bei der Leuchte *Lépingle* von Yonel Lebovici (1975), die wirklich einer Anstecknadel entspricht, oder bei der Stehleuchte *Svincolo* (1979) von Ettore Sottsass für Alchimia, die übersetzt „Autobahndreieck" heißt, ein scheinbar vollkommen aus dem Kontext gerissener Titel. (Abb. 4) Ingo Maurer hat nicht nur diese Trends verfolgt, ihn inspirierten auch künstlerische Stile wie der Dadaismus oder die bereits genannte Pop Art, deren Vertretern er Leuchten widmete: **Man Ray** (OH MAN, IT'S A RAY!), **Roy Lichtenstein** (LICHT.ENSTEIN) oder **Yves Klein** (REMEMBER YVES).

American proponents of Postmodernism. The new radical positions were also reflected in the symbiosis of form and name as in the case of *L'épingle* by Yonel Lebovici (1975), which really does resemble a safety pin, or Ettore Sottsass' upright luminaire *Svincolo* (1979) for Alchimia, which translated is called "interstate interchange", a title that is seemingly taken completely out of context. (fig. 4) Ingo Maurer not only followed these trends, he was also inspired by Dadaism and the Pop Art mentioned previously, to whose exponents he devoted luminaires: **Man Ray** (OH MAN, IT'S A RAY!), **Roy Lichtenstein** (LICHT.ENSTEIN) and **Yves Klein** (REMEMBER YVES).

A comparison with present-day German luminaire manufacturers reveals just how extravagant Ingo Maurer's approach was. Founded in 1934 in Lüdenscheid, after 1945 the company ERCO initially specialized in plastic luminaires and then in lighting systems; since 2015 it has only manufactured LED lighting. Until the 1970s the product names, which are geared specifically to architecture illumination (i.e., are not intended for living areas), had four to five-digit model numbers. Nowadays, the names are short and easy to remember, such as *Beam, Lichtmark* or *Pollux* for a ceiling spotlight – the brightest star in the constellation Gemini is popular, and in 1967 even Ingo Maurer named a table luminaire after it.

The Hamburg luminaire manufacturer Tobias Grau, which has been designing luminaires since 1987, is likewise an industrially oriented company with a matter-of-fact but technically sophisticated formal idiom. This is reflected in the classic product names through

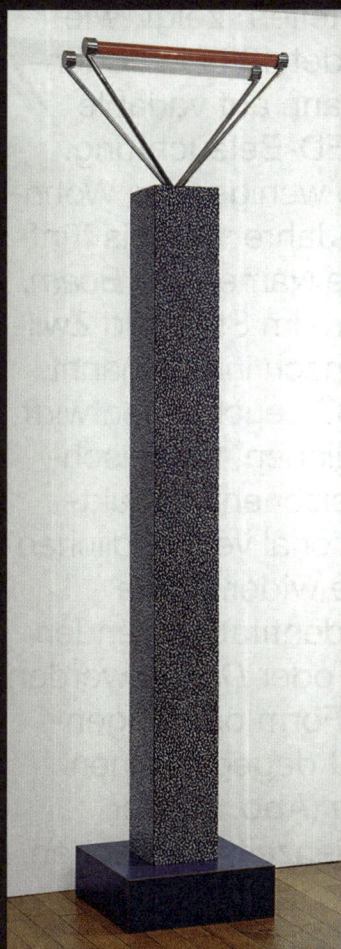

4
Ettore Sottsass
Svincolo, 1979
Alchimia, Mailand / Milan
Foto / Photo: A. Bröhan, München

5
Tobias Grau
Luja, 1987
Foto / Photo: Tobias Grau,
Michael Wurzbach

6
Diez Office
Rope Trick, 2015
Wrong.london / Hay, Horsens
Foto / Photo: Jonathan Mauloubier

Ein Vergleich mit gegenwärtigen deutschen Leuchtenherstellern zeigt, wie extravagant Ingo Maurers Ansatz ist. Die Firma ERCO, gegründet 1934 in Lüdenscheid, hat sich nach 1945 zunächst auf Kunststoffleuchten, dann auf variable Lichtsysteme spezialisiert und produziert seit 2015 nur noch LED-Beleuchtung. Die Produktnamen, die speziell für Architekturbeleuchtung – also weniger den Wohnbereich betreffend – ausgerichtet sind, hatten bis in die 1970er-Jahre vier- bis fünfstellige Modellnummern. Heute sind es kurze, leicht einprägsame Namen wie *Beam, Lichtmark* oder *Pollux* für einen Deckenstrahler – der hellste Stern im Sternbild Zwilling ist beliebt, sogar Ingo Maurer hatte 1967 eine Tischleuchte nach ihm benannt.

Der Hamburger Leuchtenhersteller Tobias Grau, der seit 1987 Leuchten entwirft, ist ebenfalls eine industriell ausgerichtete Firma mit einer sachlichen, technischausgeklügelten Formensprache. Dies spiegelt sich in den klassischen Produktnamen, zum Beispiel durch die Verwendung von kurzen, international verständlichen Vornamen wie *George, John, Bill* oder *Anna, Emma* und *Louise* wider. Diese Personalisierung des Produkts soll bei den Kund*innen einen identitätsstiftenden Moment bewirken. Mit den Namen *Eye, Falling Water, Column* oder *Dance* werden hingegen klare Bilder und Vorstellungen verknüpft, die auf die Form oder Eigenschaft Rückschlüsse geben. Graus erster Entwurf von 1987 hat dagegen einen ungewöhnlichen Namen: *Luja*, die verkürzte Form von *Halleluja* (Abb. 5). Der Hanseat Grau verewigte damit seine positiv empfundene Studienzeit in München. Es ist naheliegend, dass er Ingo Maurers Arbeiten gekannt hat, denn die Form der Standleuchte ähnelt ILIOS (1983).

the use of short, internationally comprehensible names such as *George, John, Bill* or *Anna, Emma* and *Louise*. This personalization of the product is intended to enable customers to identify with them. By way of contrast, names like *Eye, Falling Water, Column* or *Dance*, on the other hand, are associated with clear pictures and ideas that provide insight into the shape or features. The name of Grau's first design in 1987, on the other hand, is special: *Luja*, the shortened term of Halleluja. (fig. 5) Grau, a native of Hamburg, eternized his favorably perceived time as a student in Munich this way. It is nearby, that he knew Ingo Maurer's work, as the shape of the upright luminaire is also reminiscent of ILIOS (1983).

In the case of ERCO and Tobias Grau, who like Ingo Maurer manufacture their products in Germany, the names are easy to remember, as they are short, simple to read, easy to write, and to a certain extent familiar. This demonstrates that the thrust of their corporate philosophy is in no way compatible with Ingo Maurer's anti-industrial approach. Nils Holger Moormann's approach is perhaps comparable with Maurer's name philosophy. The furniture manufacturer from Germany's Chiemgau region, who has been working with external designers since 1984, reveals similar humor and astuteness with regard to word games. The simplicity and sophistication of the tables, chairs, and shelves are also reflected in their names, which are intended to make one smile. There is a bed called *Tagedieb* (dawdler), a wardrobe *Hut ab* (hats off), a lean-to deposit *Der kleine Lehner* (the small leaner), and a shelf *Egal*.

Bei ERCO und Tobias Grau, die ebenfalls wie Ingo Maurers Firma in Deutschland produzieren, haben die Namen eine hohe Merkfähigkeit, da sie knapp, einfach lesbar und leicht zu schreiben sind und einen gewissen Bekanntheitsgrad haben. Hier zeigt sich ganz deutlich, dass sich ihre firmenphilosophische Ausrichtung überhaupt nicht mit Ingo Maurers unindustrieller Herangehensweise deckt. Vergleichbar mit Maurers Namensphilosophie ist vielleicht noch Nils Holger Moormanns Ansatz. Der Möbelhersteller aus dem Chiemgau, der seit 1984 mit externen Designern zusammenarbeitet, hat einen ähnlich ausgeprägten Witz und Scharfsinn für Wortspiele. Der Schlichtheit und Raffinesse der Tische, Stühle und Regale entsprechen auch die Namen, die zum Schmunzeln bringen wollen. Ein Bett heißt *Tagedieb*, eine Garderobe *Hut ab,* eine angelehnte Ablage *Der kleine Lehner* oder ein Regal *Egal.* Die wenigen Leuchten bei Moormann heißen *La Funsel*, *Rosi* oder *Wenig*. Da stellt sich neugieriges Interesse ein.[16]

Persönlichkeiten im Design, die auf offene Hersteller treffen und nicht nur Leuchten entwerfen, haben Einfluss auf die Wahl der Produktnamen. Die bereits erwähnten Castiglioni-Brüder kreierten dadurch ihre eigene Marke. Aber ebenso der extrovertierte Philippe Starck, 17 Jahre jünger als Maurer, hat sich durch seine wilde, ironische und provokative Verknüpfung von Produkt und Bezeichnung einen Namen gemacht. Starck gefiel Maurer so sehr, dass er ihn mit der penisgeformten Tischleuchte HORNY PHILIPPE (1998) ehrte und auch noch dessen spinnenartige Alessi-Zitronenpresse *Juicy Salif* in die Leuchte BITTER LEMON (2001) verbaute. Ihrer freundschaftlichen Verbundenheit setzten der israelisch-

The few luminaires in the Moormann range go by the names *La Funsel*, *Rosi* and *Wenig*. And they are bound to conjure up interest.[16]

Design personalities who come across open-minded manufacturers and do not just design luminaires exert influence on the choice of the product names. The Castiglioni brothers mentioned earlier created their own brand this way. And the extrovert Philippe Starck, 17 years Maurer's junior, made a name for himself by giving his products wild, tongue-in-cheek and provocative names. Maurer liked Starck so much that he honored him with the penis-shaped table luminaire HORNY PHILIPPE (1998) and also incorporated his spidery *Juicy Salif* lemon squeezer for Alessi into the BITTER LEMON (2001) luminaire. Israeli-British designer Ron Arad and Ingo Maurer demonstrated their friendship through the joint design of an upright luminaire with an aluminum lampshade featuring a honeycomb structure: the AR-INGO is a clear reference to them both.[17]

But the portfolios of young designers from Munich, among them Konstantin Grcic, whose studio was formerly there, with his versatile *Mayday* luminaire for Flos (1999) and Stefan Diez with his ingenious upright luminaire *Rope Trick* (2015) (fig. 6) for Hay, have names that are good choices, humorous, and narrative.[18]

They do not see themselves in the tradition of an Ingo Maurer, who they know, they develop their own design idiom while at times relying on the manufacturer's corporate philosophy.

Ingo Maurer, however, is still the master of association, who only implies something and gives free rein to the user's imagination.

britische Designer Ron Arad und Ingo Maurer ein Zeichen mit dem gemeinsamen Entwurf aus einer Aluminium-Wabenstruktur: Stehleuchte AR-INGO verweist klar auf beide Autoren.[17]

Bei den jüngeren Designern aus München gehören Namen zum Portfolio dazu, wie vom ehemals ansässigen Büro von Konstantin Grcic mit der vielseitigen *Mayday*-Leuchte für Flos (1999) oder von Stefan Diez mit seiner pfiffigen Stehleuchte *Rope Trick* (2015) für Hay (Abb. 6), die klug gewählt, humorvoll und erzählerisch sind.[18] Sie sehen sich nicht in der Tradition eines Ingo Maurers, den sie wahrnehmen, sie entwickeln ihr eigenes Vokabular mitunter abhängig von der Firmenphilosophie des Herstellers.

Ingo Maurer aber bleibt der Meister der Assoziation, der nur etwas andeutet und der Fantasie der Nutzer*innen Spielraum lässt. Er ist Schöpfer eines einzigartigen Namenkosmos, den er über 50 Jahre aufgebaut und damit ohne Zweifel ein eigenes Feld in der sogenannten Ökonymie, der Linguistik von Produktnamen, hervorgebracht hat. Seine Leidenschaft, sein Ansatz, sein Charakter bilden sich in seinen Namen ab und geben nicht nur seinen Leuchten einen tieferen Sinn.

He is the creator of a unique name cosmos which he has built up over 50 years and as such has doubtless established a field of his own in the linguistics of product names. His passion, his approach, and his character are revealed in his names and give not only his luminaires deeper meaning.

Anmerkungen

1 Lampe ist eigentlich der korrekte Begriff für Leuchtmittel und Leuchte das Gesamtprodukt der Einzelteile. Glühbirne, eigentlich Glühlampe, wird in diesem Text umgangssprachlich verwendet.
2 Helmut Bauer (Hg.): Ingo Maurer: Making Light. Tucson, Arizona 1992, S. 10.
3 Ausst. Kat. Provoking Magic. Lighting of Ingo Maurer. Cooper-Hewitt, National Design Museum, Smithsonian Institution, New York. New York 2008, S. 48.
4 Provoking Magic 2008 (wie Anm. 3), S. 47.
5 Provoking Magic 2008 (wie Anm. 3), S. 32; Jolanthe Kuger: "Die Qualität des Lichts ist wichtiger als die Form." Gespräch mit Ingo Maurer, 13. Mai 2013, in: Ausst.Kat. Lightopia. Bd. 3, Visionen, Lichtgestaltung für morgen. Vitra Design Museum. Weil am Rhein 2019, S. 75: Leuchte ist inspiriert von fliegenden Blättern.
6 Uli Wilhelm: The Story of YaYaHo, in: Bauer 1992 (wie Anm. 2), S. 148 f.
7 Bernhard Dessecker (Hg.): Ingo Maurer. Designing with Light / Gestalten mit Licht. München et al. 2008, S. 164.
8 Susanne Latour: Namen machen Marken. Handbuch zur Entwicklung von Firmen- und Produktnamen. Frankfurt a. M. 1996, S. 20.
9 Kurt Franz, Albrecht Greule, Stefan Hackl (Hg.): Gerhard Koß. Warennamen – Marken – Kunstnamen. Transposition und Kreation in der Wirtschaft. Regensburger Studien zur Namensforschung, Bd. 5. Regensburg 2008, S. 12 f., 26, 220 f.: Weibliche Vornamen wurden vor allem für Textilien, Schuhe, Kosmetika und Porzellan- und Kristallglasservices vergeben, deren Zielgruppen Hausfrauen waren.
10 Isabell Gangkofner (Hg.): Aloys Ferdinand Gangkofner, Glas und Licht, Arbeiten aus vier Jahrzehnten. München et al. 2008, S. 96 f. Leuchten, die keine wohnliche Stimmung oder Innenraum-Atmosphären erzeugen, haben bis heute in der Regel technische Bezeichnungen.
11 Xenia Riemann: Das Werk Wilhelm Braun-Feldwegs. Industrielle Formgebung in Deutschland nach 1945. FU Berlin. Berlin 2007, Werkverzeichnis Leuchten, Nr. 194 ff. *Tegel* wird von der Firma Mawa Design reeditiert.
12 Beate Manske (Hg.): Täglich in der Hand. Industrieformen von Wilhelm Wagenfeld aus sechs Jahrzehnten. Bremen 1987, Vierte Auflage 1998, S. 320 f.
13 Die ML-Serie wurde wegen ihrer Kommerzialität auch „Puff"-Programm genannt. Siehe Thomas Bärenthaler: "Ich bin hochgeschossen wie ein Unkraut". Interview mit Ingo Maurer, in: SZ Magazin, 15. April 2019, S. 30.
14 Provoking Magic 2008 (wie Anm. 3), S. 76.

Notes

1 Lamp is actually the correct term for a lighting medium and luminaire the correct one for the sum total of the parts in a single product. Bulbs, meaning lamps, are used in the vernacular sense in this text.
2 Helmut Bauer (ed.): Ingo Maurer: Making Light. (Tucson, Arizona, 1992), p. 10.
3 Exhib. cat. Provoking Magic. Lighting of Ingo Maurer. Cooper-Hewitt, National Design Museum, Smithsonian Institution, (New York, 2008), p. 48.
4 Provoking Magic (2008), p. 47.
5 Provoking Magic (2008), p. 32; Jolanthe Kuger: "Die Qualität des Lichts ist wichtiger als die Form." Interview with Ingo Maurer, May 13, 2013, in: Exhib. cat. Lightopia. Vol. 3, Visionen, Lichtgestaltung für morgen. Vitra Design Museum, (Weil am Rhein, 2019), p. 75: Luminaire is inspired by flying sheets.
6 Uli Wilhelm: "The Story of YaYaHo", in: Bauer, 1992, pp. 148 f.
7 Bernhard Dessecker (ed.): Ingo Maurer. Designing with Light / Gestalten mit Licht. (Munich et al, 2008), p. 164.
8 Susanne Latour: Namen machen Marken. Handbuch zur Entwicklung von Firmen- und Produktnamen, (Frankfurt/Main, 1996), p. 20.
9 Kurt Franz, Albrecht Greule, Stefan Hackl (eds.): Gerhard Koß. Warennamen – Marken – Kunstnamen. Transposition und Kreation in der Wirtschaft. Regensburger Studien zur Namensforschung, vol. 5, (Regensburg, 2008), pp. 12 f., 26, 220 f.: In particular textiles, shoes, cosmetics, and porcelain, the target group of which were women, were given female first names.
10 Isabell Gangkofner (ed.): Aloys Ferdinand Gangkofner, Glas und Licht, Arbeiten aus vier Jahrzehnten, (Munich et al, 2008), pp. 96 f. Even today, luminaires which create neither a homely atmosphere nor interior moods as a rule have technical names.
11 Xenia Riemann: Das Werk Wilhelm Braun-Feldwegs. Industrielle Formgebung in Deutschland nach 1945. FU Berlin. (Berlin, 2007), luminaire catalogue raisonné, no. 194 ff. The firm Mawa Design still produces *Tegel*.
12 Beate Manske (ed.): Täglich in der Hand. Industrieformen von Wilhelm Wagenfeld aus sechs Jahrzehnten. (Bremen, 1987), fourth edition 1998, pp. 320 f.
13 The ML series was also called the Puff (brothel) program given its

15   Latour 1996 (wie Anm. 8), S. 96.
16   Firmenkataloge im Archiv der Neuen Sammlung und Websites von ERCO, Tobias Grau und Moormann, aufgesucht im Oktober 2019.
17   Ron Arad entwarf überdies Ohrringe mit dem Namen *Hot Ingo* (2015), siehe: Louisa Guinness: Art as Jewellery. From Calder to Kapoor. New York 2018, S. 257; Maurer verewigte zahlreiche, für ihn wichtige Männer in seinen Leuchten: hier seien Thomas Alva Edison als Erfinder der Glühbirne genannt (EDISON, WO BIST DU …?, 1997), der Metalrocker Alice Cooper (wenn auch nur ästhetisch: ALIZZ T. COOPER, 2008) oder Maurers Designerkollege Bruno Munari (ZETTEL'Z MUNARI, 2019).
18   Für Hinweise und Anregungen danke ich Sami Ayadi und Jan Heinzelmann, Andrea Czermak, Tobias Grau, Gabriele Kümmerlin, Stefan Diez und Hagen Szech.

commercial nature. See Thomas Bärenthaler, "Ich bin hochgeschossen wie ein Unkraut," Interview with Ingo Maurer, in: SZ Magazin, April 15, 2019, p. 30.
14   Provoking Magic (2008), p. 76.
15   Latour 1996, p. 96.
16   Company catalogs in the archive of Die Neue Sammlung and on the ERCO, Tobias Grau and Moormann websites, visited in October 2019
17   Ron Arad also designed earrings called *Hot Ingo* (2015), see: Louisa Guinness: Art as Jewellery. From Calder to Kapoor. (New York, 2018), p. 257; Maurer immortalized numerous men who were important to him in his luminaires: for example Thomas Alva Edison, the inventor of the light bulb (EDISON, WO BIST DU …?, 1997), the rock musician Alice Cooper (if only aesthetically: ALIZZ T. COOPER, 2008) and his colleague Bruno Munari (ZETTEL'Z MUNARI, 2019).
18   I would like to thank Sami Ayadi and Jan Heinzelmann, Andrea Czermak, Tobias Grau, Gabriele Kümmerlin, Stefan Diez and Hagen Szech for advice and suggestions.

XENIA RIEMANN-TYROLLER (GEB. 1973, MÜNCHEN)
ist seit 2012 Konservatorin an der Neuen Sammlung – The Design Museum. Die Kunsthistorikerin studierte an der Universität zu Köln und wurde an der FU Berlin über den Designer Wilhelm Braun-Feldweg promoviert. Sie war u. a. tätig für Glasmuseum Hentrich in Düsseldorf, Bröhan-Museum in Berlin und Glass and Ceramics Department des Victoria & Albert Museum in London.

XENIA RIEMANN-TYROLLER (BORN 1973, MUNICH)
has been a curator at Die Neue Sammlung – The Design Museum since 2012. An art historian, she studied at Cologne University and later gained a doctorate at FU Berlin with a thesis on designer Wilhelm Braun-Feldweg. Among other things, she was involved with the Glasmuseum Hentrich in Düsseldorf, the Bröhan Museum in Berlin, and the Glass and Ceramics Department at the Victoria & Albert Museum in London.

Zettel'z Munari
1997/2018

Ingo Maurer + Team
Japanpapier,
Edelstahl, Glas
Japanese paper,
stainless steel, glass

Zettel'z
1997

Ingo Maurer
Japanpapier,
Edelstahl, Glas
Japanese paper,
stainless steel, glass

BangBoom! Zettel'z
1997/2010

Ingo Maurer + Team
Japanpapier,
Edelstahl, Glas
Japanese paper,
stainless steel, glass

Zettel'z Laughing Buddha
1997/2018

Japanpapier,
Edelstahl, Glas
Japanese paper,
stainless steel, glass

Mozzkito
1996

Ingo Maurer
Metall, Kunststoff,
Gummi
Metal, plastic, rubber

Wo bist du, Edison…?
1997

Ingo Maurer
Acrylglas, Aluminium,
Hologramm 360°
Acrylic glass, aluminum,
hologram 360°

MaMo Nouchies
Gaku
1998

Dagmar Mombach,
Ingo Maurer + Team
Papier, Metall,
Edelstahl, Silikon, Glas
Paper, metal, stainless steel,
silicone, glass

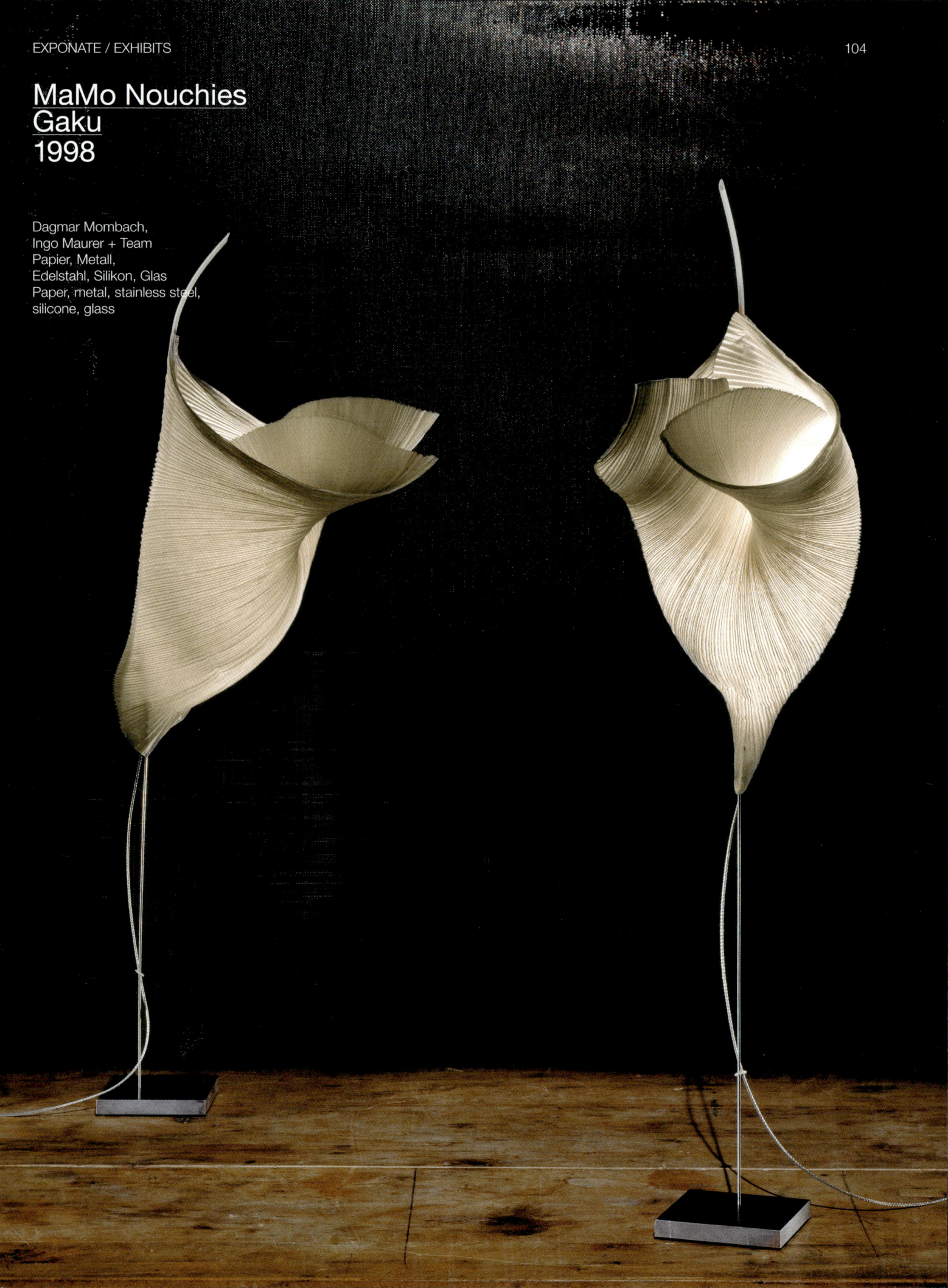

MaMo Nouchies
Kokoro
1998

Dagmar Mombach,
Ingo Maurer + Team
Papier, Metall, Glas,
Edelstahl, Kunststoff
Paper, metal, glass,
stainless steel, plastic

MaMo Nouchies
Poul Poul
1998

Dagmar Mombach,
Ingo Maurer + Team
Papier, Metall,
Silikon, Glas
Paper, metal,
silicone, glass

MaMo Nouchies
Samurai
1998

Dagmar Mombach,
Ingo Maurer + Team
Papier, Metall, Silikon, Glas,
Glasfaserblenden
Paper, metal, silicone,
glass, fiberglass panels

MaMo Nouchies
Wo-Tum-Bu 1 + 2 + 3
1998

Dagmar Mombach,
Ingo Maurer + Team
Papier, Beton, Metall,
Kunststoff, Glasfaser
Paper, concrete, metal,
plastic, fiberglass

MaMo Nouchies
Walking in the Rain
1998/2017

Ingo Maurer + Team
Papier, Metall,
Silikon
Paper, metal,
silicone

MaMo Nouchies
Yoruba Rose
1998/2017

Dagmar Mombach,
Ingo Maurer + Team
Papier, Metall,
Silikon
Paper, metal,
silicone

Oskar
1998

Ingo Maurer
Metall, eloxiertes
Aluminium
Metal, anodized
aluminum

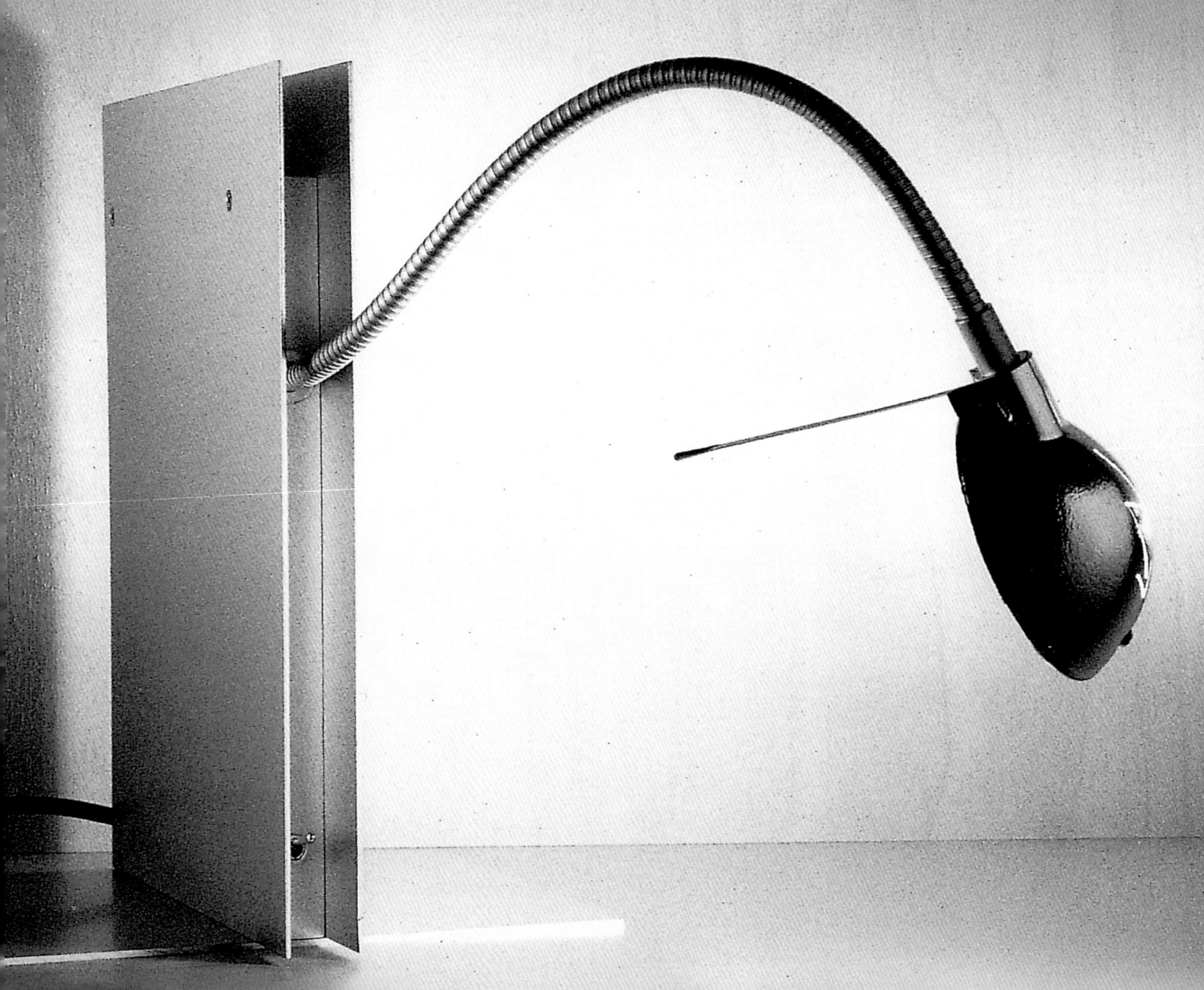

Holonzki / Dead Bulb Alive
2000

Eckhard Knuth,
Ingo Maurer
Glas-Hologramm,
Metall
Glass hologram,
metal

Wabe
2001

Ingo Maurer
Platine, LED,
Metall, Edelstahl
Circuit board, LED,
metal, stainless steel

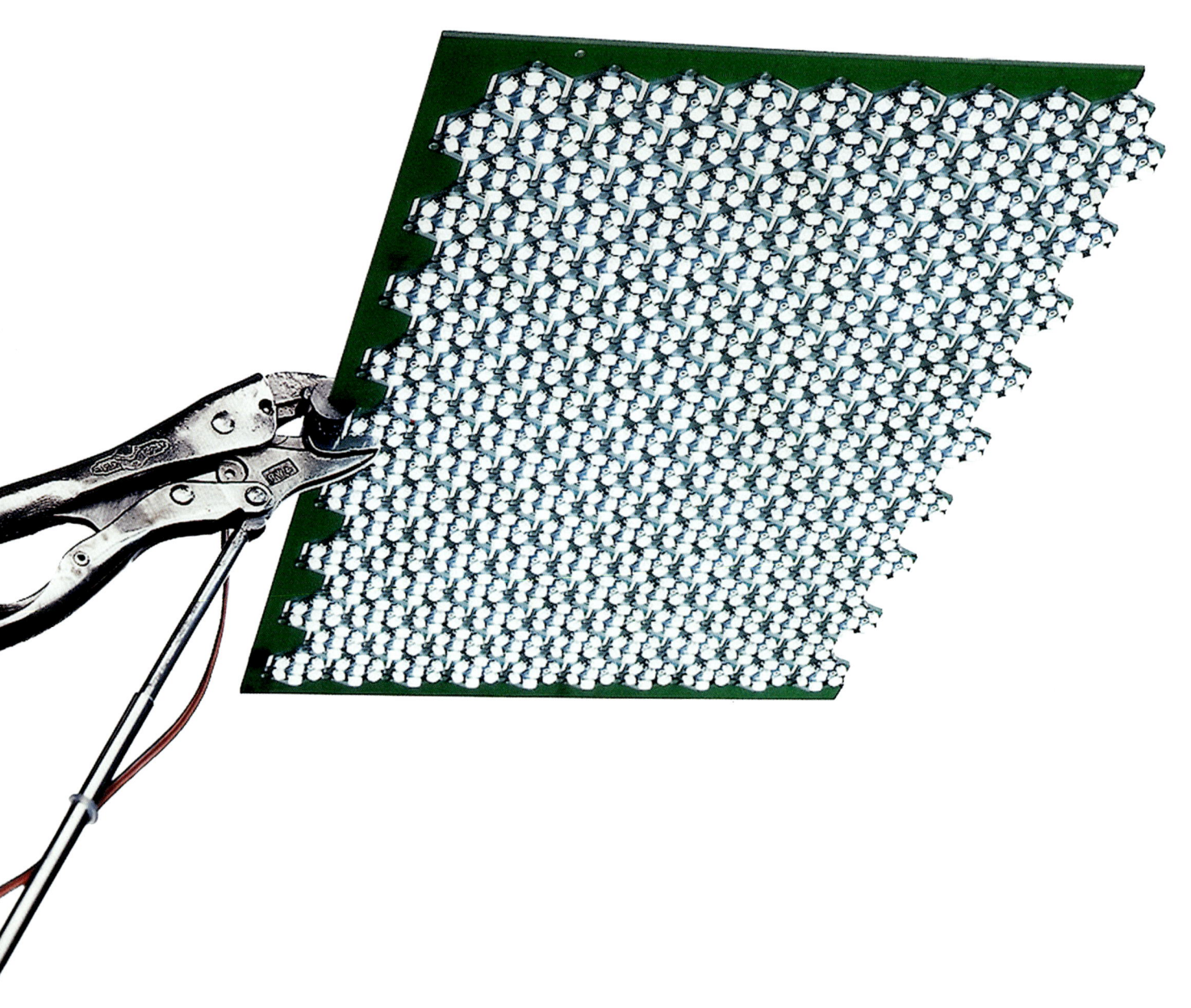

EL.E.DEE
2001

Ingo Maurer
Platine, LED,
Metall, Edelstahl
Circuit board, LED,
metal, stainless steel

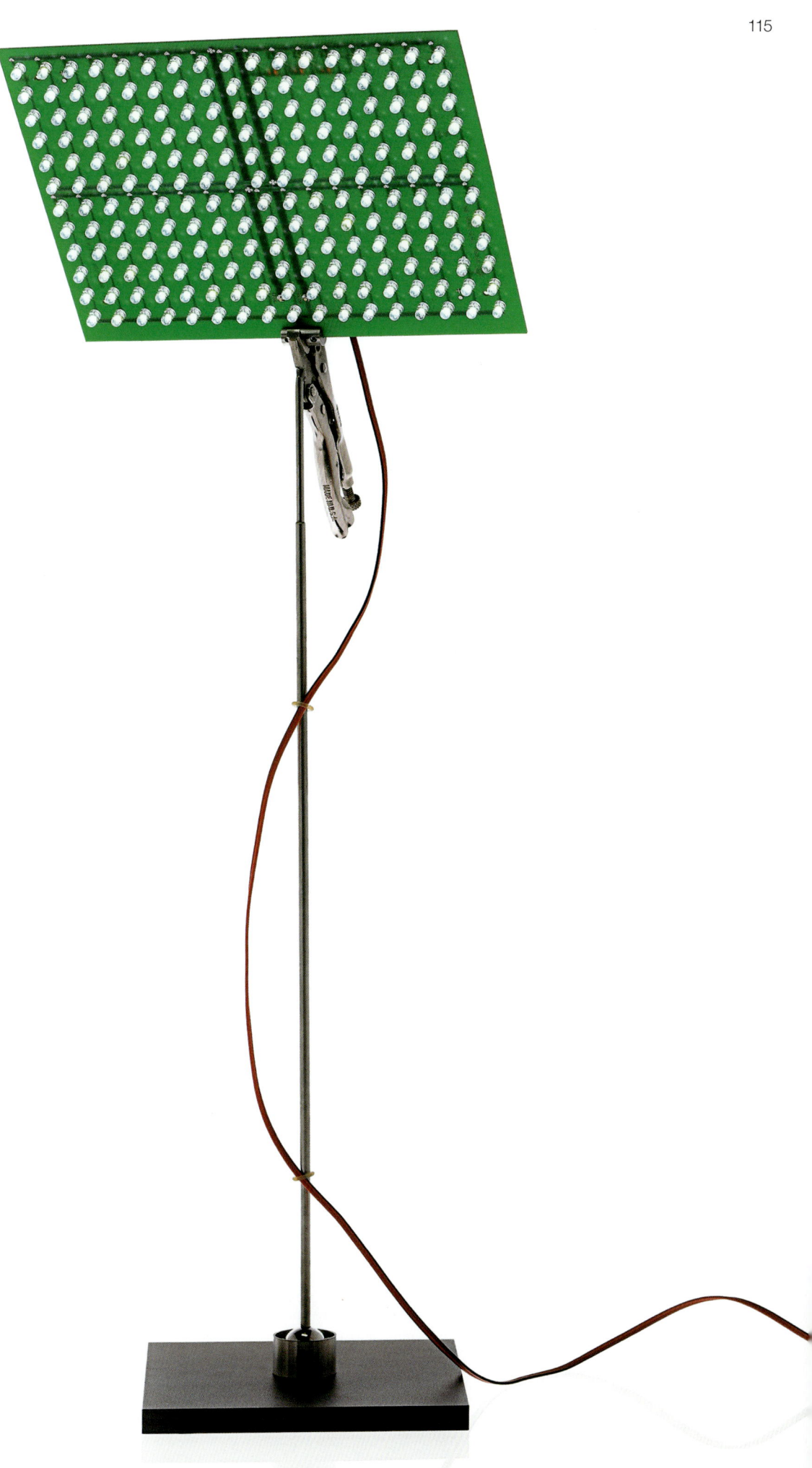

Flora Dee
2001

Ingo Maurer
Platine, LED,
Metall, Edelstahl
Circuit board, LED,
metal, stainless steel

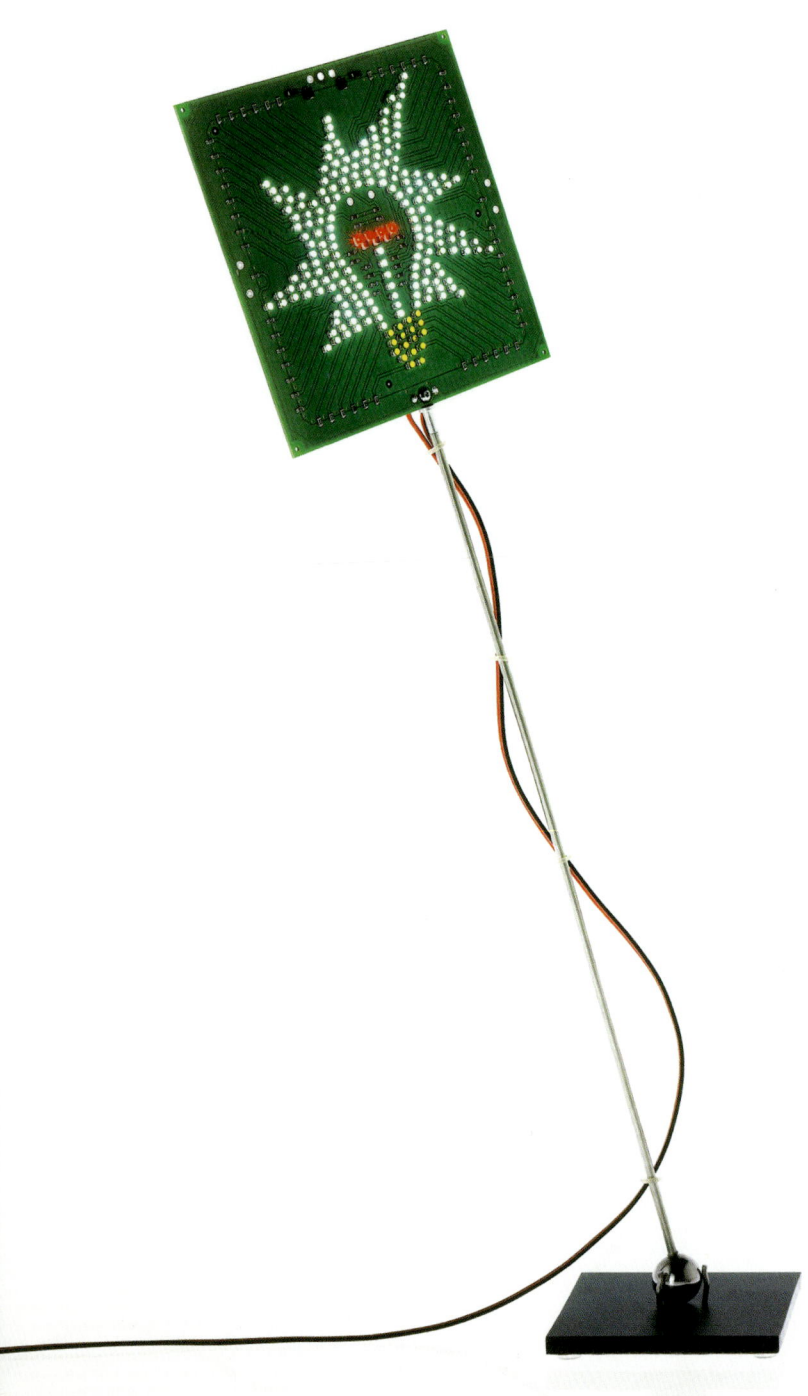

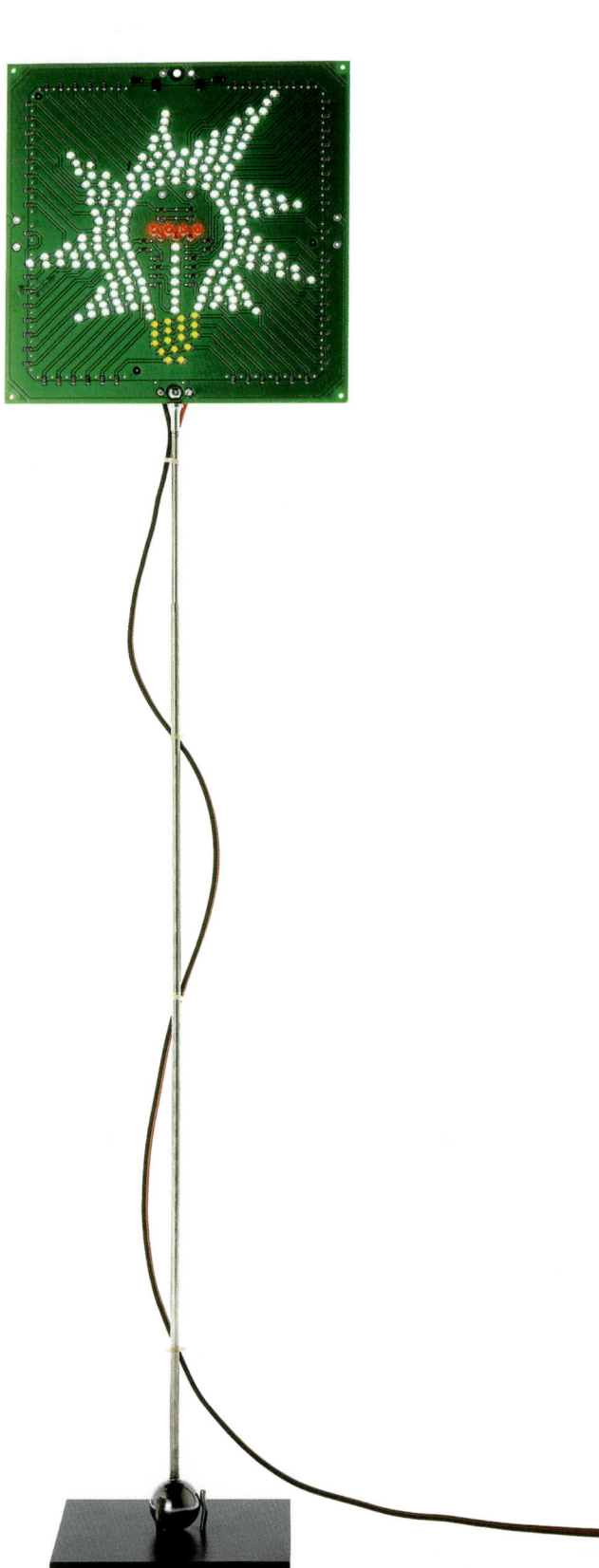

Licht.Enstein
2001

Ingo Maurer
Platine, LED,
Acrylglas, Metall
Circuit board, LED,
acrylic glass, metal

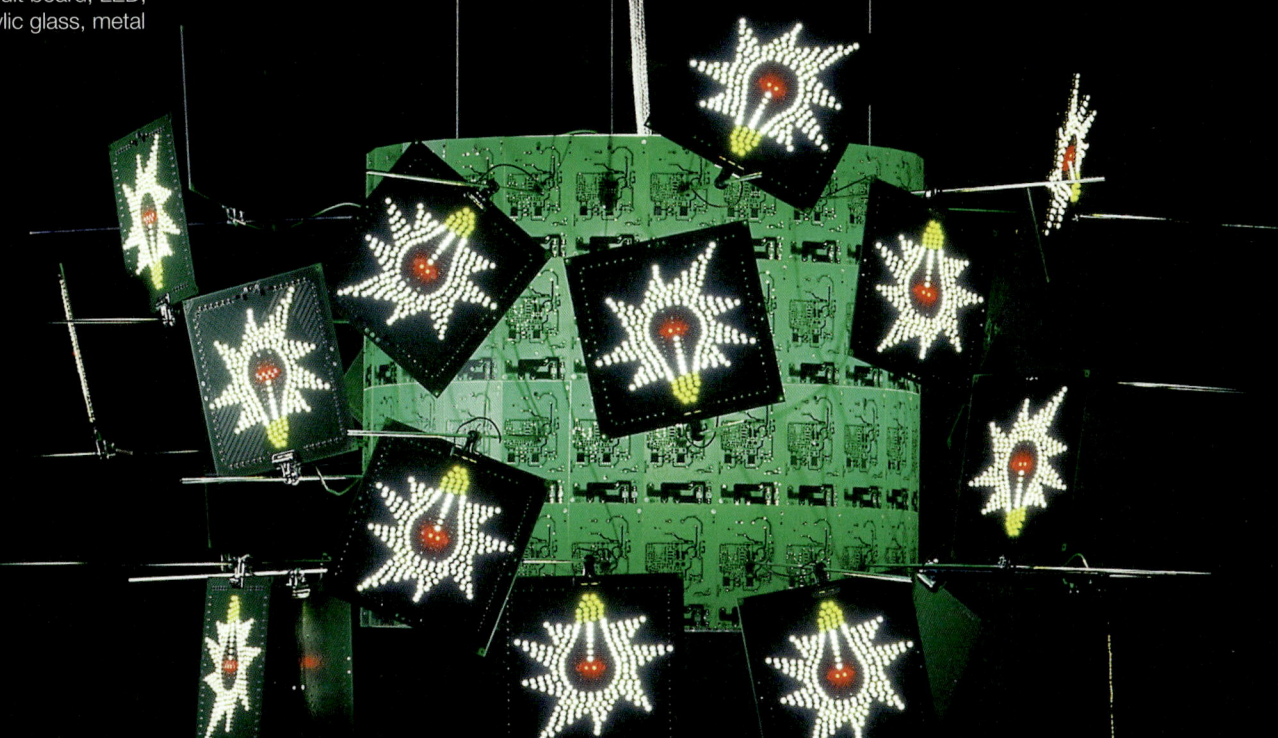

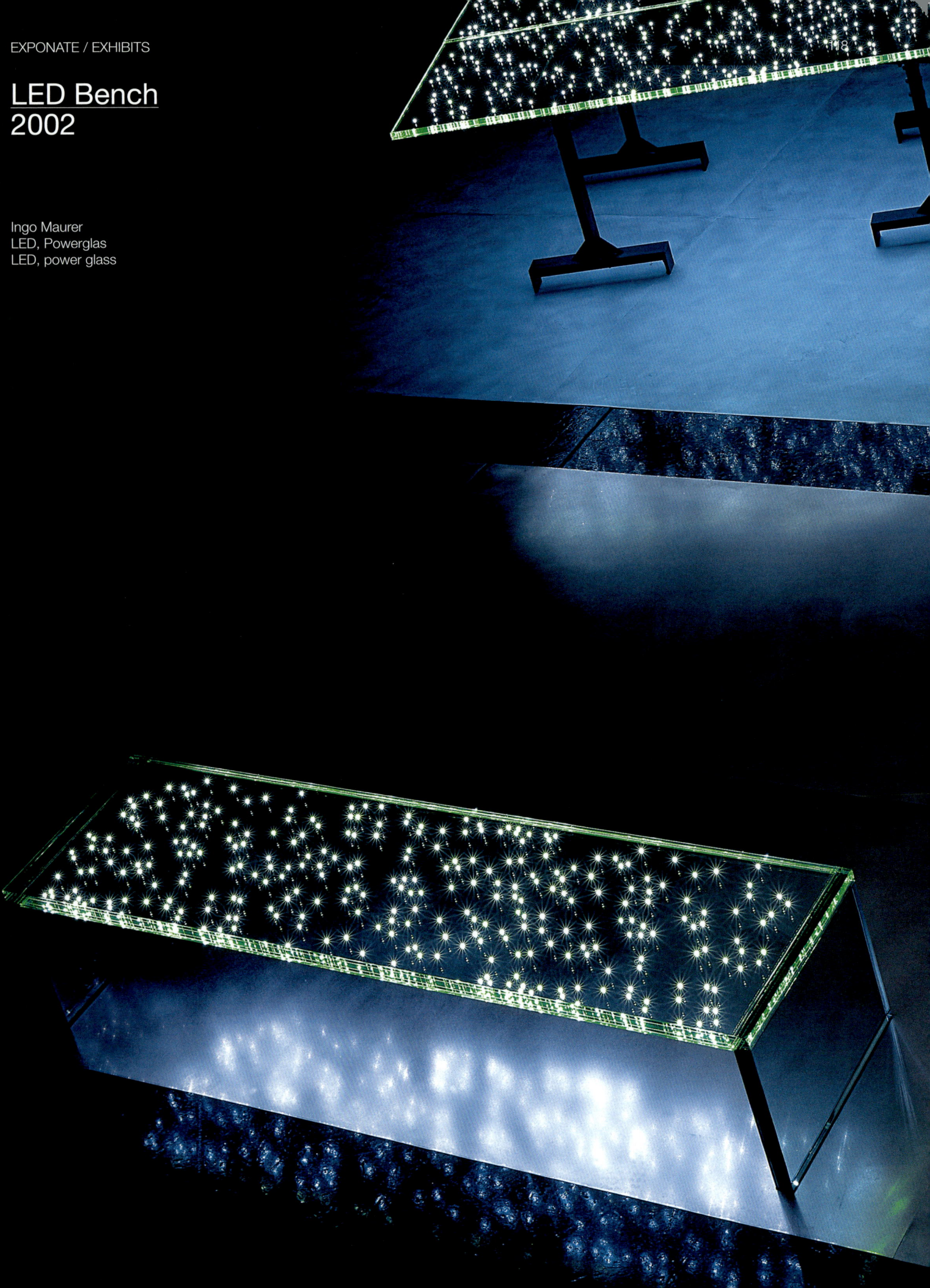

LED Bench
2002

Ingo Maurer
LED, Powerglas
LED, power glass

Lüster
2003

Ingo Maurer
LED, Powerglas
LED, power glass

24 Karat Blau T
2005

Axel Schmid
Metall, Acrylglas,
Blattgold
Metal, acrylic glass,
gold leaf

24 Karat Blau Floor
2005/2017

Axel Schmid
Metall, Acrylglas,
Blattgold
Metal, acrylic glass,
gold leaf

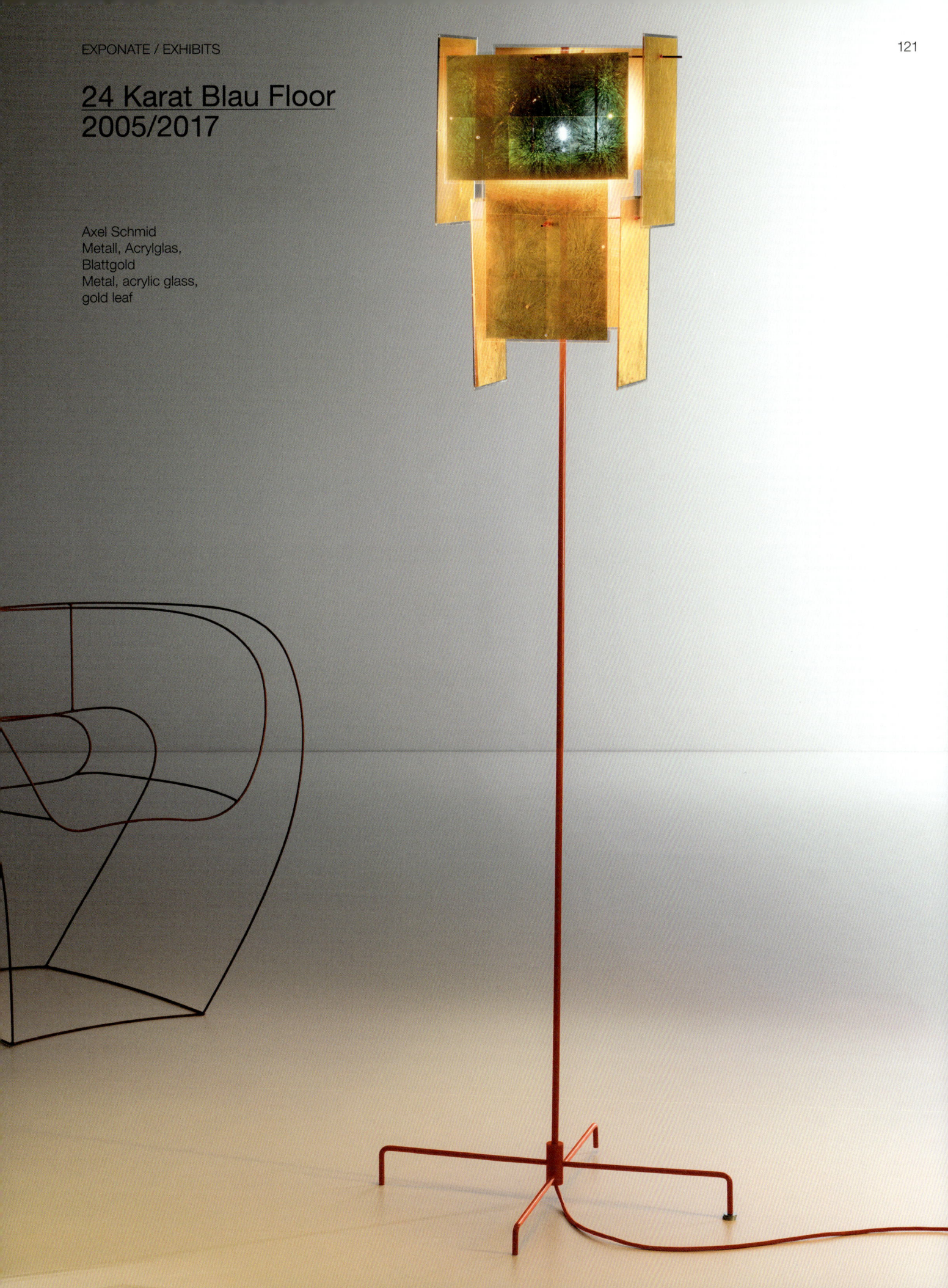

1000 Karat Blau
2009/2016

Axel Schmid
Metall, Acrylglas,
Blattgold
Metal, acrylic glass,
gold leaf

Rose, Rose on the Wall
2005

Ingo Maurer
Platine, LED, MDF,
Elektronik-Bauteile
Circuit board, LED, MDF,
electronic components

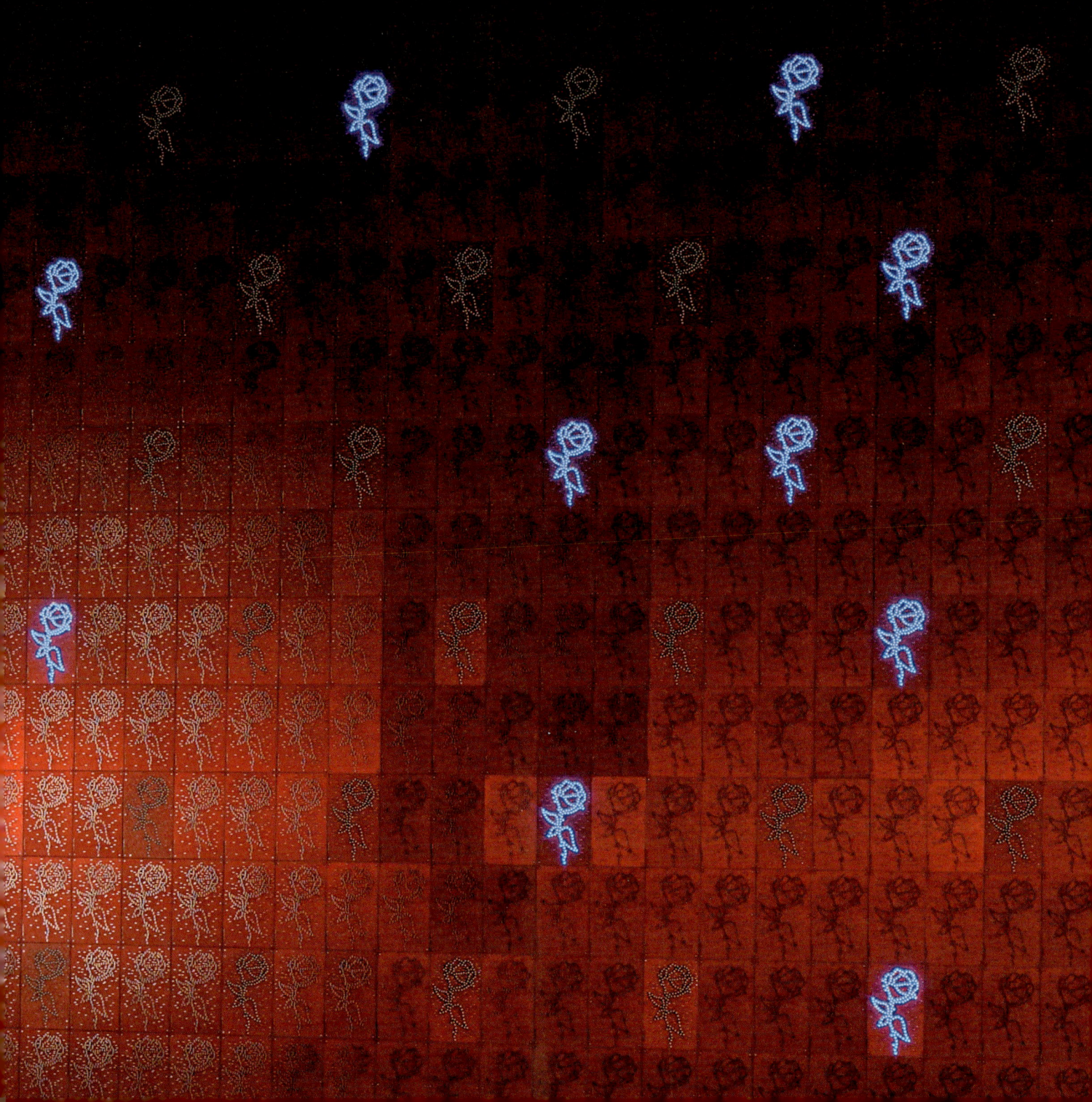

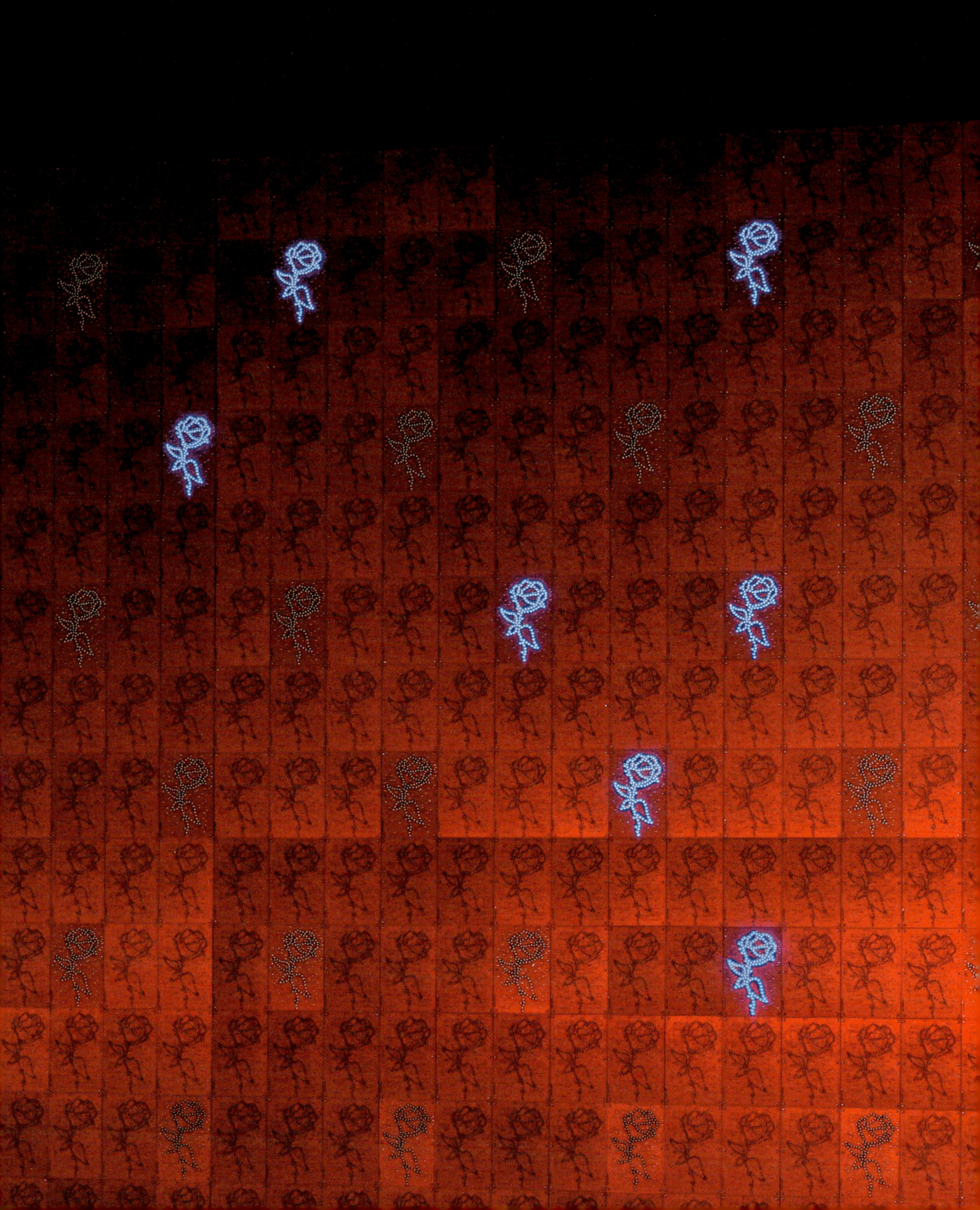

Flying Future
2006

Ingo Maurer + Team
OLED-Module,
Glas, Kunststoff
OLED modules,
glass, plastic

Remember Yves
2007

Ingo Maurer
Polyurethan, Harz
Polyurethane, resin

Nasir Kassamali
Die Welt ein bisschen schöner machen /
Ways of Making the World that Little More Beautiful

Seit dem Bauhaus gab es nur wenige Bewegungen, die einen neuen theoretischen Ansatz für das Design von Lichtobjekten angeregt haben. Ingo Maurer hat diesbezüglich wegweisende Arbeit geleistet, denn es ist ihm gelungen, die Unterscheidung zwischen bildender und angewandter Kunst aufzuheben sowie Kreativität und Produktion wiederzuvereinen. Er ist immer dem Handwerk verbunden geblieben, hat dabei aber stets konzeptuelle Ideen und technische Innovationen erkundet, um eine neue Kategorie von Lichtlösungen zu entwickeln, die die Definition der Leuchte im wahrsten Sinne des Wortes in einem neuen Licht erscheinen lassen.

Ingo entwirft nicht einfach nur Leuchten, er kreiert vielmehr Lichtkonzepte, die den Betrachter niemals unbeteiligt lassen und ihm eine poetische Meditation über die Kraft des Lichts eröffnen. Seine Projekte sind von seiner gestalterischen Klarheit, dem Gespür für die Auswahl der richtigen Materialien und der leidenschaftlichen Suche nach der jeweils ultimativen Lösung getragen.

Seine Karriere nahm vor fünf Jahrzehnten ihren Anfang; zunächst studierte Maurer in Deutschland und in der Schweiz Grafikdesign, bevor er in die USA auswanderte, wo er als freiberuflicher Designer in New York und San Francisco arbeitete. Obwohl er 1963 nach Deutschland zurückkehrte, wo er Design M, seine

Since the Bauhaus, there have been only a few movements that have shown a new theoretical approach to the design of lighting objects. Ingo Maurer, through his ability to level the distinction between fine and applied arts and to reunite creativity and manufacturing, has created the most important one. He has remained committed to handcraft, explored conceptual ideas and engaged technical innovations in his impressive œuvre to create a new category of lighting that begs the viewer to reconsider what a lamp can be.

Ingo does not just design lamps – rather, he creates lighting concepts that affect those who view them, providing the onlooker with a poetic meditation on the power of light. With a clarity in design thinking and an acute sensitivity to material selection, his projects represent a passionate search for excellence.

His journey began over five decades ago, originally as a student of graphic design in Germany and Switzerland, before emigrating to the United States where he worked as a freelance designer in New York and San Francisco. Though returning to Germany in 1963 and beginning his seminal company, Design M, graphic design has remained a compelling force in his work. In each creation, the fundamental principles of graphic composition are visible, translated into the unique forms of his work and often referencing Bauhaus ideals on proportion, form, clarity, and reduction of the unessential.

Triggering Maurer's self-taught career in lighting design was his fascination with the light bulb as the perfect meeting of industry and

zukunftsträchtige Firma gründete, blieb das Grafikdesign immer eine treibende Kraft in seiner Arbeit. In jedem seiner einzigartigen Entwürfe, die im Hinblick auf Proportion, Form, Klarheit und Reduktion auf das Wesentliche häufig auf die Ideale des Bauhauses verweisen, sind die grundlegenden Prinzipien der grafischen Komposition sichtbar.

Maurer hat sich die Grundlagen des Lichtdesigns selbst beigebracht, Auslöser war seine Begeisterung für die Glühlampe, die er als perfekte Begegnung von Industrie und Poesie empfand. Inspiriert von der Pop Art und als Hommage an Edison entwarf er 1966 BULB, eine Tischleuchte mit einer überdimensionierten Glühlampe, die sich schnell als Klassiker etablierte. Sein Hang, die archetypische Form der Glühbirne mit ihrer Funktionalität und dezenten Eleganz auszuschöpfen, entwickelte sich schließlich zum wiederkehrenden Thema seiner Arbeit und inspirierte berühmte Entwürfe wie u. a. LUCELLINO und seine Serie BIRDS.

Mit WO BIST DU, EDISON …? trieb er diese Form des Experiments auf die Spitze, es ist eine Allegorie der Immaterialität des Lichts in Form einer Hängelampe. Der zylindrische Schirm aus Acrylglas erwacht durch das Hologramm einer herkömmlichen Glühbirne zum Leben, wenn sie eingeschaltet ist. Die Fassung über dem Leuchtenschirm, in der sich die eigentliche Lichtquelle für das Hologramm befindet, hat das Profil von Thomas Edison. Maurer wollte sich ganz offenkundig auch hier die Möglichkeit einer Anspielung keinesfalls entgehen lassen. Hier kommt Ingos frappierende Fähigkeit zum Ausdruck, den Details seiner Entwürfe skurrile und oftmals witzige Elemente beizufügen.

poetry. In 1966, inspired by Pop Art and as an homage to Edison, he designed BULB, a table lamp in the form of a bulb within a giant light bulb that quickly established itself as a classic. His propensity to exploit the archetypal form of the bulb and highlight its understated utility and elegance became a running theme in his work, inspiring his iconic designs including LUCELLINO and the BIRDS series, among others.

Ingo took this study to its furthest reaches with WO BIST DU, EDISON…?, an allegory of the intangible quality of light in the form of a pendant lamp. A cylindrical drum of acrylic comes alive with the hologram of a traditional incandescent bulb when switched on. Not overlooking any details or opportunities for referential commentary, the light socket above the shade, which holds the actual light source for the hologram, is shaped like a profile of Thomas Edison. This evinces the uncanny ability Ingo has to distill whimsical and often humorous elements into the details of his designs.

Beyond his conceptual approach to lighting, Ingo never loses sight of the importance of materiality itself. In his MAMO NOUCHIES, he offers a collection of transcendent creations in an inspirational combination of paper, metal, and stainless steel that telegraphs the fine delicacy of paper sculpture. Their seductive gestures are reflective of the poetic design approach of Ingo Maurer and highlight his artful combination of material and function as well as his ability to carefully study every detail until each part of the whole is perfected. Giving a simple material a new meaning, each is created

Abgesehen von der konzeptuellen Seite eines Lichtobjekts verliert er jedoch niemals die Bedeutung der Materialität aus den Augen. So vermitteln seine MAMO NOUCHIES, eine Reihe überragender Kreationen in einer inspirierenden Kombination aus Papier, Metall und Edelstahl, die subtile Feinheit von Papierskulpturen. Ihre bestechend schönen Formen reflektieren seinen poetischen Gestaltungsansatz und unterstreichen die kunstvolle Verbindung von Material und Funktion sowie auch Maurers Vermögen, jedes Detail so lange zu studieren und zu optimieren, bis jedes Teil des Ganzen perfekt ist. Das schlichte Material erhält hier eine neue Bedeutung. Jedes Exemplar wird aus einfachen Papierbögen von Hand zu einem skulpturalen Lichtelement geformt.

Ingo Maurer ist weltweit für seine charakteristische und unverfälschte Kreativität und Erfindungsgabe bekannt, die in ihrer Einzigartigkeit sicherlich auch durch seine eigenen Reisen um die Welt beeinflusst ist. Seine Fähigkeit, das Leben anderer Menschen durch seine Arbeit zu bereichern, lässt mich seit unserer ersten Begegnung 1984 immer wieder staunen. Mit Ingo und seiner Frau Jenny verbindet und verband uns eine kostbare und enge Freundschaft, die sich aus unserer gemeinsamen Liebe zum Design und seinen Möglichkeiten, die Welt ein bisschen schöner zu machen, entwickelt hat. Wir sind Verfechter guten Designs und Ingo ist der Mittelpunkt dieses speziellen Universums.

entirely by hand, transforming plain sheets of paper into a sculptural element of light.

Renowned the world over for his unmistakable streak of pure creativity and ingenuity, Ingo operates with a decidedly individualistic approach that is in no doubt influenced by his own travels around the world. Since meeting him in 1984 I have continually been left speechless by his ability to enhance the lives of others through his work. With Ingo and his wife Jenny, we have enjoyed a precious relationship that began in a shared love of changing the world with design and has blossomed into a close friendship. We are advocates of good design, and Ingo is in the center of this special universe.

NASIR KASSAMALI
wanderte 1973 aus Kenia in die USA aus. Er spezialisierte sich auf den Handel mit europäische Leuchten und gründete das Unternehmen Luminaire. 1974 eröffnete er seinen ersten Showroom in North Miami Beach. Seit 1979 sponsert und produziert Luminaire Designausstellungen und Vortragsreihen.

NASIR KASSAMALI
emigrated to the USA from Kenya in 1973. He specialized in trading European lighting products and founded the company Luminaire. In 1974 he opened his first showroom in North Miami Beach. Since 1979 Luminaire has sponsored and financed design exhibitions and lecture series.

Michele De Lucchi
Von der Bedeutung des Lichts und der Emotionen / About the Meaning of Light and Emotions

Ich habe ein Foto von Ingo in unserem klitzekleinen Garten in Mailand im Kopf. Wahrscheinlich wurde es im späten Frühling um 1990 herum aufgenommen. Ingo hält darauf meinen Sohn Arturo, der ein Jahr oder wenig älter gewesen sein muss, hoch über dem Kopf. Es scheint, als wolle er dem Kind zeigen, wie schön die Welt von oben ist. Und das Kind, ein wenig überrascht, lacht. Und wir alle lachten froh. Eine schöne Stimmung auf diesem alten Foto! Eine friedliche Atmosphäre stiller Heiterkeit, die beste Vorbereitung darauf, das Leben mit Erfindergeist, mit Gestaltungslust anzugehen, zu überraschen und sich auszutauschen.

Ingo kenne ich seit vielen Jahren; auch wenn wir uns relativ selten gesehen haben, hielten wir doch stets den Kontakt aufrecht. Ich war immer überzeugt, dass zu diesen außergewöhnlichen Kunstwerken ein großer Geist und ein großes Herz gehören, womöglich wenig geeignet, den Zynismus und die Gewalt der Welt von heute zu verstehen, aber mit einer eindrücklichen Wahrnehmungsgabe für alles, was das Leben erwärmt.

Es wird immer schwieriger, dem Leben einen Sinn zu geben, und es sind auch immer weniger Menschen, die danach suchen. Folglich besteht immer weniger Bedarf daran, den Dingen, den Objekten, die uns umgeben, einen Wert zuzu-

In my head I have a picture of Ingo in our teeny-tiny garden in Milan. Probably taken in the late spring around 1990. In it, Ingo was holding my son Arturo, who must have been one year old or slightly older, high above his head. It looked as if he wanted to show the boy how beautiful the world looks from up there, and the child, slightly surprised, was laughing. And we were all laughing happily. A good mood on that old photo! A peaceful atmosphere of quiet cheerfulness, the best way to prepare somebody for approaching life with an inventive spirit, with a desire to shape things, to surprise and share ideas with other people.

I have known Ingo for very many years now; even if we have seen each other relatively seldom, we kept in touch. I was always convinced that behind those outstanding works of art there must be a great intellect and a big heart, possibly not one very suitable for understanding the cynicism and the violence of the world as it is today, but with an impressive perceptive faculty for everything that makes life warmer.

It is becoming increasingly difficult to imbue our lives with meaning and there are fewer and fewer people who attempt to do so. Consequently, there is less and less call to equip the things, the objects that surround us, with a value. We often forget that we are the only living beings who consciously make things, who lend their doings a meaning and look constantly for new meanings. Today's technology impressively confronts us with the realization of how important it is – with all the tangible things that we process with our

schreiben. Oftmals vergessen wir, dass wir die einzigen Lebewesen sind, die bewusst Dinge herstellen, die ihrem Tun eine Bedeutung geben und ständig neue Bedeutungen suchen. Die Technologie von heute konfrontiert uns eindrücklich damit, wie wichtig es ist – bei allem Greifbaren, das wir mit den Händen bearbeiten –, auch das Ungreifbare, das wir mit dem Geist beeinflussen, zu erkennen und zu vergegenwärtigen, dass der Geist von Gefühlen geleitet wird. Ingo hat sein Leben ganz bewusst der Suche nach der Bedeutung des Lichts und der Emotionen gewidmet, die eine Lichtquelle hervorruft.

Es gibt einen Satz von Bruno Munari, der sagt: „Es ist nicht einzusehen, dass man schöne Dinge betrachtet und hässliche Dinge benutzt".

Wir haben das kleine Haus mit dem kleinen Garten in Mailand verlassen und sind in ein großes Haus nach Angera aufs Land gezogen (eines der tausend kleinen Dörfer, die Mailand umgeben); und wie es der Zufall will, hat sich genau in Angera, dank Michel Sempels, das italienische Büro von Ingo Maurer niedergelassen. Vor Kurzem haben wir uns dort in Angera getroffen. Ingo kam mich besuchen, und ich habe ihn für die Zeitschrift Domus interviewt. Seine Arbeiten verführen und inspirieren, und die Versuchung, sein Geheimnis zu verstehen, ist

hands – to recognize those intangible things that we shape with our intellects, and to think about the fact that our minds are guided by feelings. Ingo has consciously devoted his life to the search for the meaning of light and the emotions aroused by a light source.

There is a quote from Bruno Munari that reads: "I can't understand why we should look at beautiful things and then use ugly things."

We left the little house with its little garden in Milan and moved to a large house out in the countryside, in Angera (one of the thousand little villages outside Milan); and as chance would have it, thanks to Michel Sempels, this was exactly where the Italian offices of Ingo Maurer took up residence. We met up there in Angera quite recently. Ingo came to visit me and I interviewed him for Domus magazine. His work enchants and inspires me, and the urge to try to understand his secret is always great. Ingo is honest, genuine, authentic. It is a tremendous pleasure to spend time with him. He allows us to recognize, through his eyes but with our own eyes, the marvelousness of simplicity, its colors, its shapes, its materials, in the simplest and most surprising of combinations, things that we would never have arrived at without him pointing the way. With him it is possible to recognize the poetic power of light.

Ingo, I like you a great deal and there are many people besides me who like you a great deal.

immer groß. Ingo ist ehrlich, echt, authentisch. Es ist eine große Freude, Zeit mit ihm zu verbringen. Er lässt uns durch seine Augen mit unseren Augen in allem das Wunderbare der Einfachheit erkennen, in den Farben, in den Formen, im Material, in den einfachsten und überraschendsten Kombinationen, die uns ohne seinen Hinweis niemals in den Sinn kämen. Mit ihm gelingt es, die poetische Kraft des Lichts zu erkennen.

Ingo, ich mag Dich sehr, und mit mir sind es viele, die Dich sehr mögen.

MICHELE DE LUCCHI
(GEB. 1951, FERRARA)
ist ein vielfach ausgezeichneter italienischer Architekt, Designer und Professor. Er war Mitglied und Mitbegründer der Bewegungen Alchimia und Memphis. Seit den 1970er-Jahren lehrt er Industriedesign u. a. in Florenz und seit 2001 an der Università Ca' Foscari di Venezia.

MICHELE DE LUCCHI
(BORN 1951, FERRARA)
is a multiple-award-winning Italian architect, designer and professor. He was a member and co-founder of the Alchimia and Memphis movements. He has been teaching industrial design in Florence since the 1970s and at the Università Ca' Foscari di Venezia since 2001, alongside other teaching assignments.

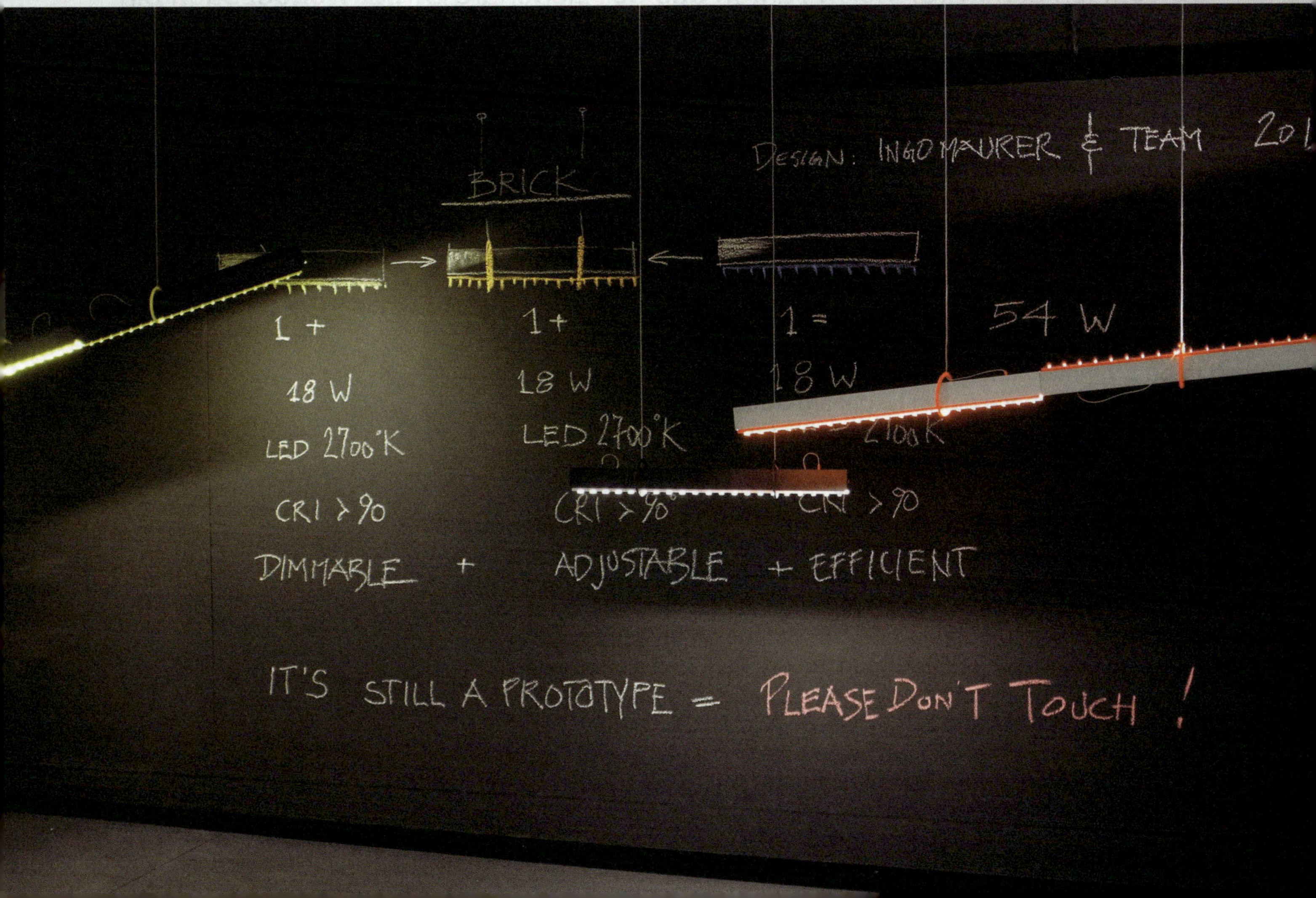
DESIGN: INGO MAURER & TEAM 201
BRICK
1 + 18 W LED 2700°K CRI > 90
1+ 18 W LED 2700°K CRI > 90
1 = 18 W 2700°K CRI > 90
54 W
DIMMABLE + ADJUSTABLE + EFFICIENT
IT'S STILL A PROTOTYPE = PLEASE DON'T TOUCH !

Kim Hastreiter
Mein wunderbarer Freund Ingo / My Amazing Friend Ingo

„HALLOOOOO!!! MEIN NAME IST INGO UND ICH MACHE LICHT!"

Das waren die ersten Worte, die ich vor vierzig Jahren von meinem neuen gut aussehenden Nachbarn, der nun ein Stockwerk über mir wohnte, zu hören bekam. An einem gemütlichen Samstagnachmittag war er in mein Loft in New York City gestürmt, begann sich wie ein Derwisch im Kreis zu drehen, schaute durch meine großen Fenster auf die Stadt, die sich vor uns ausbreitete, und rief mit seiner dröhnenden Stimme: „ICH BIN GERADE OBEN EINGEZOGEN UND ICH LIEBE NEW YORK: ES IST EINFACH UUUNGLAUBLICH HIER!" Mein erster Gedanke war: „Was ist das für ein verrückter Typ?" Als mir Ingo Maurer 1978 an jenem Tag das erste Mal begegnete, lebte ich in einem Loft in einer ehemaligen Fabrik zur Herstellung von Vitaminen. Das Gebäude befand sich in der Lispenard Street, einer etwas eigenartigen kleinen Straße in Tribeca, und wurde größtenteils von Künstlern bewohnt. Dies war der Beginn der Freundschaft zwischen meinem neuen Nachbarn und mir, einer innigen und vertrauensvollen, die über die Jahrzehnte immer fester wurde, und in so etwas wie Familie mündete.

Obwohl ich schon vor vielen Jahren aus der Lispenard Street weggezogen bin (Ingo blieb dort), war ich immer eine der Ersten, die er anrief, um mit seiner unver-

"HELLOOOOO!!! MY NAME IS INGO AND I MAKE LIGHT!"

Forty years ago, this is the first thing my new handsome upstairs neighbor announced to me in his booming voice as he barged into my New York City loft and began spinning in circles one lazy Saturday afternoon. Then, literally whirling like a dervish gasping at the city laying before us from my big windows, he continued, "I'VE JUST MOVED IN UPSTAIRS AND I LOVE NEW YORK! IT'S INCREEEDD-DIBLE HERE". My first thought was "Who is this crazy guy?" When I first met Ingo Maurer that day in 1978, I'd been living in a loft that used to be a vitamin factory, in a building filled with artists on an odd little street in Tribeca called Lispenard Street. And from that moment on, my new neighbor and I became friends. A loving trusting true friendship that grew like a weed over the decadesy, ultimately morphing beyond friendship into family.

Although I moved from Lispenard Street many years ago (Ingo remained), I was always one of his first friends to get a call announcing in that same booming voice, "HELLOOOO. I'M HEEEERE! WHEN CAN I SEE YOU?" We'd always meet for brunch immediately to catch up, then Ingo would want to come over to sit with me on my 19th floor terrace garden overlooking Washington Square Park and all of down-town, always exclaiming with his signature enthusiasm. "AAAHHH NEW YORK. ITS FANTAAAASTIC. LOOK AT ALL THE LIGHTS." We'd sit there sipping wine until long past when the sun went down. Every time I would try to turn on my terrace lights he'd slap my hand and say, "NO, NOT YET!!" He never wanted to interrupt the sunset.

kennbar dröhnenden Stimme zu verkünden: „HALLOOO, ICH BIN IN DER STADT. WANN KÖNNEN WIR UNS SEHEN?" Wir trafen uns dann immer sofort zum Brunch, um uns gegenseitig auf den neuesten Stand zu bringen. Im Anschluss kam Ingo meistens zu mir, wir saßen dann auf meiner Gartenterrasse im 19. Stock mit Blick über den Washington Square Park und Downtown und er rief mit seiner für ihn typischen Begeisterung: „AAAAH NEW YORK: ES IST FANTASTISCH. SCHAU NUR DIE GANZEN LICHTER!" Gewöhnlich saßen wir noch lange zusammen, nachdem die Sonne untergegangen war, und tranken Wein. Und jedes Mal, wenn ich die Terrassenbeleuchtung einschalten wollte, gab er mir einen kleinen Klaps auf die Hand und sagte: „NEIN, NOCH NICHT!!!" Er wollte immer warten, bis die Sonne vollständig untergegangen war.

Ich sollte vielleicht erwähnen, dass ich niemals Teil der Designszene war oder Ingo in diesem Kontext erlebt habe bzw. es spielte für mich gar keine Rolle, dass er Designer war. Für mich ist Ingo ein Künstler. Und sein Medium ist das Licht. Ingo liebt *Licht*. Nicht etwa *Leuchten*. Licht ist für Ingo so viel mehr als das, was eine Lampe verströmt. Ingo findet Licht in Menschen und in der Natur, nicht nur in der entsprechenden technischen Vorrichtung. Ich fand es immer ein wenig merk-

I should tell you now that I am not part of the design world/business, so I never knew Ingo in that context nor did I ever think of him as a designer either. Ingo, to me, was an artist. And his medium was light. Ingo loved *light*. Not *lights*. And light, to Ingo, was much more than just what came from a lamp. Ingo found light in people and nature, not just in delivery systems. I always thought it was odd that he had a company that made "lights" when objects were clearly so unimportant in his life. Ingo always lived like a gypsy with few possessions and creature comforts – happy to sleep on a mattress on the floor. He hated "things" and was very unsentimental about keeping stuff. Humanity was what was important to him. He saw light in everyone, everything, everywhere and lived for its magic… whether the drama of a long drawn out sunset or the unexpected sparkle he experienced seeing a beautiful woman, hearing a hilarious joke, meeting a new amazing person or a glint he caught in someone's eyes. He rejoiced at the mystery of reflection he saw underwater, the twinkle of a firefly or the fluorescent color hidden beneath a butterfly fluttering around a light bulb. I have even seen him applaud when he saw the psychedelic oily light made by a cheesy 60s lava lamp. Ingo was not a snob and respected both the sublime and the ridiculous. He loved a good laugh (his laugh was deep and booming) and always included humor in what he did. His drunken lamp aka the LAMPAMPE will always be my favorite and sits by my bedside making me smile every day – with its cockeyed and rumpled silhouette. Or his LOOKSOFLAT, a hilarious flattened out caricature of a

würdig, dass er eine Firma hat, die „Leuchten" herstellt, da Objekte für ihn doch so unwichtig sind. Ingo lebte schon immer wie ein Nomade mit nur wenigen Habseligkeiten und Annehmlichkeiten und gibt sich gerne auch mit einer Matratze auf dem Boden zufrieden. Er hasst „Dinge" und ist wenig sentimental, was das Aufheben von Dingen betrifft. Ihm ist hingegen Menschlichkeit ausgesprochen wichtig. Er sieht überall und in jedermann Licht und liebt seinen Zauber … sei es ein langer spektakulärer Sonnenuntergang, ein unerwartetes Funkeln angesichts einer schönen Frau, ein guter Witz, die Begegnung mit einem großartigen Menschen oder ein Glitzern, das er in den Augen seines Gegenübers wahrnimmt. Er freut sich über geheimnisvolle Reflexionen unter Wasser, flimmernde Glühwürmchen oder die fluoreszierende Farbe auf der Unterseite eines Schmetterlings, der das Licht umschwirrt. Ich habe sogar erlebt, wie er angesichts des psychedelischen ölartigen Lichts einer kitschigen Lavalampe aus den sechziger Jahren vor Begeisterung in die Hände klatschte. Ingo ist kein Snob, er weiß das Alberne ebenso wie das Erhabene zu respektieren. Er lacht gerne (ein tiefes, dröhnendes Lachen) und jedes seiner Leuchtenobjekte ist von seinem Humor beseelt. LAMPAMPE, seine betrunkene Leuchte, war schon immer meine Favoritin und steht neben meinem Bett. Mit ihrer etwas schiefen und zerknautschten Silhouette bringt sie mich jeden Tag erneut zum Lachen. Oder LOOKSOFLAT, eine urkomische, plattgewalzte Karikatur einer Tischleuchte. Oder PORCA MISERIA!, seine etwas respektlosen Deckenleuchten aus zerberstenden Porzellantellern, deren Herstellung so unanständig teuer war, dass Ingo darauf bestand, alle Einnahmen durch Verkäufe dieser Leuchte an eine

desk lamp, or his irreverent PORCA MISERIA! chandeliers made of exploding porcelain dishes that were so obscenely expensive to produce that Ingo insisted on giving all the proceeds to charity whenever he sold one because he hated their exorbitant price. Although Ingo had always been a luddite – never texting, emailing or using computers – he viewed new technology as sort of awe-inspiring magic tricks, enthusiastically embracing these new capabilities into his work, using them as Houdini-like tools to amaze the world (and himself!). Whether making lights that magically turn on if you touch a certain wire with your finger or creating a sconce of a hologram of a light bulb, an LED-flickering candle flame for an elegant dinner table or simply making lights that would only work when draped over an elegant wire strung across the room, his use of technology was always uncomplicated and humanizing.

Ingo and I laughed a lot together over the years but we also experienced sadness together. On September 11, 2001, Ingo was in town and that morning we watched our neighboring World Trade Towers and the people within them burn and fall – he from his Lispenard Street roof and me from my Washington Square Park terrace. We were on the phone together much of that morning crying as we witnessed the death and destruction in our backyard happening before our eyes. Ingo didn't know what to do so he finally walked up to my house to watch the smoke rise from our city's new broken skyline and be together. During that heavy week of sadness and fear, Ingo and a few other of our closest friends spent the time at my

Wohltätigkeitsorganisation zu spenden, da er ihren Preis als maßlos übertrieben empfand. Obwohl Ingo schon immer ein Technikfeind war – er schreibt weder Textnachrichten noch E-Mails noch verwendet er einen Computer –, nutzt er die Optionen innovativer Technologie bei seinen Projekten wie eine Art Trickkiste, um wie einst Houdini die Welt (und sich selbst!) in Staunen zu versetzen. Seine Verwendung von Technologie ist dabei immer unkompliziert und von einem ausgesprochen menschlichen Ansatz geprägt, angefangen von Leuchten, die sich nur durch die Berührung eines bestimmten Kabels wie von Zauberhand einschalten, oder einer Wandleuchte aus dem Hologramm einer Glühlampe, flackernden Kerzenlichtern aus LED für ein Candle-Light-Dinner oder Leuchten, die nur funktionieren, wenn sie an einem eleganten, im Raum aufgespannten Draht drapiert werden.

Ingo und ich haben im Laufe der Jahre sehr viel miteinander gelacht, aber wir haben gemeinsam auch Trauriges erlebt. Am 11. September 2001 war Ingo in der Stadt und wir mussten mit ansehen, wie die Türme des World Trade Centers in unmittelbarer Nähe brannten und einstürzten und die Menschen mit sich rissen. Er verfolgte das Geschehen vom Dach in der Lispenard Street und ich von der Terrasse meines Hauses in Washington Square Park.

Wir telefonierten an jenem Vormittag lange und weinten angesichts der Tode und der Zerstörung, die sich direkt vor uns abspielte. Ingo wusste nicht, was er machen sollte, also kam er zu Fuß zu mir und wir schauten gemeinsam auf die Rauchwolken, die aus der zerstörten Skyline der Stadt aufstiegen. Diese von Traurigkeit und Angst erfüllten schweren Tage haben Ingo und einige andere enge Freunde in meinem

house cooking, trying to comfort and make each other feel normal, only to look out my windows realizing in disbelief that nothing was normal, the towers were gone and smoke was still rising.

Exactly one year later, Ingo returned to New York again to be here to remember the day. At midnight on the first 9-11 anniversary, I was in bed dozing off when my phone rang and it was a very distressed, emotional Ingo shouting into his phone, "KIM, GO TO YOUR WINDOW. THE LIGHTS! SEE THE TOWERS. LOOK AT THE BIRDS. IT IS ALL THE SOULS." I had no idea what he was talking about but his voice sounded so panic-stricken that I ran to my window and looked downtown where the towers used to stand but were now replaced by two columns of light shining upwards, an impermanent monument designed to commemorate the tragic day every year. What I saw shocked me. Still on the phone, Ingo was yelling, "LOOK AT THE BIRDS! IT'S THEIR SOULS!" As my eyes focused, I suddenly realized there were thousands of birds fluttering madly within the light of the two columns beaming into the night sky. It was crazy but I saw it with my own eyes. This event was mentioned casually in the papers the next day. It turned out migrating birds attracted by the lights in the sky swarmed and went crazy in those beams of light until morning. Ingo was sure these birds were the 3000 souls who lost their lives, fluttering in the light. And I think he was right.

Haus verbracht. Wir haben gemeinsam gekocht und versucht, uns gegenseitig Trost zuzusprechen und eine gewisse Normalität aufrecht zu erhalten. Der Blick aus dem Fenster mit den noch immer qualmenden eingestürzten Türmen vor uns, führte uns allerdings vor Augen, dass uns diese Normalität abhanden gekommen war.

Ein Jahr später kehrte Ingo zum Gedenken an jenen Tag nach New York zurück. Am Jahrestag des Terroranschlags vom 11. September klingelte bei mir um Mitternacht das Telefon und Ingo schrie in einem Zustand der offenkundigen Erschütterung und Emotionalität in sein Telefon „KIM, GEH' AN DEIN FENSTER, SCHAU DIE LICHTER, DIE TÜRME UND DIE VÖGEL. ES SIND DIE SEELEN ALLER TOTEN." Ich hatte keine Ahnung, wovon er sprach, da seine Stimme so sehr von Panik erfüllt war, also rannte ich zu meinem Fenster und schaute in Richtung Downtown, wo die Türme gestanden hatten, und sah zwei Lichtsäulen, die in den Himmel strahlten, ein temporäres Monument zum jährlichen Gedenken an diesen tragischen Tag. Der Anblick schockierte mich zutiefst, Ingo schrie „SCHAU DOCH, DIE VÖGEL, ES SIND IHRE SEELEN!". Und plötzlich sah ich, dass Tausende von Vögeln aufgeregt im Licht der beiden den Nachthimmel erhellenden Säulen herumflogen. Es war völlig verrückt, aber ich habe es mit meinen eigenen Augen gesehen. Am nächsten Tag wurde das Ereignis beiläufig in den Zeitungen erwähnt. Offenbar waren Zugvögel durch das Licht angezogen worden und flogen bis in die Morgendämmerung wie von Sinnen im Licht umher. Ingo war fest davon überzeugt, dass diese Vögel die Seelen der dreitausend Menschen waren, die hier ihr Leben verloren hatten, und ich glaube, er hatte Recht.

KIM HASTREITER
(BORN 1951, WEST ORANGE, NJ)
ist Schriftstellerin, Redakteurin, Kuratorin und Kulturanthropologin. Sie war 1984 Mitbegründerin des PAPER Magazine, das sie bis 2017 herausgab. Sie gründete eine Unternehmensberatung, kuratiert Ausstellungen und arbeitet als Redakteurin beim Apartamento Magazine.

KIM HASTREITER
(BORN 1951, WEST ORANGE, NJ)
is a writer, editor, curator and cultural anthropologist. In 1984 she co-founded PAPER Magazine, of which she was editor until 2017. She founded her own consultancy company, curates exhibitions, and works as an editor for Apartamento Magazine.

Tom Vack
Arbeit für den Poeten des Lichts / To Work for a Poet Revised

Ich bin Ingo 1987 begegnet. Ein Amerikaner, der Leuchten von Ingo für Driade installierte, hatte ihn mir in Mailand vorgestellt, wo wir ebenfalls arbeiteten, und zwar an einer Sammlung mit Philippe Starck. Er hatte die Idee, dass ich als Fotograf für Ingo interessant sein könnte, und machte uns miteinander bekannt, worauf dieser sagte: „Ruf mich an, wenn du in München bist!" Bei meinem nächsten Besuch in München meldete ich mich bei ihm. Ingo kam zu mir, ich saß auf dem Boden im Eingangsbereich der kleinen Wohnung, in der ich untergekommen war. Er sah mir lange und prüfend in die Augen. Was suchte er? Was sah er? Später würde ich verstehen, dass er nach meinem „inneren Licht" suchte. Im Laufe der Jahre habe ich oft erlebt, dass er die Menschen, die er in sein Leben einließ, auf diese Weise erkundete.

Es waren weder Portfolios, Namedropping oder gemeinsame Freunde, die ihn interessierten, ihm war lediglich diese innere Dimension wichtig. Tatsächlich hatte ich bereits einmal ein Foto seines YAYAHO Systems für einen Laden namens *City* in Chicago gemacht. Es gefiel ihm nicht. Die erste Probeaufnahme, die wir für ihn anfertigten, mochte er auch nicht, meine Arbeitsweise jedoch schon. Insofern konnte ihn ein kleiner Fehlschlag nicht abschrecken.

I met Ingo in 1987. I had been introduced to him in Milan earlier by an American who was installing lighting for Driade by Ingo, where we were also working on a collection by Philippe Starck. He thought that I might be interesting as photographer for Ingo and introduced me, whereupon he said: "If you're in Munich give me a call". I was visiting Munich and called him. Ingo came over and I sat on the floor of the hall in the small apartment where I was staying. He stared me long and searchingly in the eyes. What was he looking for? What could he see? Later I came to understand he was looking for my 'inner light', as over the years I saw him do so often with others he embraced.

No portfolios, name dropping or mutual friends, it was the inner dimension that was important for him. In fact, I had taken a picture of his YAYAHO system for a store named *City* in Chicago. He didn't like it. Nor did he like the first test picture we took for him but he did like the way I worked. And so he was not to be deterred by a little failure.

I recount this story as it seems to me central to explaining who this man is who put wings on a lightbulb, or silvery Alien figures in the Atomium. While these are examples of lighting to illuminate space they are never just that, they are inner light beacons to the darkened corners of our forgotten memories. Sometimes infantile, sometimes profane, sometimes spiritual and sometimes ironic or iconic.

But I am getting ahead of myself. When I began working for Ingo he was still in his more formal period that reflected his graphic

Ich erzähle diese Geschichte, weil sie mir zu erklären hilft, wer dieser Mann eigentlich ist, der einer Glühbirne Flügel verliehen oder das Atomium mit silbernen „Alien"-Figuren ausgestattet hat. Während seine Leuchten natürlich einen Raum erhellen sollen, sind sie niemals nur das, sie sind vielmehr innere Leuchtfeuer für die dunklen Ecken unserer vergessenen Erinnerungen. Sie können mitunter infantil, manchmal profan, oder auch spirituell, ironisch oder ikonisch sein.

Aber ich greife voraus. Als ich für Ingo zu arbeiten begann, befand er sich noch in seiner etwas formelleren Phase, die auch Ausdruck seiner Ausbildung als Grafikdesigner war. Die einzige Fantasieleuchte war BIBIBIBI. Ingo hat ein ausgesprochen präzises kompositionelles Gespür (sozusagen auf den Punkt genau), vielleicht entspringt es seiner Ausbildung zum Schriftsetzer. So erinnere ich mich beispielsweise an lange Überlegungen bezüglich der Länge eines Stabs bei ECLIPSE ELLIPSE.

Als Fotograf, der Designobjekte für Designer fotografiert, stelle ich natürlich die Form in den Mittelpunkt und wähle einen Hintergrund, der sie gelungen in Szene setzt. Für die ersten Bilder habe ich mithilfe von Halogenbirnen und Folien Hintergründe aus Licht und Schatten geschaffen, um so das Licht zu gestalten.

training. The only fantasy lamp back then was BIBIBIBI. Ingo is precise in his compositional sense (to the point), probably due to his training as a typesetter. I remember long considerations of the length of a stick in ECLIPSE ELLIPSE.

As a photographer of design for designers my approach is to reveal the form and create a background that compliments the protagonist.

My first images were fashioned around light and shadow creating backgrounds using halogen bulbs and foil to shape the light. We worked in a cellar space located at his offices. It was humid and had a particular smell due to the mold that was present. In fact, my camera bag continued to smell for weeks after I returned from our time there. It was a small space and required a certain ingenuity to create the space needed for the lamps' compositions. The cellar was also used as a storage space so as time went on there was less and less space to maneuver in.

We were photographing BAKARÚ and thought that it would be good to see the light from the lamps. Not having a smoke machine back then meant that Ingo and my assistant at the time, Corinne Pfister, had to blow smoke into the lamps during the timed exposure. Neither of them being smokers meant they were giddy and nearly green by the end of the shoot. The sets were simple and did not include any furniture except for a plywood tabletop balanced on a single I-beam, both painted silver. Ingo preferred a type of design referred to as 'arte povera' to compliment his compositions rather

Wir arbeiteten im Kellergeschoss seines Büros. Es war feucht und hatte diesen charakteristischen Schimmelgeruch. Meine Kameratasche roch noch Wochen später danach. Der kleine Raum erforderte einen gewissen Einfallsreichtum, um den nötigen Platz für das Arrangement der Leuchten zu schaffen. Überdies wurde er als Lager genutzt, das heißt, im Laufe der Zeit stand uns immer weniger Platz zur Verfügung.

Wir fotografierten BAKARÚ und dachten, dass es gut wäre, wenn das Licht der Leuchten tatsächlich zu sehen wäre. Da wir keine Nebelmaschine hatten, mussten Ingo und meine damalige Assistentin Corinne Pfister während der Langzeitbelichtung Rauch in die Lampen blasen. Keiner der beiden war Raucher, gegen Ende der Aufnahmen waren sie daher ziemlich grün im Gesicht und litten unter Schwindelgefühlen. Die Kulisse war schlicht und umfasste keine Möbel bis auf eine Sperrholztischplatte, die auf einem einzelnen I-Profil balancierte. Beides war silberfarben angestrichen. Ingo bevorzugte für seine Entwürfe ein Design mit einem Bezug zur Arte povera, das Prahlerische des zeitgenössischen Designs mochte er weniger. Jasper Morrison sollte später den Begriff „Super Normal" dafür prägen. Eine Ausnahme bildete der Stuhl der Serie 7 von Arne Jacobsen. Er gehörte irgendwann fest zum Repertoire der Inszenierung. Im Übrigen sind der Tisch und bestimmte Wandtafeln dreißig Jahre später immer noch im Einsatz. Nachdem Ingos Keller schließlich zu voll war, verlegten wir unsere Arbeit in neue Räumlichkeiten, die für fotografische Zwecke, aber auch die Produktentwicklung genutzt wurden und sich in einer Kaserne in der Schwere-Reiter-Straße befanden. Ich erinnere mich, dass

than the ostentatiousness of contemporary design. This is what Jasper Morrison would later term 'super normal'. The exception being Arne Jacobsen's Series 7 chair. This became a type of repertory theater setting. In fact, the same table and wall panels are still being used thirty years later. As the cellar in the offices became ever more cramped, we switched to a new space used both for photography and prototype development that had been an army barracks on Schwere-Reiter Strasse. I remember that all the heating pipes were exposed so that in winter, even with the radiators off, it was too hot in there, to the point you needed to keep the windows open.

In 1998 we began a catalog for MAMO NOUCHIES. Ingo asked if we could do a series of images like those made with natural light by Edward Steichen of the sculptor Constantin Brâncuși's studio. We used an old store room near the offices with wooden beams and skylights, and from a stone worker friend of Ingo's, we borrowed over a ton of materials that caused wheels of the truck to touch the frame when we hit a pothole. As the pictures were to be with natural light (although in the end we also simulated it) and it was February, the time available for shooting was limited.

Consequently, the store that was rented only for four days was not enough and we needed to move everything, the full ton again, to Schwere-Reiter Strasse. We needed a different background as the space did not offer the same architecture as the store, so we rented an old canvas tent used for who knows how many Oktoberfests

alle Heizungsrohre freilagen, sodass wir selbst noch bei ausgeschalteter Heizung im Winter die Fenster öffnen mussten, da der Raum dermaßen überhitzt war.

1998 begannen wir mit der Arbeit an einem Katalog über die MAMO NOUCHIES-Kollektion. Ingo fragte, ob wir eine Reihe von Aufnahmen machen könnten, die jenen Bildern ähnelten, die Edward Steichen von Constantin Brâncuşis Atelier mit Tageslicht aufgenommen hatte. Wir nutzten einen alten Lagerraum neben den Büros mit Holzbalken und Oberlichtern. Außerdem hatten wir von einem Stein-metz, mit dem Ingo befreundet war, über eine Tonne an Materialien ausgeliehen, sodass die Räder des Lastwagens bei jedem Schlagloch an der Karosserie schrappten. Da wir im Februar und nur mit Tageslicht (obwohl wir es am Ende doch nachgestellt haben) fotografieren wollten, blieb uns nur eine begrenzte Zeit für die Aufnahmen. Die vier Tage im angemieteten Lagerraum reichten uns schließlich nicht, und wir mussten das tonnenschwere Material in die Schwere-Reiter-Straße transportieren. Hier benötigten wir aber einen anderen Hintergrund, da der Raum nicht die gleichen architektonischen Details wie das Lager hatte, also mieteten wir ein altes Zelt aus Leinwand, das schon unzählige Male auf dem Oktoberfest seinen Dienst getan hatte, und einen entsprechend penetranten Geruch verströmte.

Wir fotografierten mit einem 35mm-Polaroid Instantfilm sowohl in Farbe als auch in Schwarz-Weiß, für den Vintagelook und die abstrakte Anmutung, die damit einhergehen. Bei der Bearbeitung des Films war eine Aufnahme auf den Boden gefallen, aufgrund der Empfindlichkeit des Materials zeigte sie deutliche

which had built up, as you can imagine, a particularly pungent odor from those events.

We were shooting the pictures on a 35mm Polaroid instant film both in color and black and white for its antique, abstract feel. It was a particularly delicate material and while editing the film one frame had fallen on the floor getting walked on over the course of the day. Ingo found it and was so enamored by the scratches that we used it in the catalog. There was always room for happy accidents.

It was with the MAMO NOUCHIES catalog in 1998 that I began my collaboration with Hagen Sczech. Hagen is 'Ingo's Keeper of the Light', he is in sympathetic vibration with the many aspects of Ingo's personal aesthetics. Photography is a series of decisions where one follows another, a flow, like water running downhill and if you place an obstacle in front of it, it will divert its direction. Over the years and with mutual respect we were able to bring ourselves into focus and roll downstream together.

Together we took a series of images using styrofoam to build our sets. Hagen is incredible with styrofoam and constructed desks, tools, window frames, light switches, vases, flowers or anything you wanted. Using the lightness of the foam allowed us to float furniture or lift walls. Though you had to remember not to sit on the chairs ly-ing around, as I found out to my peril seeing one from the corner of my eye and doing just that! Luckily it was me and not Ingo.

Next we worked on a series of images using background paper rolls. Ingo is very fond of paper as a material. We used these rolls to

Kratzspuren, zumal wir mehrmals darüber gelaufen waren. Ingo hob sie auf und war so angetan von den Kratzern, dass wir sie in den Katalog aufnahmen. Es gab also immer wieder glückliche Zufälle.

Im Rahmen des MAMO NOUCHIES-Katalogs begann ich 1998 meine Zusammenarbeit mit Hagen Sczech. Hagen ist sozusagen der Hüter von Ingos Licht und hegt ein tiefes Verständnis für die vielen Aspekte von Ingos persönlicher Ästhetik. In der Fotografie folgt eine Entscheidung auf die nächste, es gleicht einer fließenden Bewegung oder abwärts fließendem Wasser, und wenn man ein Hindernis davorlegt, ändert es seine Richtung. Im Laufe der Jahre haben wir in gegenseitigem Respekt füreinander gelernt, uns gemeinsam mit einer klaren Intention im Strom treiben zu lassen.

So haben wir beispielsweise zusammen eine Bilderserie mit Settings aus Styropor gemacht. Hagen kann großartige Dinge aus Styropor zaubern, angefangen von Tischen, Werkzeugen, Fensterrahmen und Lichtschaltern bis zu Vasen, Blumen etc. Durch die Leichtigkeit des Styropors konnten wir Möbel schweben lassen oder Wände anheben. Man durfte sich nur nicht versehentlich auf einen solchen Stuhl setzen, wie es mir, glücklicherweise nicht Ingo, in einem unbedachten Moment passiert ist.

Für das nächste Projekt verwendeten wir Rollen mit Hintergrundpapier. Ingo mag Papier als Material sehr gerne. Wir haben damit den Raum unterteilt bzw. definiert und als Hommage an Lucio Fontana auch mal aufgeschlitzt. Danach arbeiteten wir mit Drahtmöbeln. Werner Berthold – der schon viele Jahre für Ingo

divide or define the space. Or even to slit it as an homage to Lucio Fontana. After that we worked with wire furniture: Werner Berthold – who has worked for Ingo for years – was able to take a picture of any chair and create a line drawing in wire, perfectly proportioned. Tables and chairs were the repeating props as the tabletop was the stage to be lit by the lamp. In the case of a wire table, we needed to place a panel over the wire frame and then keep the light and object while eliminating the panel in Photoshop. Of course, there was a Jacobsen chair too.

To work with Ingo you have to accept that he will morph you into his vision. That seems to me correct. We definitely had our differences. He would cajole me about my tendency toward drama. There was a logic to my darkness, a lamp on a white background is like a candle in the sunlight, it lacks glow, and the function of a wabi sabi lamp is to bring light to the darkness. Never mind that. Darkness was heavy for Ingo, however too much lightness made a banal image as well. In the end I understood that our work together was about the tension between our opposing views and we found the balance between the two. It sometimes happened that he would ask for that darkness but you never could predict when that would be. Predictability for Ingo was not acceptable either.

He would often flip my image as the tension of the composition seemed better balanced to him. We decided it was because I was left-handed.

arbeitete – konnte jedes Bild irgendeines Stuhls in eine perfekt proportionierte Drahtkonstruktion desselben verwandeln. Tische und Stühle setzten wir immer wieder als Requisiten ein, da die Tischplatte die Bühne für das Licht der Leuchte war. Im Falle des Drahttischs mussten wir eine Platte auf den Drahtrahmen legen, die wir dann in Photoshop entfernten, wobei wir Licht und Objekt beibehielten. Natürlich gab es auch einen Jacobsen-Stuhl.

Wenn man mit Ingo zusammenarbeitet, muss man sich bewusst sein, dass er einen nach und nach in einen Teil seiner Vision verwandelt. Ich finde das in Ordnung. Wir hatten sicherlich unsere Differenzen, so hat er mich zum Beispiel wegen meines Hangs zum caravaggesken Drama aufgezogen. Diese Dunkelheit hat aber für mich eine gewisse Logik, denn eine Leuchte vor weißem Hintergrund gleicht einer Kerze im Sonnenlicht, sie leuchtet eben nicht. Die Funktion einer Lampe ist es ja schließlich, Licht in die Dunkelheit zu bringen. Ingo empfindet Dunkelheit als bedrückend, zu viel Licht ergibt jedoch ein banales Bild. Am Ende verstand ich, dass es diese Spannung zwischen unseren gegensätzlichen Ansichten war, die unsere Zusammenarbeit prägte, die wir aber immer auszugleichen wussten. Manchmal verlangte er sogar explizit nach mehr Dunkelheit, allerdings wusste man nie, wann dies der Fall sein würde. Vorhersehbarkeit wollte Ingo ebenfalls unbedingt vermeiden.

Häufig kippte er meine Bilder einfach, wenn ihm die Komposition so ausgewogener erschien. Wir kamen zu dem Schluss, dass es offenbar etwas mit meiner Linkshändigkeit zu tun hatte.

Ingo also felt that a small camera gave you more spontaneity than the 4 × 5 camera I usually worked with. However, to do controlled lighting with multiple exposures on a constructed set in a limited space you do not have the freedom like a fashion photographer to shoot freely and then later choose a moment that convinces you more. Working in large format I am used to choosing my angle and constructing my composition around it. I do not like to make versions, I like to make decisions. There was also the economics of film and Polaroids to consider here.

Another central aspect to Ingo's aesthetics is wabi sabi. This describes the acceptance of imperfection that guided the compositions away from formal perfection and also the use of materials.

The sense of wonder is also an important ingredient. Many times I heard the word "Wahnsinn" when Ingo and the team were working on an installation or prototype. I tried to put this wonder – in varying degrees of success – into my work as well.

Digital photography changed the economic aspect but added a new concession. When we worked on film there would be a final Polaroid that would be the picture to put on film. In the digital process you work in pieces that have to be put together in post-production. This proved to be frustrating for Ingo in the beginning and he would pine for the days of the Polaroid. Eventually he warmed to the post-production phase and loved the plasticity of the process, sometimes asking to move an object in the composition two millimeters down, refining colors and space. It would be remiss

Ingo vertrat überdies die Ansicht, dass eine kleine Kamera eine größere Spontaneität erlaube als die 4 × 5-Kamera, mit der ich gewöhnlich arbeitete. Bei einer kontrollierten Beleuchtung mit mehreren Belichtungen und einem konstruierten Setting auf beschränktem Raum hat man jedoch nicht die Freiheit, einfach wie bei Modeaufnahmen drauflos zu fotografieren, um später eine überzeugende Aufnahme auszuwählen. Bei der Arbeit mit dem Großformat wähle ich den Blickwinkel und baue dann meine Komposition darauf auf. Ich mache nicht gerne verschiedene Versionen, sondern treffe lieber Entscheidungen. Außerdem spielte ja auch ein ökonomischer Umgang mit Filmen und Polaroids eine Rolle.

Ein anderer zentraler Aspekt von Ingos Ästhetik ist Wabi-Sabi. Es bezeichnet die Akzeptanz der Unvollkommenheit, bei der die formale Perfektion der Komposition in den Hintergrund tritt, und eine spärliche Verwendung der Materialien. Der Moment des Staunens ist ebenfalls ein wichtiger Aspekt. So habe ich oft das Wort „Wahnsinn" gehört, wenn Ingo und das Team an einer Installation oder einem Prototyp arbeiteten. Ich habe versucht, dieses Staunen in meinen Arbeiten aufzugreifen – mit unterschiedlichem Erfolg.

Die digitale Fotografie hat den ökonomischen Aspekt verändert, aber neue Zugeständnisse mit sich gebracht. Wenn wir mit Filmen arbeiteten, nutzten wir ein endgültiges Polaroid, welches wir dann als Bild analog umsetzten. Beim digitalen Verfahren arbeitet man mit Teilen, die in der Nachbearbeitung zusammengesetzt werden. Ingo empfand das anfänglich als frustrierend und sehnte sich nach den Zeiten des Polaroids zurück. Irgendwann lernte er aber diesen Schritt der Nach-

not to mention the contribution of Stefan Geisbauer in the post-production phase. His mastery and precision in Photoshop and printing reproduction were essential to my transition from film to digital photography.

We often made references or homage to the vocabulary of some of our revered artists: Cy Twombly, Andy Warhol, Lucio Fontana, Robert Rauschenberg, Donald Judd, Roy Lichtenstein, Man Ray, László Moholy-Nagy, Edward Steichen, and Jan Vermeer for his light. We use these out of respect for the contribution they have made to opening and defining our perspectives. Perhaps someday some new poet of lighting will create an homage to Ingo.

bearbeitung zu schätzen, vor allem die Flexibilität, die dies eröffnete. Manchmal bat er mich zum Beispiel, ein Objekt im Entwurf zwei Millimeter nach unten zu rücken, oder die Farben und den Raum anzupassen.

Es wäre ein großes Versäumnis, Stefan Geisbauer im Zusammenhang der Nachbearbeitung nicht zu erwähnen. Seine Präzision sowie die meisterhafte Beherrschung von Photoshop und in der Druckwiedergabe waren für meinen Wechsel von der analogen zur digitalen Fotografie wesentlich.

In unserer Arbeit ließen wir oft die Wertschätzung für bestimmte Künstler anklingen: Cy Twombly, Andy Warhol, Lucio Fontana, Robert Rauschenberg, Donald Judd, Roy Lichtenstein, Man Ray, Lázló Moholy-Nagy, Edward Steichen und Jan Vermeer für seinen Umgang mit Licht. Wir wollten damit zum Ausdruck bringen, dass diese Künstler unseren Horizont und unsere Sicht auf die Dinge bereichert haben. Vielleicht wird eines Tages ein junger Lichtpoet eine Hommage an Ingo schreiben.

TOM VACK
(GEB. 1948, CHICAGO)
Der Fotograf Tom Vack studierte Gegenwartskunst, Architektur, Industrie- und Grafikdesign. Im Laufe der Jahre arbeitete er u. a. für Ron Arad, Aldo Cibic, Antonio Citterio, Michele De Lucchi, Massimo Iosa Ghini, Alessandro Mendini, Marc Newson und Philippe Starck. Seit 1987 fotografiert er für Ingo Maurer.

TOM VACK
(BORN 1948, CHICAGO)
Photographer Tom Vack studied contemporary art, architecture, industry and graphic design. Over the years he worked on photography commissions for Ron Arad, Aldo Cibic, Antonia Citterio, Michele De Lucchi, Massimo Iosa Ghini, Alessandro Mendini, Marc Newson, and Philippe Starck, among others. Since 1987 he has photographed for Ingo Maurer.

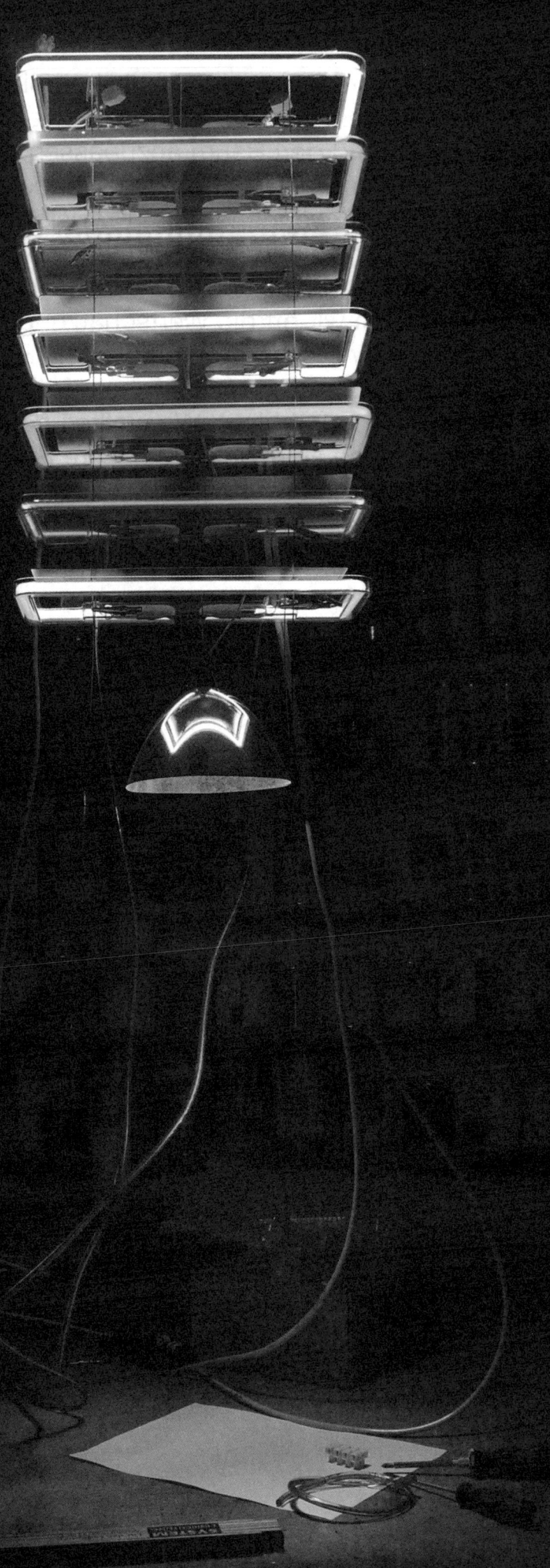

Hi Bruce
2007

Ingo Maurer
Kunststoff, Metall,
Chrom, Neonröhren
Plastic, metal, chrome,
neon lights

Living Vegas
2007

Ingo Maurer
Kunststoff, Metall, Chrom,
Neon-Röhren
Plastic, metal, chrome,
neon lights

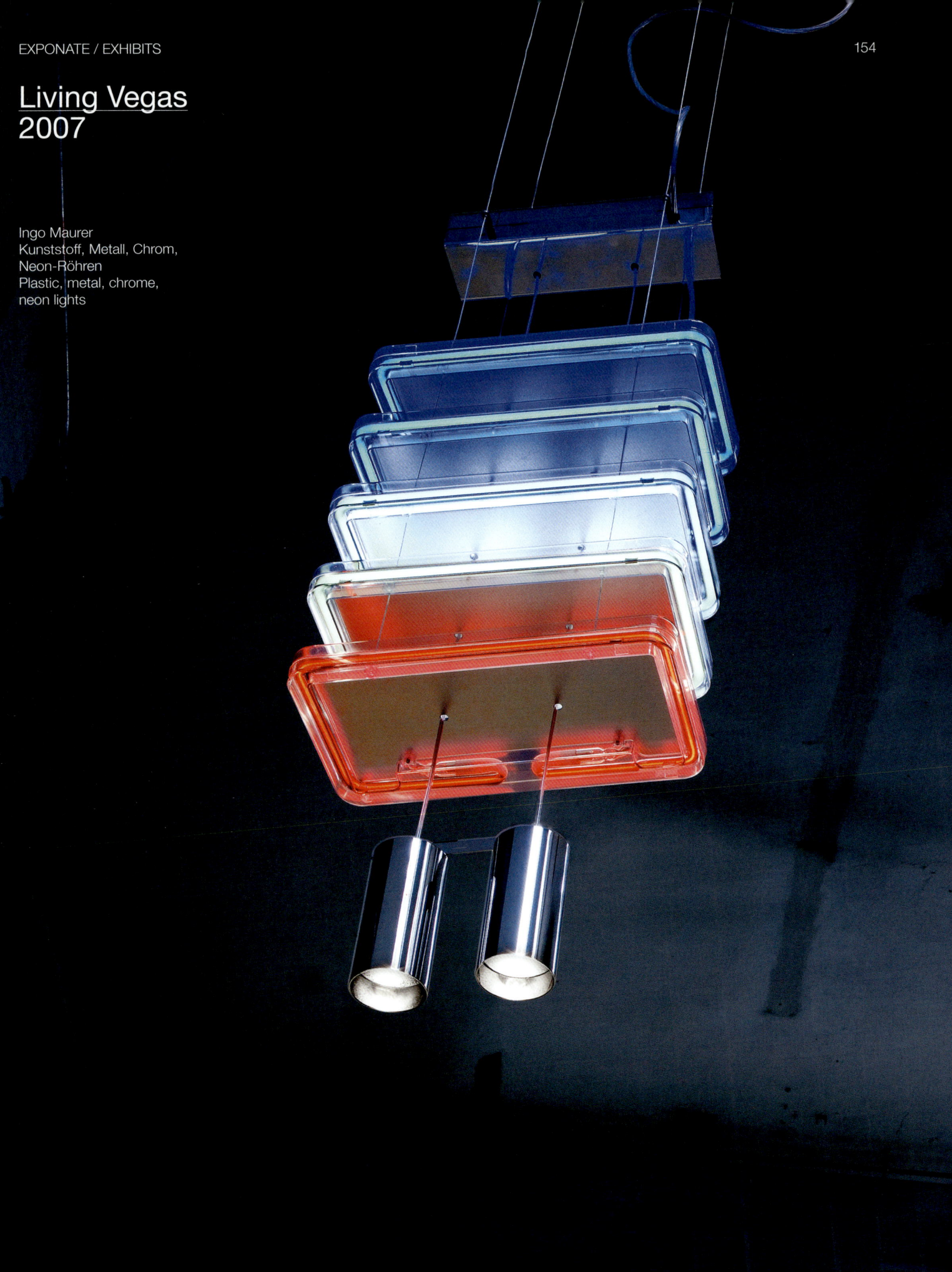

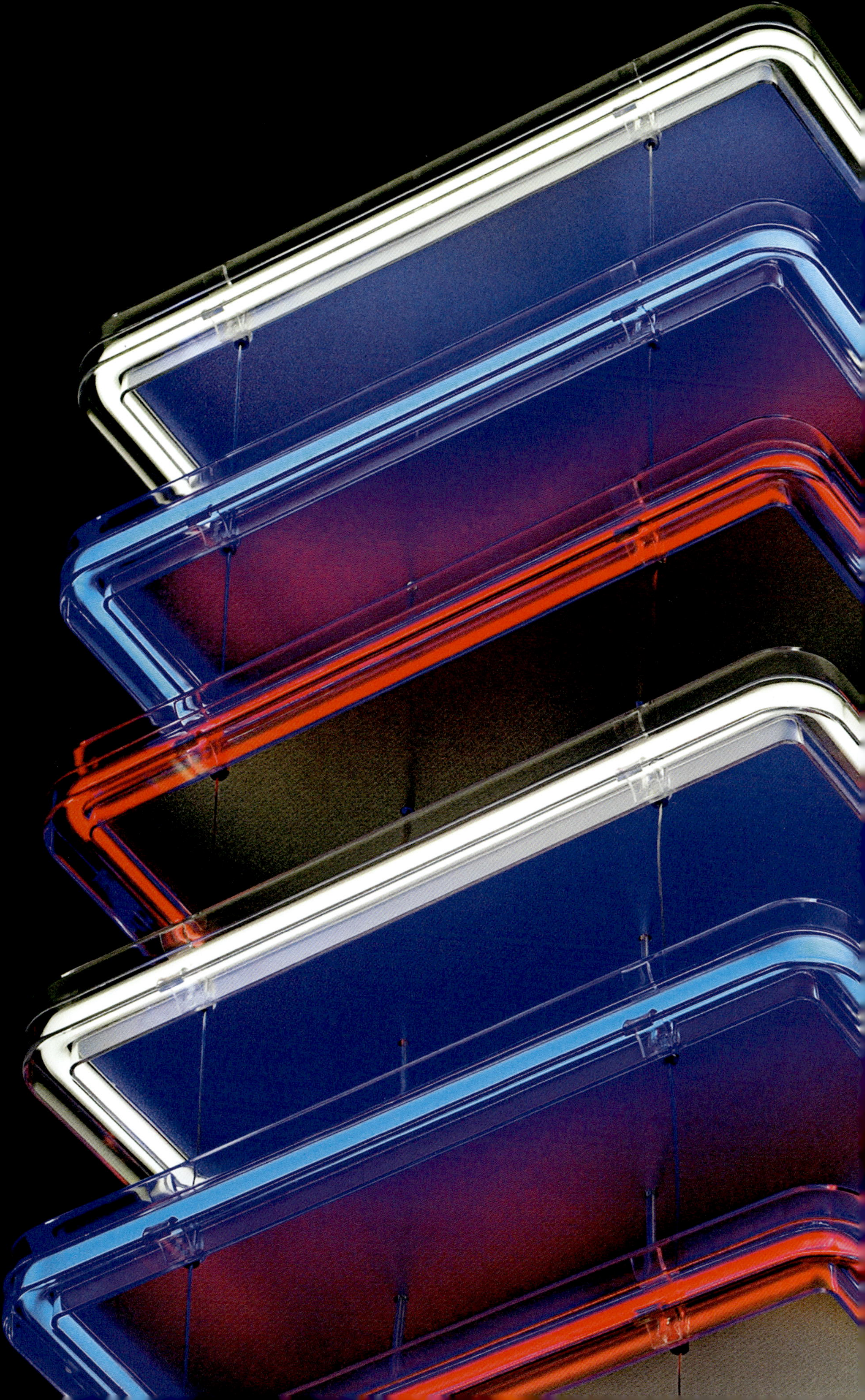

Tu-Be Two
2007

Ron Arad,
Ingo Maurer
Aluminium-Tuben, Stahl
Aluminum tubes, steel

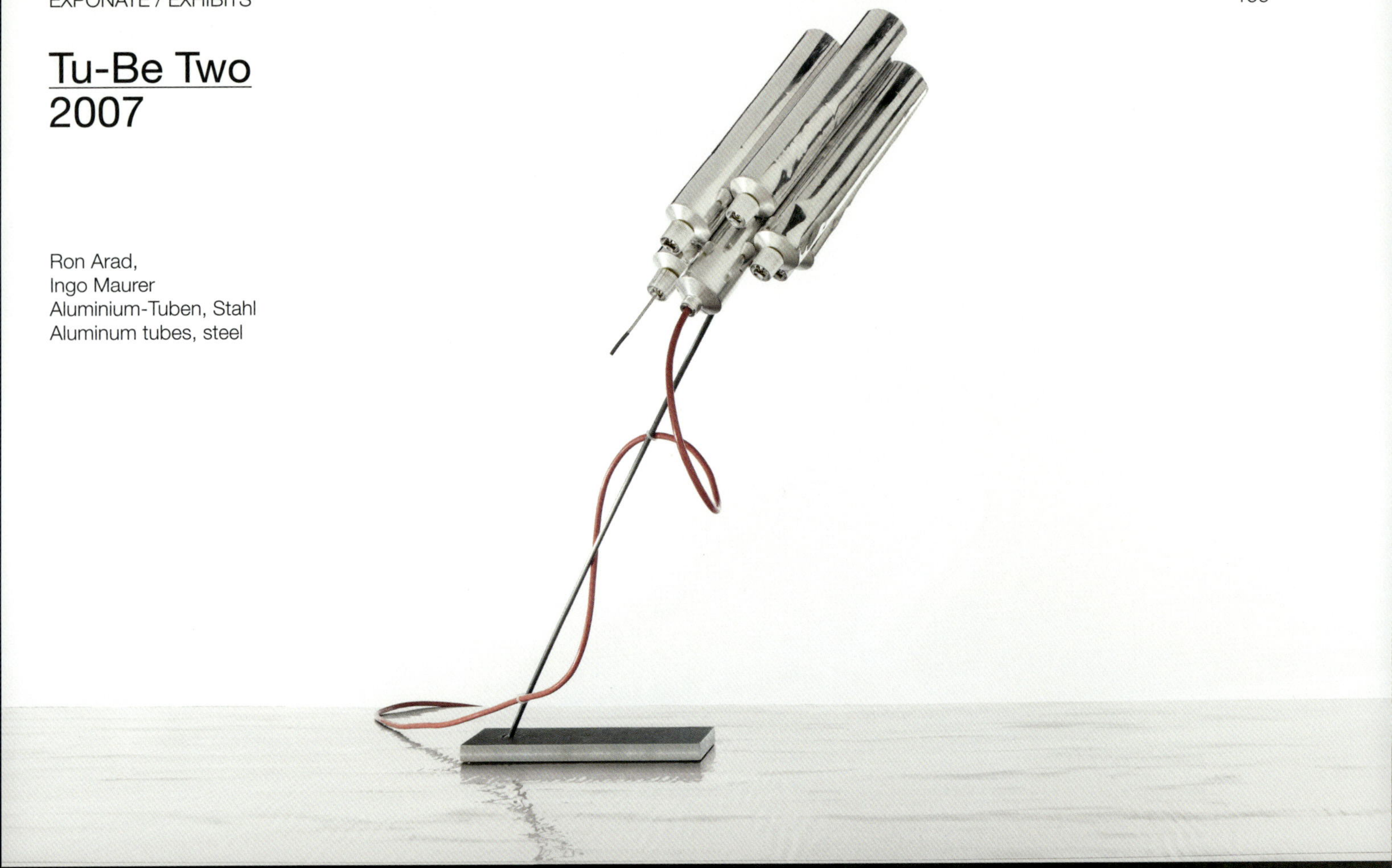

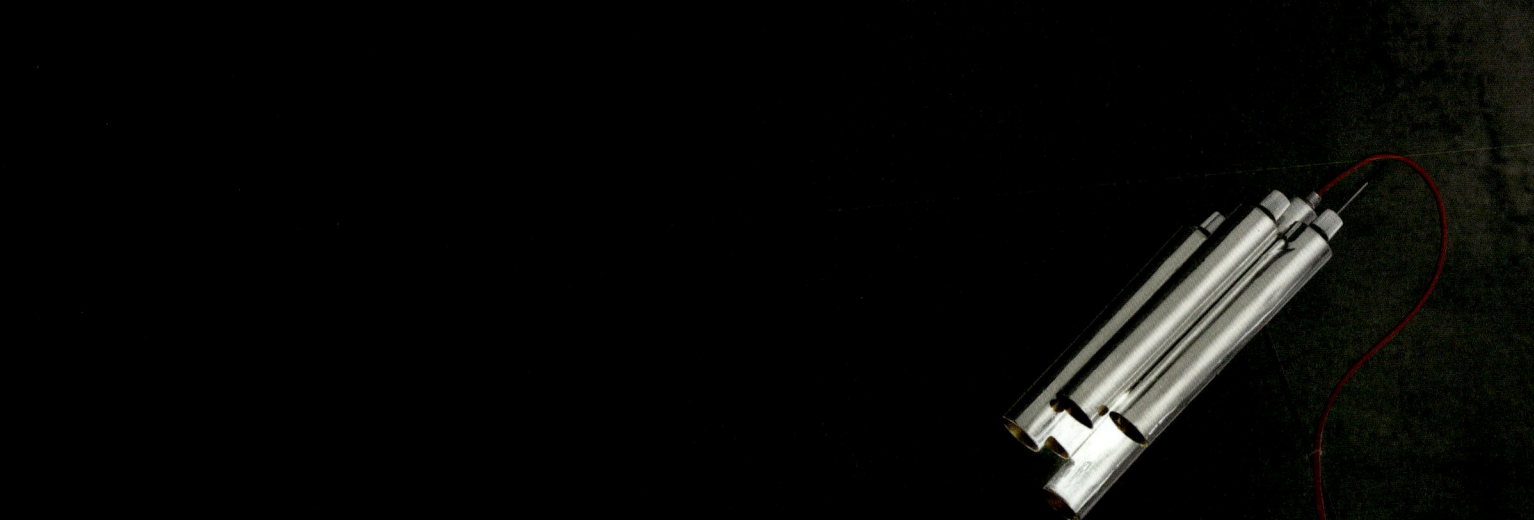

Early Future
2008

Ingo Maurer
OLED-Module,
Metall, Glas
OLED modules,
metal, glass

Zufall T
2008

Ingo Maurer + Team
Silikon, Corian,
Aluminium
Silicone, corian,
aluminum

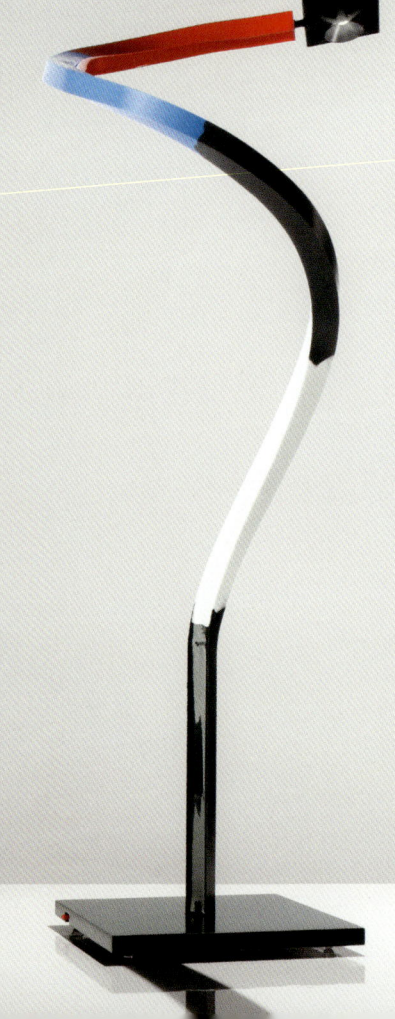

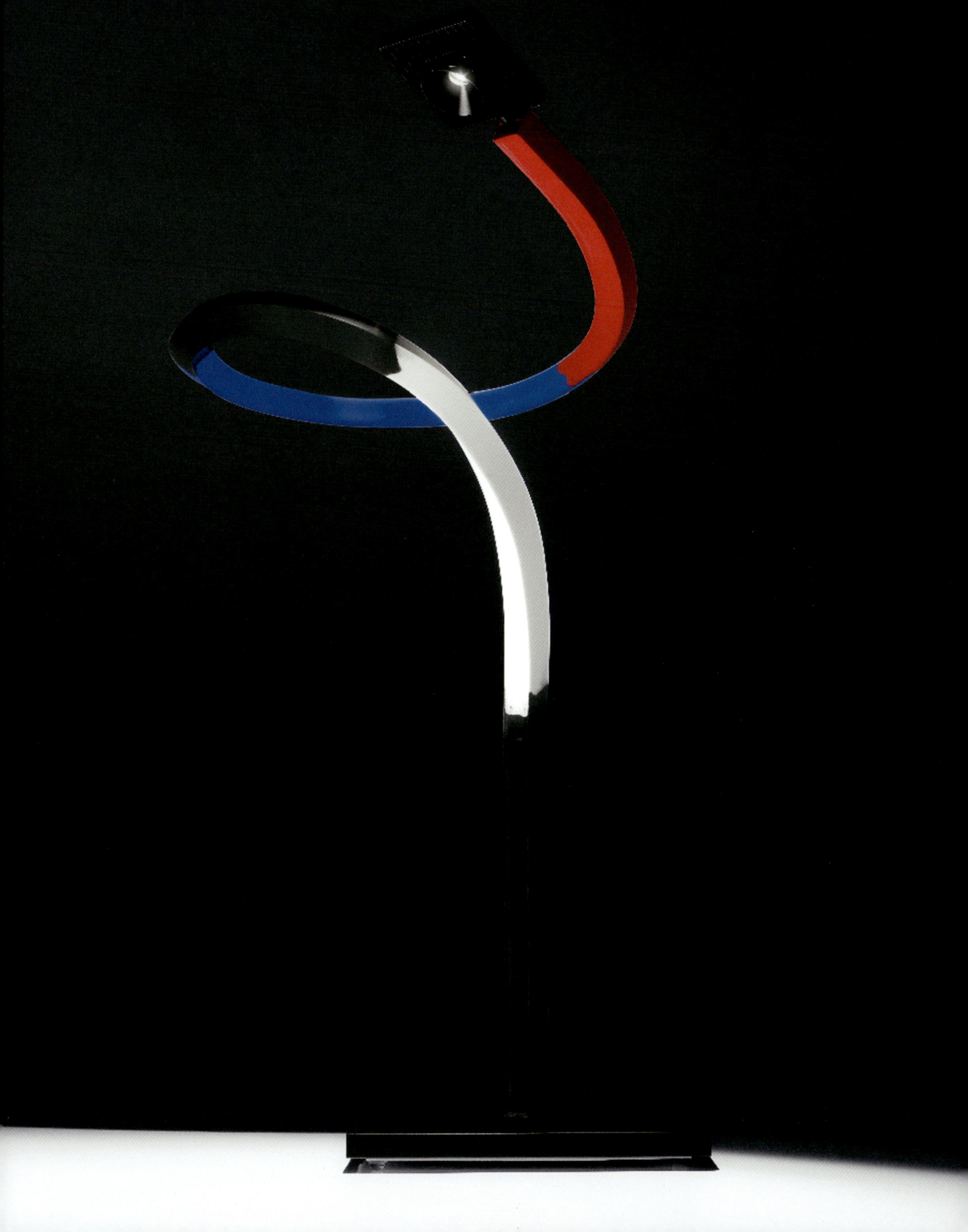

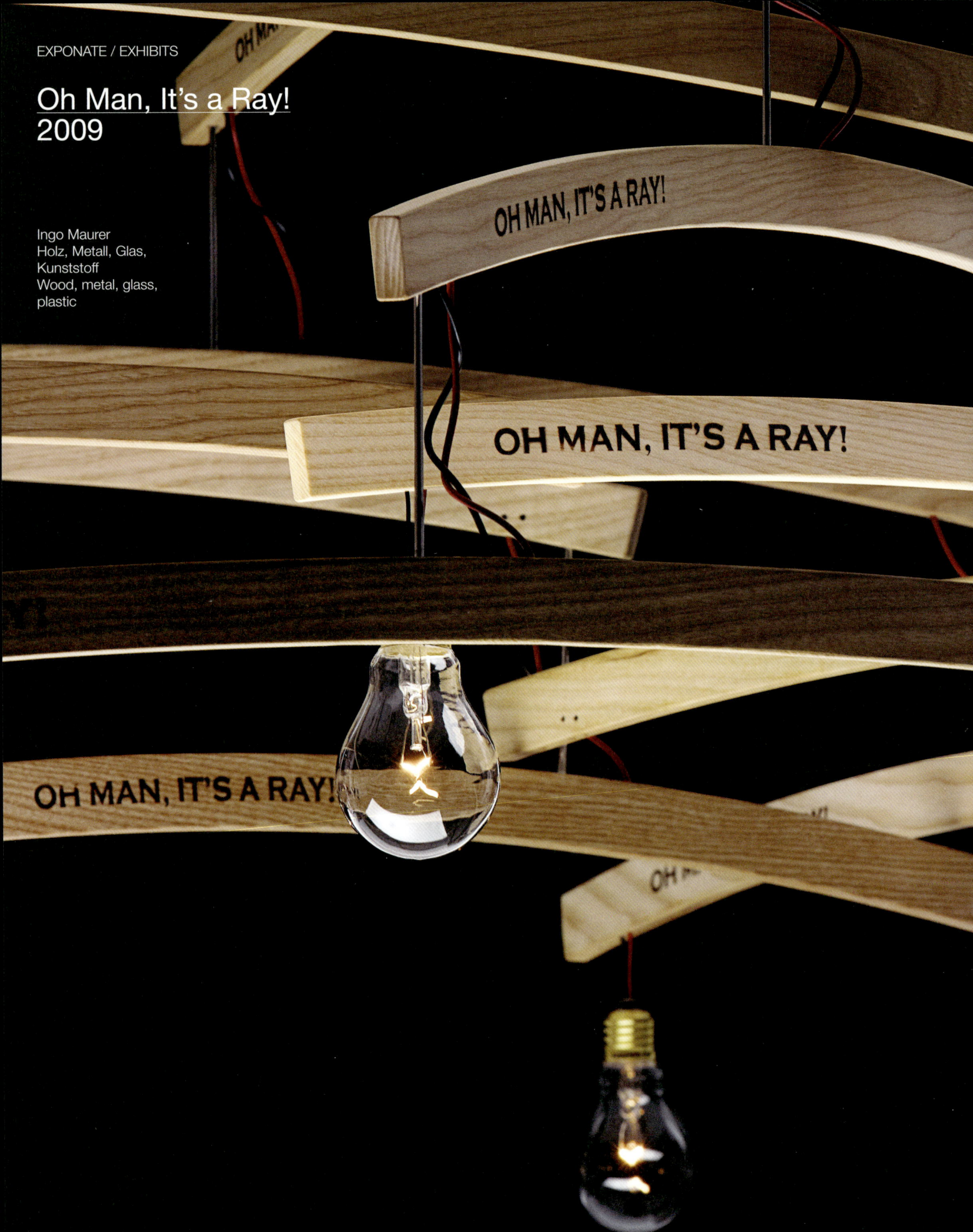

Oh Man, It's a Ray!
2009

Ingo Maurer
Holz, Metall, Glas,
Kunststoff
Wood, metal, glass,
plastic

Double T. Future
2010

Ingo Maurer + Team
OLED-Module,
Aluminium, Stahl
OLED modules,
aluminum, steel

Double C. Future
2010/2011

Ingo Maurer + Team
OLED-Module,
Aluminium, Stahl
OLED modules,
aluminum, steel

Looksoflat
2010

Stefan Geisbauer
Eloxiertes Aluminium
Anodized aluminum

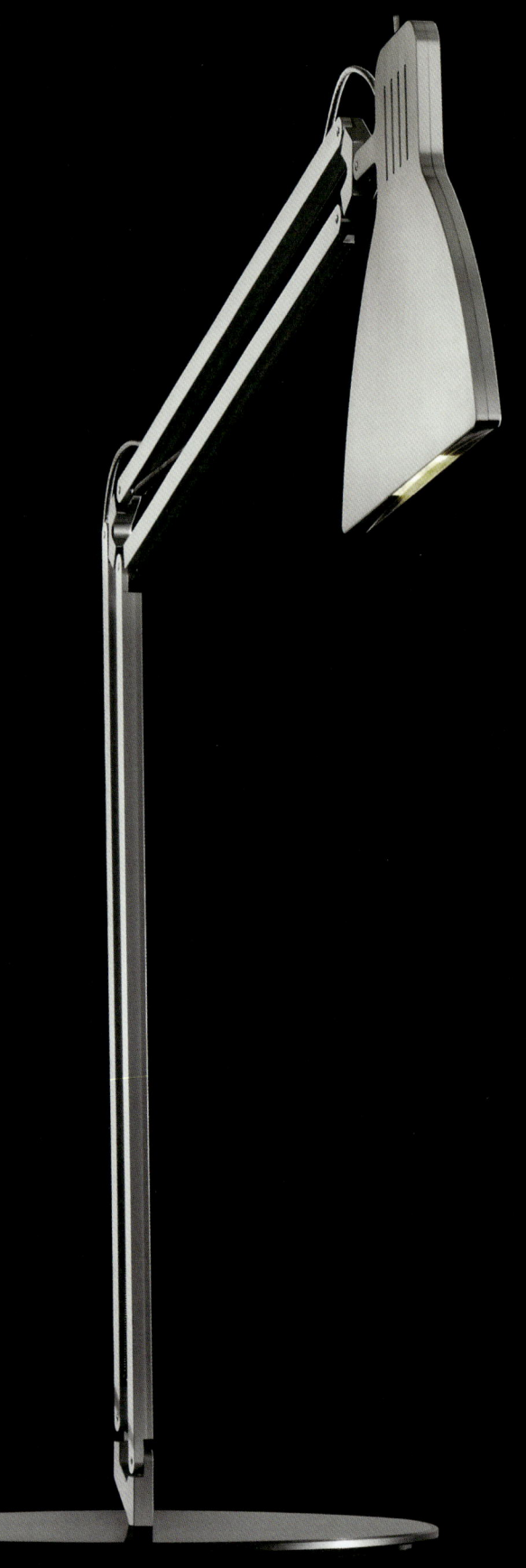

LED Wallpaper
2011

Ingo Maurer + Team
LED, Kunststoff
LED, plastic

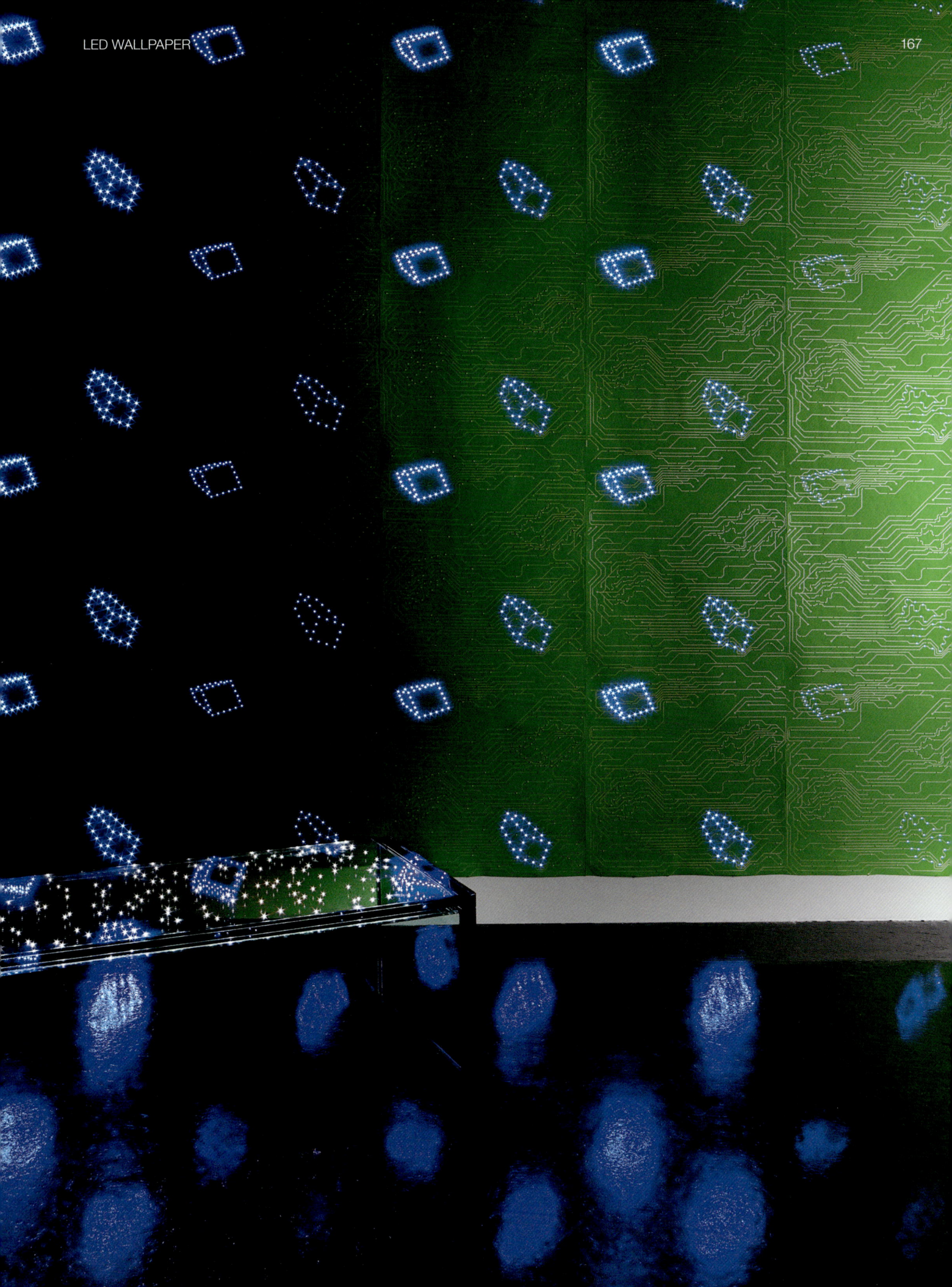

My New Flame
2012

Moritz Waldemeyer,
Ingo Maurer + Team
Platine, LED, Metall,
Kunststoff
Circuit board, LED,
metal, plastic

Flying Flames
2013

Moritz Waldemeyer,
Ingo Maurer + Team
Platine, LED, Metall,
Kunststoff
Circuit board, LED,
metal, plastic

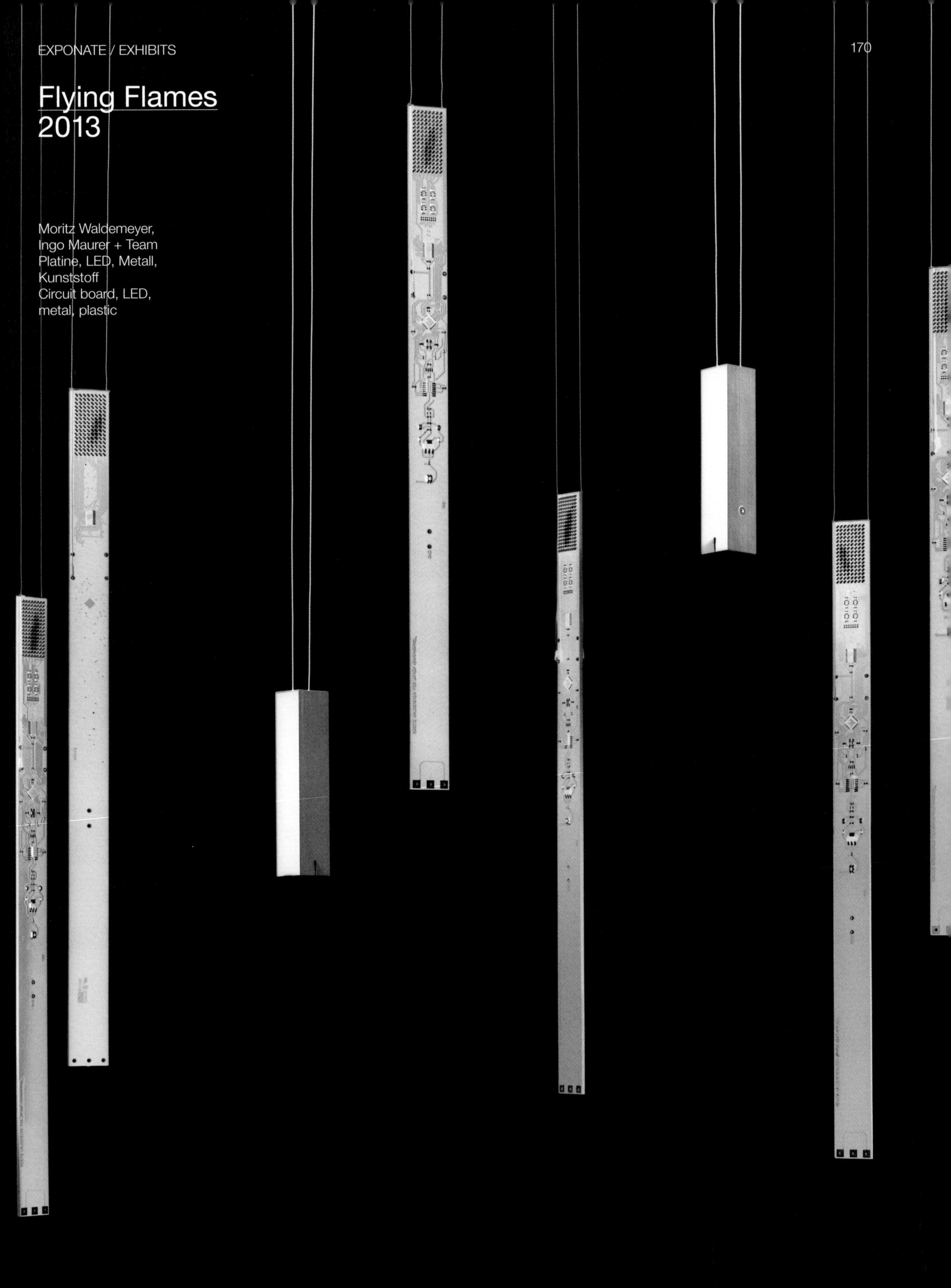

The Humblies
2014

Ingo Maurer
Papier, Metall, Blattgold,
Edelstahl
Paper, metal, gold leaf,
stainless steel

I Ricchi Poveri
Five Butterflies
2014

Ingo Maurer
Niedervolt-Halogen-Glühlampe,
Stahl, Messing,
Schmetterlingsmodelle
Low-voltage halogen bulb,
steel, brass, butterfly models

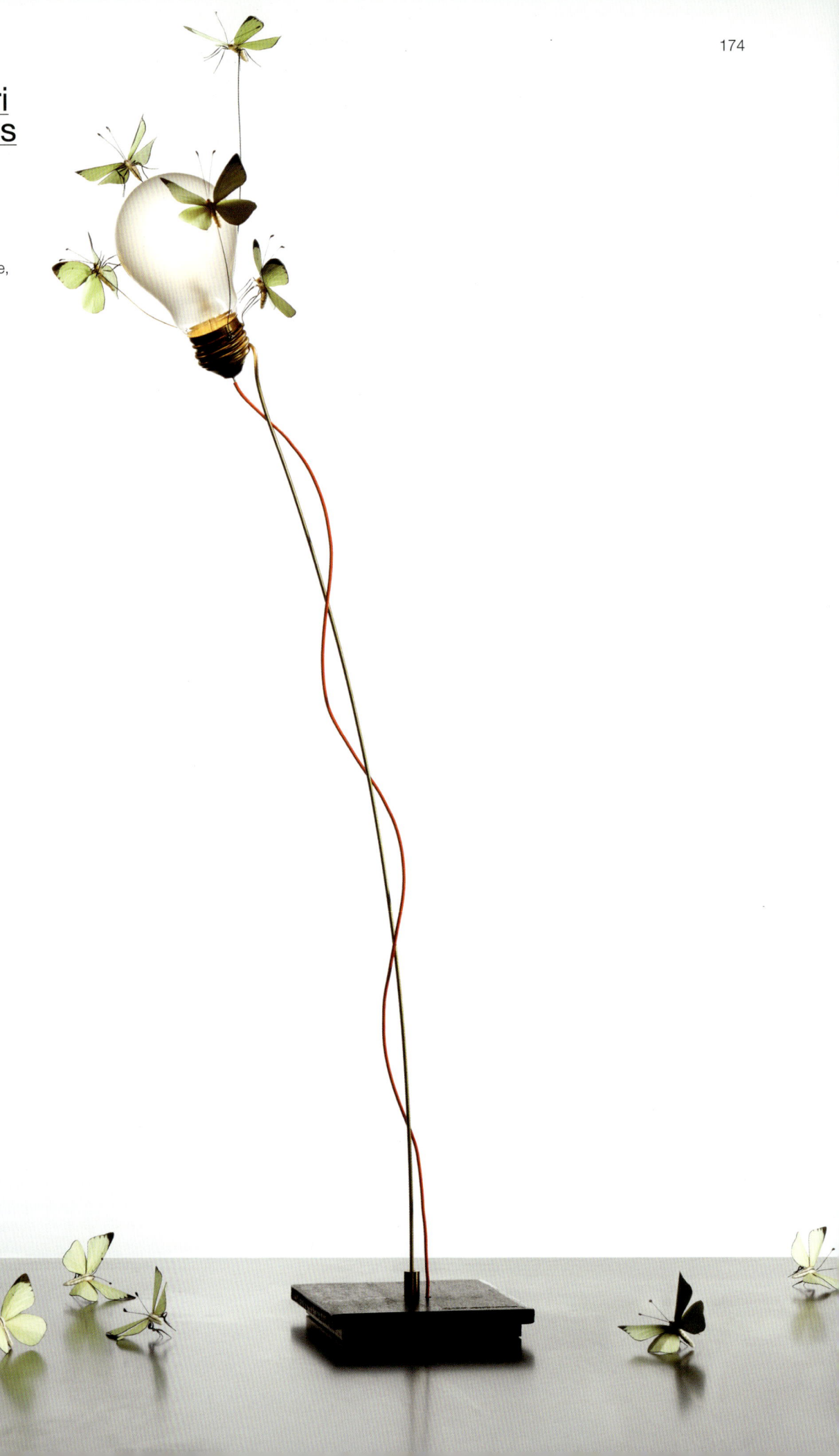

I Ricchi Poveri
Bzzzz
2014

Ingo Maurer
Niedervolt-Halogen-Glühlampe,
Stahl, Messing, Libellenmodell
Low-voltage halogen bulb,
steel, brass, dragonfly model

I Ricchi Poveri
Fly
2014

Ingo Maurer
LED-Glühlampe,
Stahl, Fliegenmodell
LED bulb, steel,
fly model

I Ricchi Poveri
Monument for a Bulb
2014

Ingo Maurer
Niedervolt-Halogen-Glühlampe,
Neusilber, Stahl, Messing, Figuren
Low-voltage halogen bulb,
nickel silver, steel, brass, figures

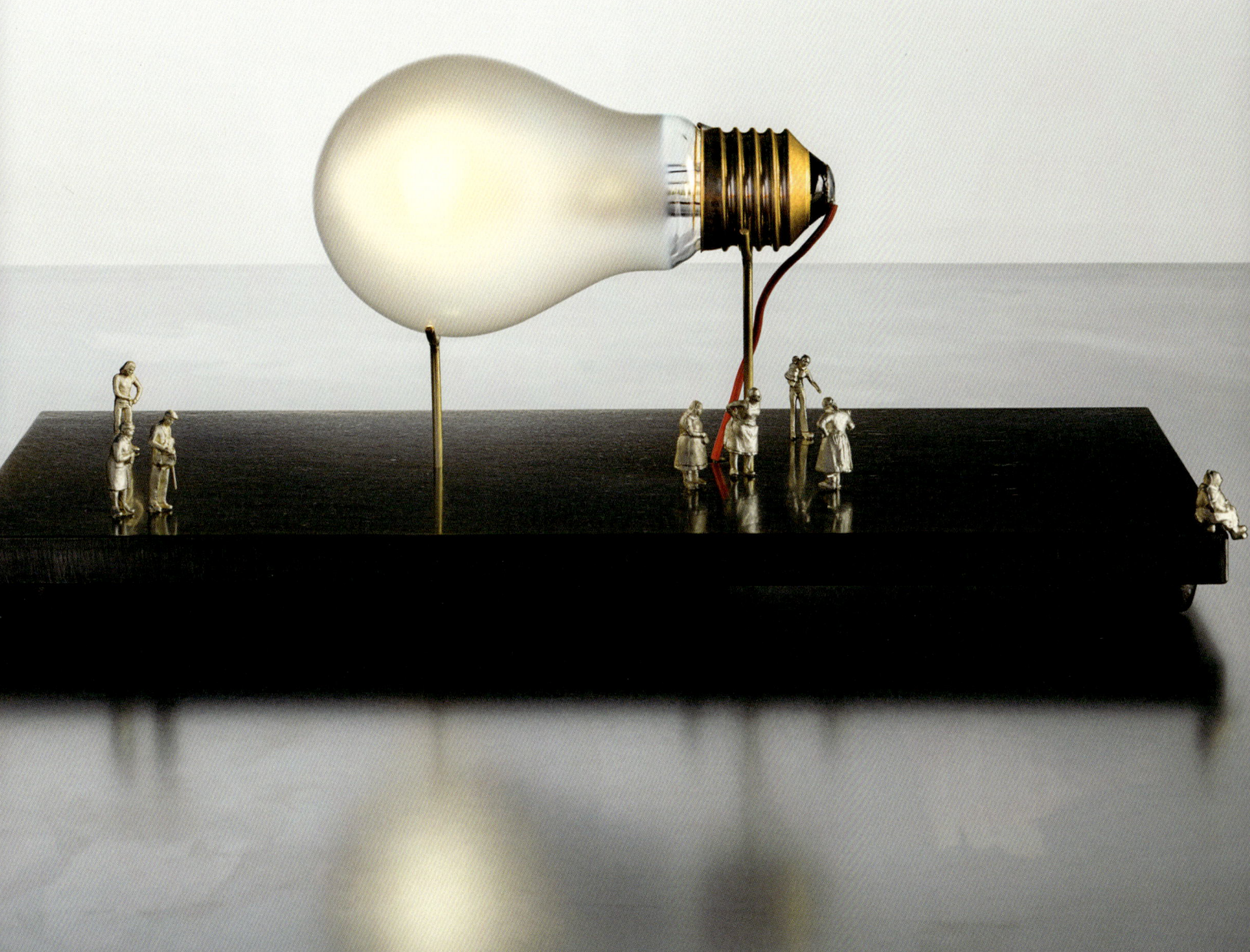

I Ricchi Poveri
Toto
2014

Ingo Maurer
Niedervolt-Halogen-Glühlampe,
Stahl, Messing
Low-voltage halogen bulb,
steel, brass

T.T. Moon
2014

Ingo Maurer + Team
Platine, Metall,
Aluminium
Circuit board, metal,
aluminum

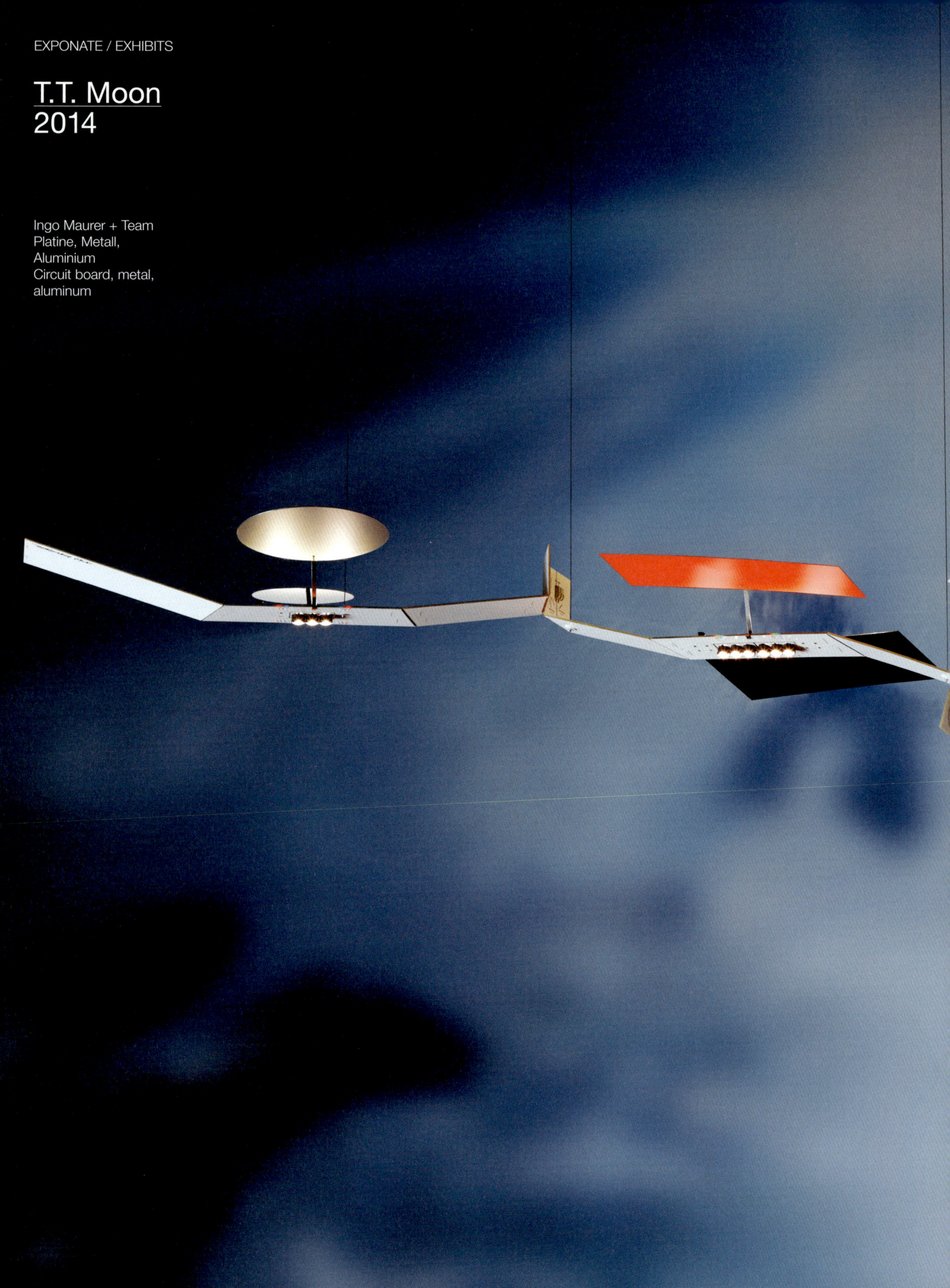

Whisper Wind
2014

Ingo Maurer + Team
OLED-Module, Metall,
Kunststoff
OLED modules, metal,
plastic

Oh·LED·One
2015

Ingo Maurer
OLED-Module, Glas,
Edelstahl, Kunststoff
OLED modules,
glass, stainless
steel, plastic

Dew Drops
2014

Ingo Maurer + Team
Kunststofffolie, Metall
Plastic foil, metal

What We Do Counts
2015

Ingo Maurer
Aluminium, Stahl
Aluminum, steel

Flatterby
2016

Ingo Maurer
Glas, Kunststoff,
Schmetterlingsmodelle
Glass, plastic,
butterfly models

Ru Ku Ku
2016

Ingo Maurer
Metall, Glas, Kunststoff,
Silikon
Metal, glass, plastic,
silicone

Ringelpiez
2017

Ingo Maurer + Team
Aluminium, Kohlefaser,
Papier
Aluminum, carbon fiber,
paper

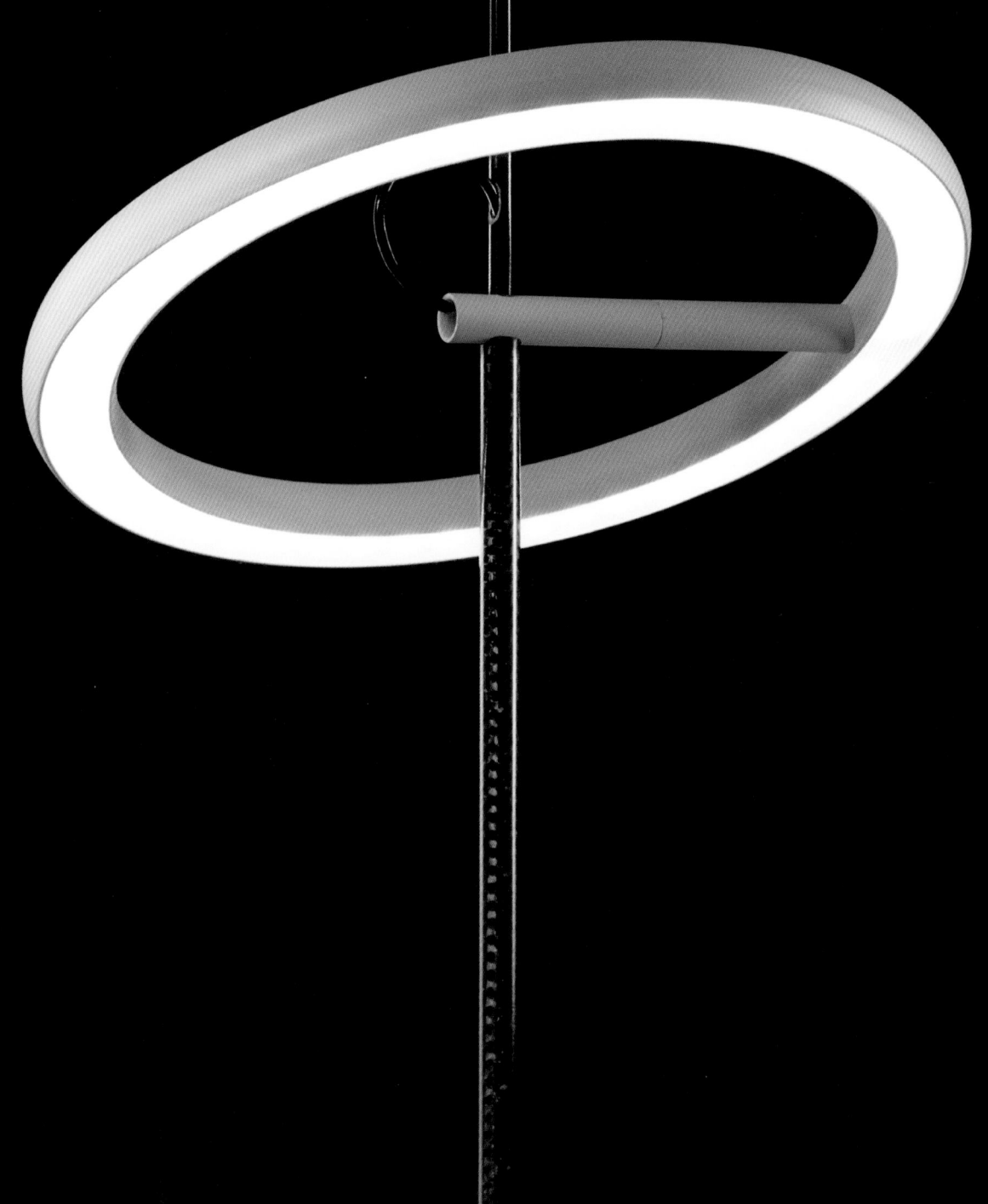

Ingo Maurer + Team
Papierschirm Frivoloso
Kohlefaser, Metall,
Kunststoff
Pleated paper diffuser Frivoloso
Carbon fiber, metal, plastic

Eclipse Ellipse
2017

Ingo Maurer
Stahl, Aluminium
Steel, aluminum

Blue Luzy
2018

Ingo Maurer
Niedervolt-Halogen-Glühlampe,
Kunststoff, Metall
Low-voltage halogen bulb,
plastic, metal

Luzy On The Wall
2018

Ingo Maurer
Niedervolt-Halogen-Glühlampen,
Kunststoff, Metall
Low-voltage halogen bulbs,
plastic, metal

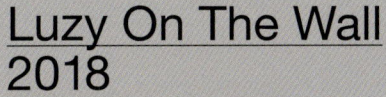

Koyoo
2018

Axel Schmid
Aluminium, Stahldraht,
Papier
Aluminum, steel wire,
paper

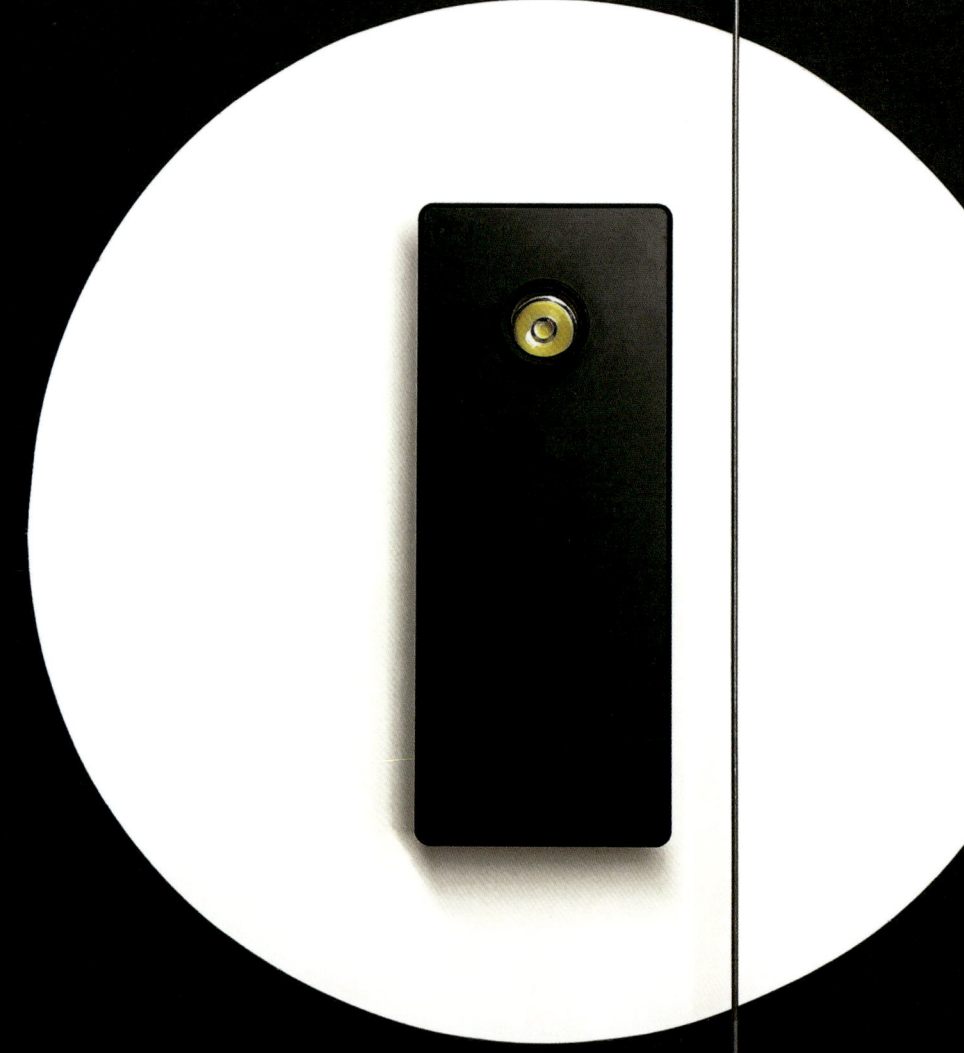

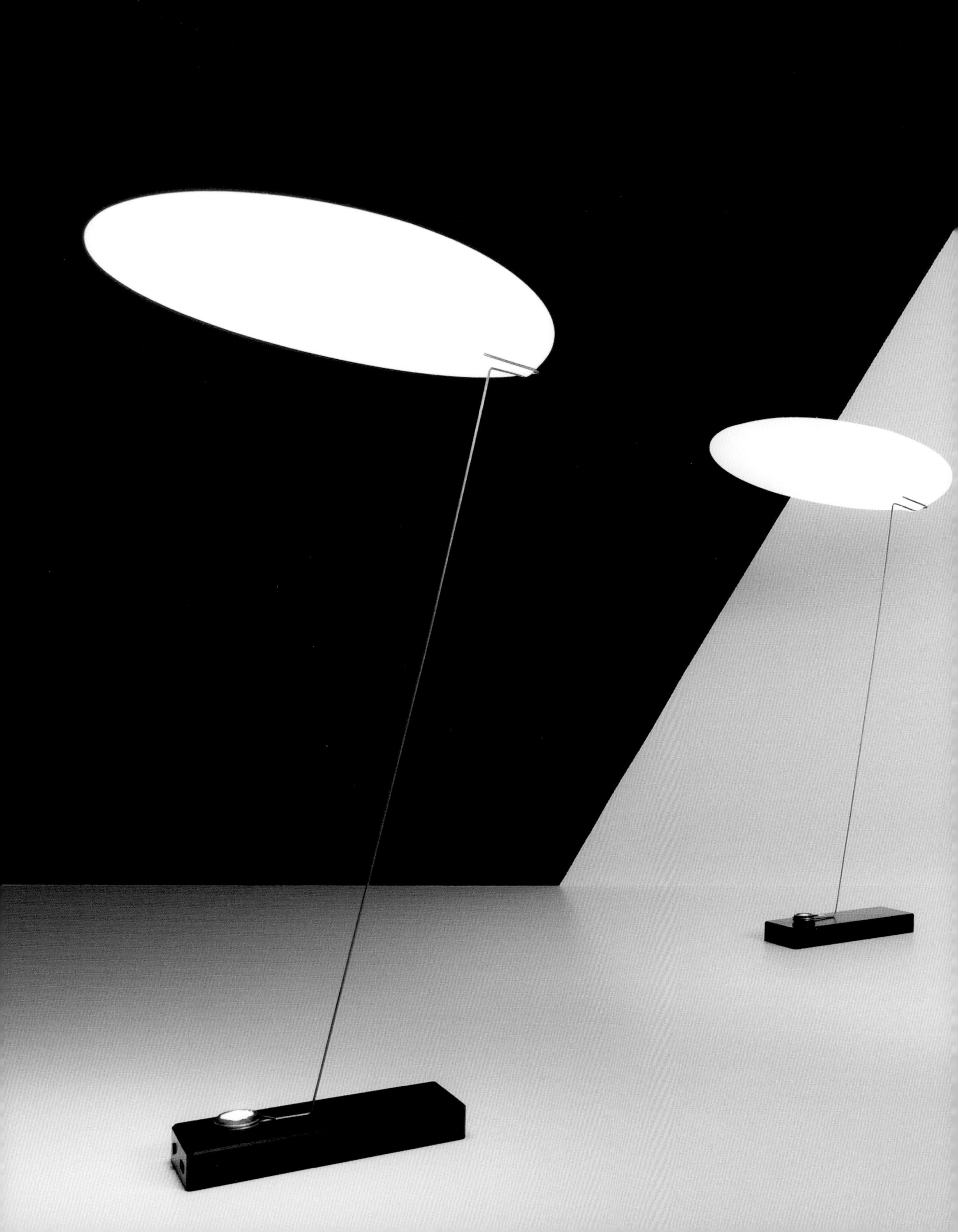

La Festa delle Farfalle
2019

Ingo Maurer + Team
Niedervolt-Halogen-Glühlampe,
Papier, Metall, Porzellan
Low-voltage halogen bulb,
paper, metal, porcelain

Oop's
2019

Ingo Maurer + Team
Papier, Metall, Kunststoff
Paper, metal, plastic

Xenia Riemann-Tyroller + Rosa Carole Rodeck
Teamgespräch / Team Talk

XENIA RIEMANN-TYROLLER – WAS IST LICHT FÜR EUCH?

MARISA MARISCAL Licht ist mein Leben. Ich habe mich immer schon mit Licht beschäftigt. Für mich ist es eine gute Symbiose von Mathematik, Kunst und Biologie.

AXEL SCHMID Licht ist erst einmal etwas im Raum. Aber wenn man es genau zerlegt, ist es eine Übereinanderstaffelung von physikalischen oder andersartigen Eigenschaften, die letztendlich das Sehen ermöglicht. Wenn man Licht und Mensch gegenüberstellt, dann ist es das Sehen. Es ist viel mehr als Helligkeit oder „an und aus".

DAVID ENGELHORN Für mich hat Licht zwei Seiten. Es bedeutet für mich Leben, Licht kann aber auch negativ sein. Das find ich das Spannende am Licht: Denn ist es ja etwas Immaterielles. Eigentlich lebt Licht nur durch andere Materialien. Man kann es nur erkennen, wenn es reflektiert wird. Licht hat auch immer einen Schatten, hat also immer einen Gegenpart.

SEBASTIAN HEPTING Licht ist für mich Stimmung und Emotion. Wenn ich an Sonnenuntergänge oder Gewitter mit Blitzen denke, an die Stimmung von

XENIA RIEMANN-TYROLLER – FOR YOU, WHAT DOES LIGHT MEAN?

MARISA MARISCAL Light is my life. I've always concerned myself with light. For me, it is a great symbiosis of mathematics, art, and biology.

AXEL SCHMIDT Light is, first up, something in space. However, if one dissects it carefully, then it is the superimposition of physical and other types of properties that in the final instance enable vision. And if light and humans are juxtaposed, then that is vision. It is much more than just a matter of brightness or "on and off".

DAVID ENGELHORN To my mind, there are two sides to light. For me, light signifies life. That said, light can also be negative. That's what I find exciting about light: Because it is something immaterial. In fact, light only exists through other materials. It can only be discerned when it is reflected. Light also always comes with shadow, meaning its opposite and counterpart.

SEBASTIAN HEPTING For me, light is mood and emotion. If I think of sunsets or storms with lightning, the mood of streetlights in fog or the strobe lights in a disco, then these are forms of light that move me spontaneously.

GABI KÜMMERLIN Personally, I think light primarily has a utilitarian function. You use it to create mood or a space, or to enable you to work at night. The decorative side to it is beautiful, but

Straßenleuchten im Nebel oder den Stroboskopeffekt in der Disko, das ist Licht, das mich spontan bewegt.

GABI KÜMMERLIN Licht hat für mich in erster Linie eine dienende Funktion. Man macht damit Atmosphäre, schafft einen Raum, aber auch die Möglichkeit, bei Nacht zu arbeiten. Das Schmückende ist schön, aber ein Beiwerk. In erster Linie muss das Licht funktionieren für das, was ich damit machen will.

„Licht ist Luxus"

SEBASTIAN UTERMÖHLEN Licht ist Luxus. Wir sind es alle gewohnt, Schalter zu drücken, zu drehen und zu dimmen.
Ich denke aber auch an die Kerze, das Flutlicht, den gedeckten Tisch mit zwei Glühbirnen darüber; die Dörfer und Städte nachts von einem Flugzeug aus, Las Vegas, das Oktoberfest (noch zu den Zeiten der Glühbirne), ein Meer von Glühwürmchen, Biolumineszenz im Meer, der Gewitterblitz, der Sternenhimmel, der Autoscheinwerfer, die Großstadtstraßenflucht und vieles mehr ist Licht. Und die Dunkelheit braucht es dazu natürlich auch.
Die Rolle des Lichts im privaten Leben ist für mich am spannendsten, da hier individuell auf die Bedürfnisse des Nutzers eingegangen werden kann. Eine U-Bahn-Station, ein Arbeitsplatz, der Sportplatz usw. unterliegen Notwendigkeiten und technischen Normen.
Und dann denke ich natürlich an die Verpackung dazu: die Lampe.

an ancillary. First and foremost, light has to function for what I want to do with it.

"Light is a Luxury"

SEBASTIAN UTERMÖHLEN Light is a luxury. We are all used to pressing, turning or dimming the switch.
However, candles also come to mind, floodlights, a dining table with two lamps above it; villages and cities at night, seen from an airplane, Las Vegas, the Oktoberfest (back in the days of the incandescent lightbulb), a sea of glowworms, bioluminescence in the sea, sheet lightning, the stars at night, car headlights, the lines of a street in a big city, and much more besides – are all light. And, you need darkness, too, of course.
For me, the role of light in private life is the most exciting topic of all, as here you can address the personal needs of the user in question. A subway station, a place of work, a sports ground, etc. – they are all subject to specific constraints and technical norms.
And then I think of course about the right packaging for the light, namely the luminaire.

ROSA CAROLE RODECK – WHAT TERMS SUM UP YOUR WORK WITH INGO MAURER?

DE Differentness. Ingo has a very specific approach. Of combining the artistic and design, something no doubt also attributable to

ROSA CAROLE RODECK – WELCHE BEGRIFFE VERBINDET IHR MIT EURER ARBEIT BEI INGO MAURER?

DE Andersartigkeit. Ingo hat einen sehr speziellen Ansatz. Das Künstlerische und das Design miteinander zu verbinden, was sicher auch am Team liegt mit seinen unterschiedlichen Hintergründen und Ingo Maurer als Künstler. Eine gute Mischung.

„Ingo geht es immer um Leichtigkeit, was mit *lightness* im Englischen noch besser passt."

AS Ich habe mal einen Text ausgeschnitten, den ich an meinen Tisch geklebt habe. Eine Ansammlung von Worten – aufgelistet von Italo Calvino – die ich ganz passend finde: Schnelligkeit, Leichtigkeit, Genauigkeit, Anschaulichkeit, Konsequenz, Vielseitigkeit. Und das fand ich irgendwie passend. Ingo geht es immer um Leichtigkeit, was mit *lightness* im Englischen noch besser passt. Es geht immer um „noch dünner". Und Schnelligkeit in Kombination mit Flexibilität. Wir sind für eine circa 60-köpfige Firma wahnsinnig schnell. Wir haben Projekte mit großen Firmen gemacht und da merkt man, was für Vorteile eine kleine Firma hat, in der jeder jeden kennt und man auch selbst produziert. Und die Vielseitigkeit muss gegeben sein, weil man als Designer*in nur ganz wenig entwirft. Man ist immer im Gespräch mit den Zulieferern, mit den Kunden, auf der Leiter oder in der Werkstatt oder macht beim Kunden eine Präsentation. Es ist eine unglaubliche Vielseitigkeit, die gefordert wird.

the team with its different backgrounds, and Ingo Maurer as an artist. A good mixture.

"Ingo's work is always about lightness in the dual sense."

AS I once cut out a piece of text I found in print and stuck it to my desk. The text is extremely apt, I think. It consisted of six words by Italo Calvino: Swiftness, Lightness, Accuracy, Vividness, Consistency, Versatility. And I somehow found that very fitting. Ingo's work is always about lightness in the dual sense, of making things "thinner and thinner". And swiftness in combination with flexibility. For a company with a payroll of about 60 people we are incredibly fast. We've done projects with large companies and you quickly notice what the advantages of a small company are, where everyone knows everyone else and you make the items in-house.

And diversity is a must, because as a designer you actually spend very little time designing. You're busy discussing things with suppliers, with clients, up a ladder, or in the workshop or presenting to clients. In other words, you have to be incredibly versatile.

GK Deliberations, spontaneity, and freedom.

At first sight, Ingo's deliberations always seem very spontaneous and surprising, whereas in truth an awful lot of thought has gone into them. Down through the years, when you have seen a lot of his things, you'll no longer be so taken by surprise by an

GK Überlegungen, Spontaneität und Freiheit.
Auf den ersten Blick wirken Ingos Ideen immer sehr spontan und überraschend, allerdings steckt eine ganze Menge an Überlegung dahinter. Im Laufe der Jahre, wenn man schon viele seiner Sachen gesehen hat, schafft er es nicht mehr so oft, einen mit einer Idee zu überraschen, aber trotzdem kommt es auch nach 25 Jahren noch vor, was auch den Reiz ausmacht, dort zu arbeiten.
Die Freiheit liegt bei Ingo indessen im sich Freimachen von der technischen Machbarkeit und von Kosten. Wenn er eine Vision hat, setzt er sie zum Teil gegen große Widerstände durch, oder er bedauert es, wenn er es nicht geschafft hat.

SH Begeisterung. Die Begeisterung der Mitarbeiter*innen oder der Designer*innen wird dadurch hochgehalten, dass Ingo auf dich zukommt und dir sagt, hier ist ein Projekt, das ist dein Baby, dafür bist du von der Idee bis zur Realisierung verantwortlich. Das begleitest Du vom Entwurf über die Ausführungsplanung. Dann endet dieser Prozess eigentlich mit der Montage des Objekts im Privathaus oder Ausstellungsraum. Das ist nicht nur vielseitig, das fördert auch das eigene Herzblut und die Begeisterung, weil man ein Projekt bis zum Abschluss begleiten kann. Das Team ist dadurch immer extrem motiviert.

„… und einen Häuptling akzeptieren können, der am Schluss immer eine noch bessere Idee hat als man selber."

SU Aufregung, Freude, Stress, Familie, Freundschaft, Erfolg, Überraschungen, Menschen.

idea of his, and yet even after 25 years that element of surprise is still alive and kicking, which makes working with him so engaging. For Ingo, freedom is a matter of making sure you are free from thinking only about technical feasibility and costs. When he has a vision, he realizes it, in part despite fierce opposition, or he regrets not realizing it.

SH Enthusiasm. The staff and designers' enthusiasm are maintained by the fact that Ingo comes up to you and says, here's a project, it's your baby now, you're responsible from the first idea through to the realization. You'll manage the process from the first design through to planning realization. And the process actually ends with the assembly of the object in a private home or an exhibition space. Not only is that a highly varied set of tasks, it also encourages you to treat the job as truly yours and kindles your enthusiasm because you can manage the project right through to the end. As a result, the team is always highly motivated.

"… and happy accepting that you work for the Big Chief who at the end of the day always has an even better idea than the one you had."

SU Excitement, joy, stress, family, friendship, success, surprises, people.
To be open and inquisitive, to be a team player, to be flexible and happy accepting that you work for the Big Chief who at the end of the day always has an even better idea than the one you had. Ingo is not just an employer, he is also a mentor, a father, a friend, and a teacher.

Offen und neugierig sein, Teamfähigkeit besitzen, Flexibilität und einen Häuptling akzeptieren können, der am Schluss immer eine noch bessere Idee hat als man selber. Ingo ist nicht nur ein Arbeitgeber, er ist auch Lehrmeister, Vater, Freund und Mentor.

XRT – SEIT WANN GIBT ES EIN TEAM INGO MAURER?
WIE SETZT ES SICH ZUSAMMEN, WIE IST ES STRUKTURIERT?

GK Im Prinzip hat Ingo 1966 die Firma gegründet und relativ schnell Leute eingestellt, die ihn produktionstechnisch unterstützen konnten.
In den 1980er-Jahren gab es das Team, das mit Ingo u. a. die YAYAHO entwickelt hat. Danach gab es einen ziemlichen Umbruch. Das war auch in der Zeit, in der Ingo an der Kunstakademie Stuttgart gelehrt und nach neuen Leuten gesucht hat.
Ich habe schon viele kommen und gehen gesehen, weil die meisten fünf bis zehn Jahre bleiben, was in einem Kreativberuf schon eine wahnsinnig lange Zeit ist.

„Ingo ist keiner, der theoretisiert, in Konzepten denkt und arbeitet, sondern immer an der Sache selbst.“

AS Meines Wissens gab es ein Team von Anfang an, seit Ingo in München angefangen hat, denn unter dem Team versteht Ingo nicht nur die Entwurfsabteilung. Neben den beiden Bereichen „Designerei" und „Projekt" versteht er

XRT – SINCE WHEN HAS THERE BEEN AN INGO MAURER TEAM?
WHAT'S THE MAKE-UP AND STRUCTURE?

GK Basically, Ingo founded the company back in 1966 and pretty swiftly hired people who could support him both in technical terms and as regards the production technology.
In the 1980s, the team was in place that together with Ingo developed the YAYAHO, among others. Then there was a massive change. It was the time when Ingo was teaching at the Stuttgart Academy of Art and was on the lookout for new staff members.
I've seen many come and go, because most people stay for between five and ten years, which is a hell of a long time in the creative professions.

"Ingo is not someone who theorizes, someone who thinks and works in concepts, but someone who always focuses on the thing itself."

AS To my mind, there was a team from Day One, from the time when Ingo settled in Munich onwards, because Ingo does not only view the design development section as the team. Alongside the two Designing and Projects section he views everyone who takes part to be a team member. And there are also staff members who have been along for the ride since the very early days. First and foremost, among them Werner Berthold, who is now over 80. He started out in the workshop, having trained as a decorative metal worker, and has immense experience with brass. All the things that arise physically involve the input of

als Team alle, die mitmachen. Und es gibt auch noch Mitarbeiter, die von den ganz alten Zeiten mit dabei sind. Vor allem Werner Berthold, der jetzt auch schon über 80 Jahre alt ist. Er arbeitete in der Werkstatt, ist gelernter Gürtler von Beruf und hat viel Erfahrung mit Messing. Die ganzen Dinge, die physisch entstehen, haben den Input von demjenigen, der sie in der Werkstatt umsetzt. Und da ist der Ingo offen.

Wenn man von einem Entwurfsteam spricht, dann hat das in den 1980er-Jahren einen Schub bekommen, mit YAYAHO, aber auch mit der großen Ausstellung im Centre Pompidou. Seitdem sind diese Denklabore immer da gewesen. Es gab da ein Bild, als ich angefangen habe. Das hat einer vor vielen, vielen Jahren an die Tür der Designerei geklebt. Es waren zwei, die Tischtennis spielen. Die Designerei – das Wort setzt sich übrigens aus Design und Schreinerei, also Werkstatt, zusammen – war auch manchmal als Spielzimmer verschrien. Es sieht dort ungewöhnlich aus, mit den ganzen Modellen. Aber das ist auch der Denk- und Probierraum, der wichtig ist für die Firma. Und weil man mit Licht arbeitet, kann man sehr wenig theoretisch oder mit Lichtsimulationen machen, sondern man muss von Anfang an in die drei Dimensionen gehen und Modelle bauen. Das ist auch Ingos Ansatz, dass er erst entscheidet, wenn er Ideen greifbar vor sich hat. Ingo ist keiner, der theoretisiert, in Konzepten denkt und arbeitet, sondern immer an der Sache selbst.

SU Ingo Maurer ist der beste Träumer und größte Visionär, alles andere ist das Team.

the person who makes them in the workshop. And Ingo is completely open in this regard.

If one speaks of a design team, then that got a real boost in the 1980s, with YAYAHO, not to mention the major exhibition at Centre Pompidou. These thinking labs have existed ever since. There was a picture there when I started. Someone tacked it onto the Design section door years before. It showed two people playing ping-pong. The Design section is like a sports table for design, and the Cabinetmaking section, which stands for the workshop, was sometimes notorious for being a games room. Things look pretty unusual there, with all the models. However, it's also the thinking and testing area, which is crucial to the company. And because we work with light, you can do very little at the theoretical level, or using light simulations, you need from the outset to delve into three dimensions and make models. That's also Ingo's method, and he first takes a decision when he has ideas in tangible form before him. Ingo is not someone who theorizes, someone who thinks and works in concepts, but someone who always focuses on the thing itself.

SU Ingo Maurer is the best dreamer and greatest visionary; the team does everything else. Sub-divided into Sales, Production, Design, Development, Planning although ultimately everything forms a unit and is closely inter-related.

Aufgeteilt in Verkauf, Produktion, Design, Entwicklung, Planung und am Schluss ist doch alles eine Einheit und hängt eng zusammen.

„Die Arbeit bedeutet, sich einzumischen,
sich Bälle zuzuspielen."

SH   Deswegen umgibt sich Ingo auch mit so vielen Menschen, die anders denken als er, mit Handwerkern, mit Physikern, mit Menschen, die emotional oder realistisch denken. Die Arbeit bedeutet, sich einzumischen, sich Bälle zuzuspielen, so ergeben sich im Team auch unterschiedlichste Richtungen. Je nachdem, wer sich wo einbringt.

AS   Streng genommen arbeiten die Designer*innen in der Designerei und im Projektbereich die Architekt*innen. Sie befassen sich mit Lichträumen, Beleuchtungskonzepten, architekturgebundenen Lichtinstallationen wie zum Beispiel dem TORRE VELASCA oder Münchener U-Bahn-Stationen. Letztendlich ist es aber nur eine räumliche Trennung. Denn fast jeder, der in der Designerei arbeitet, arbeitet auch an Projekten. Und ab und zu arbeiten Leute, die an Projekten arbeiten, auch an Produkten. Das ist in der Firma auch nicht leicht trennbar. Zum Beispiel kann das Projekte-Team für eine Hotellobby-Gestaltung auf ein Serienprodukt zurückgreifen oder manchmal entsteht was Neues bei einem solchen Projekt, das zum Produkt wird.

DE   In der Kaiserstraße sitzen die Gestalter und ihre Arbeit ist sehr verflochten mit der Produktion. Wir nennen uns auch Produktentwickler, da wir nicht nur gestalten, sondern es gibt viele Tabellen, Nummern und Prozesse, die einfach

"The work means intervening in things,
bouncing ideas around."

SH   Which is why Ingo surrounds himself with so many people who do not think the way he does, with craftspeople, with physicists, with people who think emotionally or realistically. The work means intervening in things, bouncing ideas around, and the team therefore often develops ideas that go in all manner of different directions. Depending on who weighed in with what.

AS   Strictly speaking, the designers all work in the Design section and the architects work in the Projects section. They concern themselves with illuminated spaces, illumination concepts, architecture-based light installations, such as the TORRE VELASCA or the Munich subway stations. In the final instance, all this is simply a spatial division. As almost everyone working in the Design section will also be working on projects. And now and then those who work on projects will find themselves working on products. It's hard to separate the two inside the company. For example, the Projects team may resort to a mass product for the design of a hotel lobby or sometimes during a project something new arises that results in a product.

DE   The designers are based at Kaiserstrasse and their work is closely bound up with that at Production. We also call ourselves product developers, as we not only design things,

da sind, wenn man produziert. Auch zwischen der Produktion, die in Aubing sitzt, und dem Verkauf besteht eine enge Verbindung.

„Das ist eine Stärke von uns,
dass die Produktentwicklung und Produktion
unter einem Dach sitzen."

SH Das ist eine Stärke von uns, dass die Produktentwicklung und Produktion eigentlich unter einem Dach sitzen. Wenn ich eine Leuchte entwerfe, gehe ich in die Produktion und schaue, was können meine Kollegen produzieren, was gibt es für Produktionsprozesse. Damit habe ich gleichzeitig auch eine Qualitätskontrolle. Da zeigt mir jemand, wie er es machen würde, und im Prozess entsteht eine gemeinsame Lösung.

AS Die Produktion ist vor zehn Jahren umgezogen, weil es in der Kaiserstraße zu eng wurde. Der Showroom war der Raum, in dem die Produktion und der Versand stattgefunden haben. Es ist für uns ein großer Vorteil, selbst zu produzieren. Wenn man nur entwerfen und an eine Produktionsstätte weitergeben würde, und diese sagt, so können wir es nicht machen, würde der ganze Prozess gebremst. Wenn bei uns die Produktion sagt, so können wir es nicht machen, können wir hingehen und einen bestmöglichen Kompromiss finden. Kompromisse sind schließlich nichts Schlechtes. Da wir mit der Produktion eins sind, kommen wir weiter und können Dinge auf den Markt bringen, die sonst nicht den Weg auf den Markt finden könnten.

but there are countless tables, numbers and processes that invariably arise if you are producing something. And there are close links between the Production section, which is based in Aubing, and Sales.

"That's one of our strengths, the fact that
product development and production are basically under
one and the same roof."

SH That's one of our strengths, the fact that product development and production are basically under one and the same roof. If I'm designing a luminaire then I go over to Production and take a look at what my colleagues are able to produce, at the production processes there. This also means I have an inbuilt quality assurance system. Someone there shows me how he or she would make the object in mind and during this process a joint solution evolves.

AS The Production section relocated ten years ago as space got cramped at Kaiserstrasse. The showroom was also the space where Production and Dispatch were located. One of our great advantages is that we make our products ourselves. If all you did was design and then pass something on to a production facility that then says, "No we can't do it" then the whole process would grind to a halt. If in our case the Production section say, "No we can't do it" then you go over to them and find the best possible compromise. After all, compromises are not bad per se. Since we and Production are one and the same

RCR – BETRACHTET MAN SICH ALS MANUFAKTUR ODER WIE UNTERSCHEIDET SICH INGO MAURER VON EINEM KLASSISCHEN HERSTELLER?

SU Entwurf, Entwicklung, Produktion, Vertrieb ist alles unter einem Dach (oder ein paar Dächern) und sehr viele Produkte, die nicht ausschließlich maschinell hergestellt werden können. Also eindeutig Manufaktur.

SH Wir unterscheiden uns dadurch, dass wir Einzelstücke, also Kunstwerke, machen, und dass es einen fließenden Übergang zur Serienproduktion einer Leuchte gibt, die mehrere Tausend Mal im Jahr verkauft wird. Dazwischen ist alles möglich: Kleinserien, limitierte Editionen. Dadurch sind wir eine Manufaktur, weil diese Einzelstücke nur in einer großen Halle mit genialer Werkstatt hergestellt werden können – und die haben wir glücklicherweise. Wir haben das nie definiert, aber das ist unsere Stärke: mit handwerklichen und mit digitalen Hilfsmitteln (3D-Software) zu arbeiten. Wir unterscheiden uns von anderen Herstellern dadurch, dass wir diese Produktion noch haben, dass wir alle Materialien testen können und über ein Lichtlabor verfügen. Bei uns wird eine Idee sofort in Bezug auf Licht ausprobiert.

„Jede Lampe ist ein Unikat, komplett handgemacht."

MM Da ich vorher bei anderen Leuchtenherstellern als Lichtplanerin gearbeitet habe, bei denen nur digital gearbeitet wurde, hat es mich als jüngere Mitarbeiterin erst einmal erschrocken, dass so viel in Handarbeit gemacht wird. Bei

company, we have an edge and can bring things to market that would otherwise not find their way there.

RCR – DO YOU SEE YOURSELVES AS A MANUFACTURING WORKSHOP OR HOW DOES INGO MAURER DIFFER FROM A CLASSICAL MANUFACTURER?

SU Design, Development, Production, Sales, they're all under one roof (or a few roofs) and very many products that cannot exclusively be made by machine. So, it's really a manufacturing workshop.

SH We differ by virtue of the fact that we make one-offs, meaning artworks, and that there is a fluid transition to the mass production of a luminaire that sells several thousand a year. In-between, all manner of things is possible: Mini-series, limited editions. In this way, we are a manufacturing workshop because these one-offs can only be made in a large hall with ingenious craftspeople – and fortunately we have both. We never defined this, but our strength is combining crafts skills and digital tools (3D software). We differ from other manufacturers by still having our Production section, being able to test all the materials, and having our own light lab. We can immediately try out an idea in relation to light.

"That means every object is unique, completely made by hand."

der Firma, von der ich kam, habe ich nur mit Robotern und Maschinen gearbeitet. Bei Ingo Maurer wird alles mit den eigenen Händen gemacht. Ich habe
mich gefragt, wieso. Aber mit den Jahren habe ich gelernt, dass dieser
Prozess zwar langsam ist, aber gute Qualität erzeugt. Eine Person setzt die
Leuchte zusammen, jedes Teil an die richtige Stelle. Jede Lampe ist dadurch
eigentlich ein Unikat, komplett handgemacht. Das ist das Schönste bei Ingo
Maurer.

„Es gibt eigentlich keine andere
Leuchtenfirma, die so arbeitet."

AS Es ist ein Firmenmodell aus den 1960er-Jahren. Es war damals nicht unüblich,
dass man Dinge entwarf und sie gleich gefertigt hat. Aber dass wir diese Praxis
hinübergerettet haben in die jetzige Zeit, das ist ein Alleinstellungsmerkmal
von Ingo Maurer. Es gibt eigentlich keine andere Leuchtenfirma, die so arbeitet. Ingo wollte immer die Produktion nah an sich dran haben, um die Dinge
aus seinem Kopf genauso zu machen, wie er sich diese vorstellt.

MM Wir hatten zum Beispiel vor Kurzem einen Fall, bei dem ich eine Lampe
entwickeln sollte, und digitale Prozesse nutzen wollte, weil wir wussten, dass
es machbar ist. Doch alle angefragten Firmen haben abgesagt, weil keine
Maschine es umsetzen konnte. Dann sind wir zu unserer Produktion gegangen
und ein Mitarbeiter hat es in Handarbeit gemacht. Da merkst du, wie es
manchmal ist, sich von Technologie leiten zu lassen. Wenn wir eine andere
Firma wären, in der wir ausschließlich mit Technologie arbeiten würden, müssten

MM As I had previously worked as a light planner for other luminaire
manufacturers who rely solely on digital methods as a younger
colleague I was initially shocked by how much is done by hand.
At my last company I only worked with robots and machines.
At Ingo Maurer everything is done using your own hands.
I often wondered why. But over the years I have realized that
though this process is slow it does produce excellent quality.
One person assembles the luminaire, puts every part in the
right place. That means every object is unique, completely
made by hand. That is the best thing about Ingo Maurer.

"There are not really any other
luminaire firms that work this way."

AS It is a business model from the 1960s. It was not unusual at the
time to design things and then manufacture them immediately.
But the fact that we have transferred this practice into the
present day is something that sets Ingo Maurer apart. There
are not really any other luminaire firms that work this way. Ingo
always wanted to keep the Production section close at hand
so that the things he thought up could be made exactly the way
he envisaged them.

MM We recently had a situation where I was to develop a luminaire
and was to use digital processes because we knew it was
feasible. But all the firms we approached turned us down
because they didn't have the right machine to realize our ideas.
So, we consulted the Production section and a colleague there

wir ständig sagen, das können wir so nicht realisieren.

SH Gleichzeitig habe ich Respekt vor den Handwerkern. Aber auch Angst, weil keine Handwerker mehr nachkommen. Handwerker, die spezielle Kenntnisse und Fähigkeiten haben, findest du nicht mehr. Auf Nachfrage heißt es sofort, das ginge nicht.

DE Unsere Methode funktioniert aber auch nur, weil unsere Produktionszahl nicht so hoch ist. Wenn wir in eine höhere Stückzahl gehen müssten, würde das Handwerkliche verloren gehen oder gar nicht mehr funktionieren. Weil dieses System dann an seine Grenzen stößt.

RCR – WIE ENTSTEHT EINE LEUCHTE ODER EINE INSTALLATION:
WIE ENTSTEHEN DIE IDEEN?

„Am Anfang gibt es immer eine Serviette."

SU Am Anfang gibt es immer eine Serviette. Eine Skizze von Ingo. Sie ist an sich eigentlich schon ein kleines Kunstwerk. Wenn man Ingo nicht schon eine Zeit lang kennt, kann man mit ihr erst einmal wenig anfangen oder muss sehr viel mit ihm reden. Bei Ingo muss man erst mal Servietten lesen lernen. „Serviet-tisch!"

„Ich bin kein Telepath.
Ich kann dir nicht in den Kopf schauen."

made it by hand. That makes you realize what it can be like to be guided by technology. If we were a different company that worked exclusively with technology we would constantly have to say "we can't realize it that way".

SH Simultaneously, I have great respect for artisans. But I am also worried because vacant positions are not being filled in this area. You no longer find craftsmen who have the requisite specialist knowledge and skills. As soon as you ask, the answer is: we can't help you.

DE That said, our method only works because we don't go for high production runs. If we had to move to a higher roll-out then the manual aspect would no longer work so well or wouldn't work at all. Because then the system would come up against its limits.

RCR – HOW DOES A LUMINAIRE OR AN INSTALLATION COME ABOUT:
HOW ARE IDEAS BORN?

"It always starts with a paper napkin."

SU It always starts with a paper napkin. A sketch by Ingo. It is really a small work of art in its own right. If you haven't known Ingo very long then you can't do much with it to begin with or you need to talk to him a lot. With Ingo you have to learn to read serviettes. "Serviettan!"

"I'm not telepathic.
I can't look inside your head."

GK Ingo bringt zum Beispiel Ideen von seinen Reisen mit. Früher hat er viel im Flugzeug gezeichnet, weswegen wir eine ganze Menge an Lufthansa-Servietten mit seinen Zeichnungen haben. In seiner Jackentasche hatte er oft einen bestimmten Stift, wir nennen ihn auch den Ingo-Stift, und einige Servietten, damit er immer etwas zum Zeichnen hatte. Der Vorteil von Servietten ist, dass sie nicht kaputt gehen, man kann sie rollen und knittern, und wenn einem ein Entwurf nicht taugt, wischt man sich den Mund ab und wirft sie weg.
Ingo hat am Anfang eine konkrete Vorstellung, aber wie man dahin kommt, ist noch unklar. Ich sage immer: „Ich bin kein Telepath. Ich kann dir nicht in den Kopf schauen".
Am Anfang hat es auch eine Weile gedauert, seine Sprache zu sprechen. Es war unklar, was er meinte, wenn er etwa sagte: „Ich stell mir etwas vor, und da zischt so ein Licht raus."
Oder eine Skizze auf einer Serviette, bei der man gleich wissen muss, wie groß der Entwurf ist, weil er das für einen bestimmten Raum im Kopf hat, und wehe, du weißt jetzt nicht sofort, was für einen Raum er meint.
Über die Zeit entwickelt sich ein Dialog. Man macht irgendetwas, was grob in die Richtung geht, um zu testen, ob man überhaupt verstanden hat, was er meint. Anfangs liegt man noch relativ oft auf der falschen Spur, aber im Laufe der Zeit weiß man, was er will.
Und insbesondere bei Licht stellt sich die Schwierigkeit, dass man es nicht wirklich zeichnen kann, weswegen wir auch direkt ins Modell gehen.

GK For example, Ingo brings ideas back from his travels. Years ago, he did a lot of drawings on the plane which is why we have a whole lot of Lufthansa serviettes with his drawings. He often had a certain pen in his jacket pocket, we call it the Ingo pen, and a few serviettes so that he always had something to draw with. The advantage of serviettes is that they are indestructible, you can roll and crumple them and if a design is no good you use it to wipe your mouth and throw it away.
Ingo has a specific idea at the start but it remains unclear how it can be achieved. I always say: "I'm not telepathic. I can't look inside your head".
It also took a while at the beginning to speak his language. It wasn't clear what he meant when he said for example: "I can imagine something with a light that fizzes out."
Or with a sketch on a napkin where you have to realize immediately how big the design is, because he has it in mind for a certain room, and woe betide anyone who doesn't know straight away which room he means.
Over time you develop a dialog. You do something that might roughly fit in order to test whether you have understood what he means. To begin with you are way off track relatively often but as time goes by you know what he wants.
And especially with light you have the problem that you can't really draw it so we tend to move straight to the model.

„Mit dieser skizzierten Idee wählt Ingo die Person aus,
mit der er sie umsetzen möchte."

DE Er zeichnet eigentlich auf alles, was er gerade zur Verfügung hat. Der Start
    sind diese Zeichnungen. Mit dieser skizzierten Idee wählt Ingo die Person aus,
    mit der er sie umsetzen möchte.
    Und wenn man diese Skizze sieht, dann interpretiert jeder sie auf seine Weise.
    Jeder Gestalter von uns hat andere Vorstellungen.

MM Oder Geschmack. Jeder hat einen unterschiedlichen Geschmack und Ingo
    weiß, wie jeder tickt. Und je nach Projekt wählt er einen Mitarbeiter, weil er
    mehr technisch orientiert oder verspielter gestaltet. Und manchmal bildet er
    auch ein Team aus zwei Personen.

SH Wichtig ist auch die Zusammenarbeit mit Mitarbeiter*innen, die über
    bestimmtes Wissen verfügen, sich z. B. schon einmal mit LED-Montage
    auseinandersetzen mussten. Und so ist der, der das Projekt leitet, umgeben
    von vielen, die er sich dazu holt.

AS Wir arbeiten im Großraumbüro, das heißt, die Leute sind in Bewegung und
    arbeiten sehr selbstständig. Man kann, wenn etwas an die Firma heran-
    getragen wird, sogar entscheiden, ob man es annimmt oder ablehnt.

„Ingo hat einmal gesagt, wir sind so etwas wie ein Teig."

SH Ingo hat einmal gesagt, wir sind so etwas wie ein Teig, in den ganz viele ver-
    schiedene Zutaten kommen, und das ergibt dann das Besondere. Wir arbeiten
    in einer flachen Hierarchie.

"And then Ingo chooses the person he wants
to implement this sketched idea."

DE He simply draws on anything he happens to have to hand.
    It begins with these drawings. And then Ingo chooses the
    person he wants to implement this sketched idea.
    And when you see this sketch everyone interprets it in their
    own way. Each of us designers has different ideas.

MM Or taste. Everyone has different taste and Ingo knows
    how each of us ticks. And depending on the project he
    selects a colleague because his design is more technically
    oriented or more playful. And sometimes he has teams of
    two people.

SH It is also important to collaborate with colleagues who have
    specific know-how, for example ones already familiar with
    LED assembly. So, the person who heads the project is always
    surrounded by lots of people he calls on board.

AS We work in an open-plan office, which means people move
    around and work very independently. And if the firm is asked
    to do something you can even decide whether to accept or
    reject it.

"Ingo once said we are a bit like a dough."

SH Ingo once said we are a bit like a dough that requires many
    different ingredients and this is what makes it special. We work
    with a flat hierarchy.

AS Und da wir nicht nur mit Computern arbeiten, die man ja nur von vorne betrachtet, sondern vor allem mit Modellen, ist jeder Tisch voll mit irgendwelchen
Sachen. Man läuft ständig dran vorbei. Das heißt, ich sehe, was bei den anderen
auf dem Tisch liegt, und gebe einen Kommentar dazu. Oder umgekehrt,
jemand geht an meinem Tisch vorbei und ich frage denjenigen. So ist die
Kommunikation innerhalb des Teams gut und wichtig. Und dadurch entsteht,
saublöder Name, eine Firmenkultur. Auch wenn jeder anders ist. Durch diese
Gleichzeitigkeit, Offenheit und Flexibilität wird alles miteinander verknetet,
wenn wir wieder auf den Teig zurückkommen wollen.

RCR – KOMMEN DIE IDEEN NUR VON INGO MAURER
ODER AUCH VON ANDEREN DES TEAMS?

SU Zum ganz großen Teil kommen die Ideen von Ingo. Aber wenn man ein Haus
baut, braucht es eine ganze Menge von Menschen, die ihre Qualitäten einbringen und dadurch den Entwurf beeinflussen. Auch eigenständige Ideen aus
der Mannschaft werden gesehen und umgesetzt. Da ist Ingo immer offen.

GK Axel hat zum Beispiel einige Leuchten im Portfolio, die er autark in der Werkstatt entworfen und Ingo gezeigt hat. Dann wird abgewogen, ob es passt oder
nicht, und ob die Idee Ingo erwärmen kann. Vor allem, wenn es nicht in die
Kollektion passt, ist es sehr unwahrscheinlich, dass es produziert wird.
Am Ende steht der Name Ingo Maurer und Team darauf, weil Ingo Maurer

AS And as we don't work with computers, that you can only look at
from the front, but with models – every desk is full of various
items. You're always walking past them. That means I can see
what is on other people's desks and I comment on it. Or somebody walks past my desk and I ask what they think. So, there is
excellent communication within the team and that is important.
And as a result, you get something with a really stupid name
called corporate culture. Even though everyone is different. And
to return to this idea of dough these parallel activities, the
openness and flexibility are all kneaded together.

RCR – DO THE IDEAS ONLY COME FROM INGO MAURER
OR ALSO FROM OTHER PEOPLE IN THE TEAM?

SU Most of the ideas come from Ingo. But when you build a house
you need a lot of people who bring their own qualities to bear
and consequently influence the design. And ideas that come
from the team are often considered and implemented. Ingo is
always open in that respect.

GK For example, Axel had a few luminaires in his portfolio that he
had designed in the workshop and then showed them to Ingo.
Then we weigh up whether something fits or not and whether
Ingo can warm to the idea or not. But if it doesn't fit in the
collection it is highly improbable that it will be produced. In
the end the object bears the name Ingo Mauer and team on it

in dem Zusammenhang als Firma fungiert, aber das hat mich noch nie gestört.

AS Ingo ist da sehr offen. Wir stehen in einem Innenhofkomplex, der ist wie ein weißes Blatt Papier, und dann heißt es, alle Ideen auf den Tisch. Und jeder gibt seinen Senf dazu.

MM Du kannst Vorschläge machen, dann machen wir gemeinsam ein Brainstorming und diskutieren darüber. Wenn sich alle für diese Idee begeistern, weißt du, dass es in die richtige Richtung geht. Dann liefert man dem Kunden Vorschläge und er entscheidet. Wenn Ingo eine Idee hat, die er unbedingt umsetzen will, dann arbeiten wir alle daran.

XRT – INGO MAURER HAT ÜBER SEINE ARBEIT MIT DEM TEAM GESAGT:
„I ENJOY WORKING WITH MY TEAM. AND I
ALSO FIGHT THEM ONCE IN A WHILE. I AM IMPATIENT."
WIE SEHT IHR DAS?

AS Impatience ist immer da. Das ist eine Kombination aus Vorfreude und Ungeduld. Und derjenige, der mit dem Projekt betraut ist, stößt eben auf Grenzen, an die er vorher nicht gedacht hat.

DE Wenn Ingo uns eine Idee ausschüttet, hat er schon lange darüber nachgedacht. Dann kann er es uns nicht so schnell erklären, wie er es möchte, weder mit Worten noch mit Skizzen. Er wird meist wahnsinnig ungeduldig, weil er es eben in seinem Kopf bereits fertig hat.

because Ingo Maurer acted as the firm in that context, but this has never bothered me.

AS Ingo is very open in that respect. We are standing in a courtyard complex, which is like a blank sheet of paper, and then it's a matter of putting all the ideas on the table. And everyone has their say.

MM You can make suggestions, then we have a joint brainstorming and discuss everything. If everyone is happy about the idea then you know you're moving in the right direction. Then you deliver the ideas to the customer and he decides. If Ingo has an idea that he is bent on implementing then we all work on it.

XRT – INGO MAURER ONCE SAID: "I ENJOY WORKING WITH MY TEAM.
AND I ALSO FIGHT THEM ONCE IN A WHILE. I AM IMPATIENT."
HOW DO YOU SEE THAT?

AS There is always impatience. It's a combination of anticipation and eagerness. And the person who's in charge of the project can come up against obstacles he didn't think about before.

DE When Ingo pours out an idea to us he has usually thought about it for a long time. And then he can't explain it to us as quickly as he would like, either with words or with sketches. That makes him incredibly impatient because the thing is already finished in his mind.
Something that always works is the model. Then we assemble

Was immer funktioniert, ist das Modell. Danach wird so schnell wie möglich etwas zusammengebaut, damit Ingo was Handfestes hat, womit er spielen kann und bei dem er sagen kann, wo sich etwas ändern muss.

„Hey, what's cooking?"

SH Es ist wie eine interne Präsentation. Ingo bespricht etwas mit dir. Ein paar Tage später kommt er wieder, und dann passiert etwas Klassisches, er stürmt herein und fragt: „Hey, what's cooking?" Er will wissen, was in der Zwischenzeit passiert ist. Wenn du dann sagst, du recherchierst immer noch, wird er nervös. Daher ist es immer gut, etwas auf dem Rechner oder ein Modell zu haben, das man zeigen kann.

AS Die Ungeduld ist ja auch auf unserer Seite. Ungeduld ist eine Supersache, weil dadurch die Dinge Fahrt aufnehmen. Wir rasen manchmal durch Stadien der Entwicklung. Wenn wir das mit einem Tennisspiel vergleichen, ist es so, als würden wir die Bälle immer Volley nehmen. Der Ball kommt nie runter, er ist dauernd in der Luft. Zack, zack, zack. Links, rechts, links, rechts. Das fordert uns, aber es gibt dem Ganzen Schwung. Und manchmal, zum Glück nicht so oft, kommt es vor, dass ein Projekt eine Delle erhält, weil es zu einem Stillstand kommt. Es kostet Energie, das wieder auszubügeln. Für ein Projekt ist es sehr wichtig, dass es durchflutscht. Daher braucht es die Ungeduld bei allem, auch, wenn das Nerven kostet.

XRT – INWIEWEIT SPIELT DER ZUFALL EINE ROLLE IM PROZESS?

something as quickly as possible so that Ingo has something specific he can play around with and say what has to be altered.

"Hey, what's cooking?"

SH It is like an internal presentation. Ingo discusses something with you. Then a few days later he comes again, and then something classic happens, he bursts in and asks: "Hey, what's cooking?" He wants to know what has happened in the intervening time. If you then say you're still researching something he gets nervous. So, it is always good to have something on the computer or a model you can show him.

AS Well, impatience is also to our advantage. Impatience is a wonderful thing because it means things get moving. We sometimes rush through stages of development. If you compare that with a tennis match it's as if we keep volleying the balls to each other. The ball never touches the ground, it is always in the air. Wham, wham, wham. Left, right, left, right. That's demanding but it adds a certain dynamism. And sometimes, luckily not that often a project gets a dent because things come to a standstill. It takes a lot of energy to smooth that out again. It is very important for a project to move smoothly and quickly. So, you need impatience in everyone even though nerves get frayed.

SH Da möchte ich nochmals auf unsere Tische zurückkommen, auf denen unsere
Fundstücke liegen. Wenn wir etwas finden, was uns persönlich begeistert und
bei dem wir uns wünschen, dass Ingo mit aufspringt, ein spannendes Material,
ein toller Effekt, ein Bild, nehmen wir das mit und legen es auf unseren Tisch.
Ingo, der immer alle Tische scannt und Dinge in die Hand nimmt, spricht
mit uns über diese Fundstücke. Wenn sie in ihm eine Flamme erzeugen, kann
er schon mal sagen: „Lass uns das weiterverfolgen!" Der Zufall begleitet uns
die ganze Zeit. Wir tüfteln, wir forschen und es passieren auch Dinge, die man
nicht vorhersieht.

GK Ein sehr gutes Beispiel dafür ist die Leuchte ZUFALL. Ursprünglich sollten mit
dem Material Tischkanten verdeckt werden, die uns sehr hässlich erschienen.
Als das Silikon, das wir zuvor in die Tischkante hineingegossen hatten,
herausfiel, nahm Ingo die Streifen in die Hand und meinte: „Das ist cool!
Daraus machen wir was!"

RCR – ENTWIRFT MAN BEI DEM PROZESS UM DAS LICHT HERUM?
ODER IST DIE FORM ZUERST DA?

„Das Umhüllen hat etwas mit Entblenden zu tun."

GK Das ist unterschiedlich. In der Halogenzeit war es so, dass man einen starken
Blendeffekt hatte, weil es sich um eine kleine, starke, punktförmige Lichtquelle

XRT – HOW BIG A ROLE DOES CHANCE PLAY IN THE PROCESS?

SH To answer that I'd like to return to our desks with all our
found items. If we find something that we consider exciting
and hope that Ingo might feel the same way, say a fascinating
material, a great effect, a picture, then we take it with us and
put it on our desk. And Ingo being someone who always scans
the desks and picks up things on them, talks to us about these
items.
If they spark a flame in him he might well say: "Let's take that
up!" Chance is our permanent companion. We tinker, we re-
search and sometimes things happen that you can't foresee.

GK An excellent example of this is the luminaire aptly called ZUFALL
(coincidence). Originally, the material was to be used to conceal
table edges we found very ugly. But when the silicon we had
poured into the table edge fell out Ingo picked up the stripes
and said: "That's cool! We'll make something from that!"

RCR – DO YOU DESIGN AROUND THE LIGHT?
OR IS THE FORM THERE FIRST?

"So, shrouding has to do with avoiding the glare."

GK It depends. In the halogen era you had a very strong dazzling
effect because it is a small, strong, point light source that
produces a lot of light. It is unpleasant looking directly into it.

handelt, die sehr viel Licht macht. Es ist unangenehm, direkt hineinzuschauen. Aber man will auch eine gewisse Menge an Licht haben, damit der Raum so hell wird, wie er sein soll. In solchen Fällen mache ich zuerst die Menge Licht und umhülle sie dann. Bei LED ist das Licht eher flächig oder linear. Ich muss dadurch mehr den Blendeffekt umhüllen. Das Umhüllen hat etwas mit Entblenden zu tun. Mit der PORCA MISERIA! lässt sich das gut erklären. Bei ihr ist das helle Zentrum von Anfang an da und darum herum werden die Scherben so gesetzt, dass man möglichst nicht mehr in die Lichtquelle reinschauen kann und dass sich das Licht nach außen durcharbeiten muss. Die Lichtquelle muss allerdings weiterhin so stark sein, dass genügend Licht herauskommt.

SU Meistens ist erst der Traum, die Vision oder die Form da und das „gute" Licht wird integriert. Manchmal ist aber auch eine neue Technologie maßgebend für den Entwurf wie die DEW DROPS zum Beispiel.

SH Ich würde schon sagen, dass wir das Licht früh anschalten. Wir überlegen uns, was für eine Lichtquelle infrage kommt. Zum Beispiel bei der LED hat man das Problem der Entwärmung, die Größe des Kühlkörpers spielt dann ästhetisch eine Rolle. Und man lässt sich auch davon überraschen, ob die Wirkung so ist, wie man es sich gewünscht hat. Es können Schatten und Reflexionen entstehen, die man nicht möchte.

MM Ich persönlich denke immer an das Licht und wie es aussieht. In unseren Modellen bauen wir ganz kleine Spots ein, um zu überprüfen, wie das Licht wirkt. Danach schauen wir, welche Leuchtmittel passen können. Das Licht ist

But you also want a certain amount of light so the room is as bright as it needs to be. In such cases I make the amount of light first and then I enclose it. With LED the light is flatter or -linear – meaning it's more necessary to shroud the dazzle effect. So, shrouding has to do with avoiding the glare. A good example of that is PORCA MISERIA!.
In this luminaire the bright center is there from the start and the porcelain shards are arranged around it so that ideally you can no longer look into the light and the light has to work its way out through them. However, the light source still has to be so strong that enough light is emitted.

SU Usually, it begins with the dream, the vision or the design and then the "good" light is integrated. But sometimes a new technology is decisive for the design, as with DEW DROPS for example.

SH I would say that we switch the light on at an early stage. We consider which source of light might be suitable. For example, with LED you have the problem of removing the heat, the size of the cooling mechanism also plays a role in the overall appearance. And you see for yourself whether the effect is as you would like it. You may get shadows and reflections that you don't want.

MM Personally, I always think about the light and what it looks like. We add really small spotlights to our models to test the light's effect. Then we look at which kind of lamp would be

sehr wichtig, denn es geht darum, ob man eine gleichmäßige Beleuchtung haben möchte oder eine dramatische Stimmung.

DE Es kommt immer darauf an, ob man von einer Technologie oder einer Innovation ausgeht. Denke ich an die OLEDs, gehe ich von einem Lichtelement aus. Das heißt, am Anfang hat man das Licht, das man kennt. Aber ich muss gestehen, dass Ingo erst einmal nicht ans Licht denkt, sondern er eine Idee hat, wie die Leuchte aussehen könnte. Wir müssen das Licht aber relativ schnell einsetzen, damit er weiß, wie es wirkt.

MM Genau. Bei Produkten geht es Ingo darum, dass es schön aussieht und manchmal lustig ist, und dass die Leute sagen „Wow! Das würde ich gerne haben!" Aber wenn es um Projekte geht, möchte er eine gute Stimmung im Raum erzeugen, damit sich die Leute wohlfühlen.

RCR – MACHT IHR IN DER PRODUKTENTWICKLUNG AUCH KOMPROMISSE?

„Aber insgesamt sind die Objekte immer bis zum technisch Möglichen ausgereizt und noch ein kleines bisschen darüber hinaus."

GK Schwerlich. Manchmal, wenn etwas zu heiß wird und die LED ausfällt, muss man den Kühlkörper größer machen oder die LED schwächer. Das sind Sachen, denen sich Ingo nicht entziehen kann. Aber insgesamt sind die Objekte immer bis zum technisch Möglichen ausgereizt und noch ein kleines bisschen darüber hinaus.

suitable. The light is very important because it is a matter of whether you want even lighting or a dramatic mood.

DE It always depends on whether you have a technology or an innovation as your starting point. When I think of OLEDs, I begin with a light element. In other words, you begin with a light that you know. But I had to admit that Ingo does not think of the light first but has an idea of how the luminaire might look. However, we have to integrate the light relatively quickly so that he knows what sort of an impact it will have.

MM Exactly. With products Ingo is always keen for it to look attractive or sometimes funny and for people to say "Wow! I'd like to have that!" But when it is about projects he would like to produce a good mood in the room so that people feel comfortable.

RCR – DO YOU ALSO MAKE COMPROMISES IN PRODUCT DEVELOPMENT?

"But on the whole the objects are always taken to the limits of what is technically possible and a bit beyond."

GK Only grudgingly. Sometimes if something is too hot and the LED doesn't work you have to make the cooling device bigger or the LED weaker. Those are things Ingo can't get around. But on the whole the objects are always taken to the limits of what is technically possible and a bit beyond.

XRT – HABT IHR SPEZIELLE KONTAKTE FÜR DIE PRODUKTION, DIE AUCH AUSSER-
HALB EURER FIRMA LIEGEN? LEGT IHR WERT DARAUF, DASS SIE LOKAL SIND UND
NICHT ZU WEIT WEG?

GK Es ist mittlerweile so, dass fast alle Elektronik-Bauteile aus Fernost kommen.
Wir importieren aber nicht selber, weil es sehr mühsam mit der Zulieferung ist,
sondern haben Importeure, von denen wir wiederum kaufen. Früher war das
anders, da gab es den *TouchTronic*, bei dem man durch eine Berührung das
Licht an- und ausschalten konnte. Das wurde hier in München exklusiv für
Ingo Maurer produziert.
„Wir nutzen den Markt für das, was wir brauchen,
und wenn etwas nicht zu bekommen ist, machen wir es selbst."
AS In München haben wir den Vorteil, dass es sehr viele Werkstätten gibt, die
auch gut sind! Wir arbeiten mit Schlossern, Metallbauern, Kulissenbauern,
Lackierern und Fachleuten, die sich mit Kunststoff auskennen. Dadurch, dass
die Firma seit über 50 Jahren existiert, haben wir ein gutes Netzwerk. Wir
haben persönliche Verhältnisse zu Handwerkern in der Umgebung, die uns
hilfreich sind. Es hat aber auch mit den Stückzahlen zu tun. Wenn wir woanders
fertigen lassen, ist eine Mindeststückzahl gefordert. Wir kommen dann
immer wieder an den Punkt, Reflektoren und Fassungen selber zu machen.
Wir nutzen den Markt für das, was wir brauchen, und wenn etwas nicht zu
bekommen ist, machen wir es selbst.

XRT – DO YOU HAVE SPECIAL CONTACTS FOR THE PRODUCTION THAT
ARE OUTSIDE YOUR OWN FIRM? IS IT IMPORTANT FOR YOU TO ACT
LOCALLY AND NOT GET SUPPLIES FROM TOO FAR AWAY?

GK These days almost all electronic components come from the
Far East. So, we import, or rather we don't because the delivery
is very arduous but we work with importers from whom we then
buy stuff. Years ago, it was different, we had *TouchTronic,*
which allowed you to switch the light on and off through touch.
It was produced here in Munich exclusively for Ingo Maurer.
"We use the market for what we need and if we can't get it
we make it ourselves."
AS The advantage of Munich is that we have many workshops that
are really good! We collaborate with fitters, metalworkers, set
designers, painters and specialists who work with plastics. And
as the firm has existed for over 50 years we have an excellent
network. We have personal relationships to tradespeople in the
region who can help us. This of course also has to do with the
numbers. If we have things made somewhere else they ask for
a minimum production run. So, we often end up making our
own reflectors and sockets. We use the market for what we
need and if we can't get it we make it ourselves.
SH Often, we make our suppliers go all out. Can we have this
bigger, faster, brighter and better? We had one supplier a tube
manufacturer who makes 100,000 tubes every day. But we only

SH Oft bringen wir die Lieferanten an ihre Grenzen. Gibt es dieses größer, schneller, heller und besser? Wir hatten einen Lieferanten, einen Tubenhersteller, der 100.000 Tuben täglich produziert. Wir brauchten aber nur 2.000 Stück und noch dazu speziell gefertigt. Er meinte, dann müsse er seine ganze Produktionsstraße stoppen, das rechne sich nicht für ihn. Aber wenn er hinterher eine Leuchte für seinen Eingangsbereich bekomme, mache er es.

RCR – DIE EU-POLITIK BESTIMMT NEUERUNGEN IN DER LICHTTECHNOLOGIE. WIE GEHT IHR DAMIT UM?

AS Kreativ!

DE Sie machen uns viel Arbeit.

AS Es gibt in dem Bereich, in dem wir arbeiten, Konstellationen, für die keine Norm greift. Da suchen wir den Dialog mit den Experten. Aber die Normen sind schon eine Hürde!

SH Wir müssen Leuchten umbauen, weil plötzlich Leuchtmittel nicht mehr erhältlich sind. Sie haben dann aber einen anderen Lichteffekt. Dann müssen wir weiter eingreifen, nur, um eine Leuchte, die gut läuft, halten zu können.

AS Probleme machen auch Bauteile, die verboten werden oder genormt sind. Ich erinnere mich an eine Lampe, die sehr wenig Strom verbraucht hat. Man

needed 2,000 and needed them custom made. He said that would mean halting the entire production line and it wouldn't be worth it for him, but if he could have a luminaire afterwards for his entrance areas he would do it.

RCR – EU POLICIES DEFINE INNOVATIONS IN LIGHT TECHNOLOGY. HOW DO YOU HANDLE THAT?

AS Creatively!

DE They cause us extra work.

AS In the field we operate in there are constellations for which no standard applies. Then we have to consult the experts. But the standards are always an obstacle!

SH We have to convert luminaires because suddenly certain light sources are no longer available. But using the alternative means they have a different light effect. Then we have to make further changes just to be able to keep a luminaire that sells well.

AS Components that are banned or standardized can also cause problems. I remember a lamp that used very little electricity. We could have used a very thin cable but the norm states that for safety reasons the leads for luminaires that are moved around must have a certain cross-sectional area. When I researched it, I found out that there's a children's toothbrush that runs on a high voltage but whose lead has a much thinner cross section.

hätte ein sehr dünnes Kabel verwenden können, aber die Norm besagt, dass ortsveränderliche Leuchten aus Sicherheitsgründen einen bestimmten Querschnitt brauchen. In der Recherche sah ich dann aber, dass es eine Kinderzahnbürste gibt, die auch mit Hochvolt läuft, mit viel dünnerem Querschnitt. Wo doch die Gefahr in einem Badezimmer ungleich höher ist als für jemanden im Wohnzimmer! Das war einfach die Norm, die für Zahnbürsten anders gilt als für Leuchten. Deswegen konnten wir das dünne Kabel nicht verwenden, sondern mussten da eine fette Wurst dranmachen.

SH Man hätte die Lampe auch mit Borsten ausstatten und als Zahnbürste verkaufen können.

XRT –WIE ENTSTEHEN DIE PRODUKTNAMEN?

„Und wie soll es heißen?"

AS Ingo sind die Namen wahnsinnig wichtig. Wenn man mit einer neuen Idee an ihn herantritt, fragt er als Zweites oft „Und wie soll es heißen?". Was ich nachvollziehen kann, denn mit dem Namen kann man dem Kunden ein Bild in den Kopf setzen.

SH Ingo ist brilliant darin, einen Namen zu finden. Wenn man selbst eine Leuchte entwickelt, überlegt man immer, wie sie heißen könnte. Und jedes Mal, wenn Ingo seine Meinung dazugibt, fragt man sich, warum man da selber nicht darauf gekommen ist.

Yet the danger in a bathroom is much higher than for someone in a living room. The standards for toothbrushes are simply different to those for luminaires. So we couldn't use the thin cable but had to add a really thick one.

SH We could have added bristles to the luminaire and sold it as a toothbrush.

XRT – HOW DO THE PRODUCT NAMES COME ABOUT?

"And what's it to be called?"

AS The names are incredibly important to Ingo. When you approach him with a new idea the second thing he often asks is "And what's it to be called?". Which I can appreciate because with names you can plant an image in the customer's mind.

SH Ingo is brilliant at finding names. When you develop a luminaire yourself you always think about what to name it. And every time Ingo makes a suggestion you wonder why you didn't think of it yourself.

SU Often a name is found during development and is then altered shortly before the first presentation. That is also work that demands a great deal of creativity and imagination.

GK Generally speaking the names come from Ingo and should have something to do with the design and transport emotions. Often names are borrowed from foreign languages, Arabic or Japanese, for example. Or come from a saying or a song.

SU Oft gibt es einen Namen auf dem Weg der Entwicklung, der kurz vor der Erstpräsentation noch geändert wird. Auch dies ist eine Arbeit, die hohe Kreativität und Fantasie erfordert.

GK In der Regel kommen die Namen von Ingo und sollten etwas mit der Form zu tun haben und Emotionen transportieren. Oft sind Namen auch aus Fremdsprachen entliehen, dem Arabischen oder Japanischen zum Beispiel. Oder aus einem Sprichwort oder einem Song.
Die T.T. MOON kommt von „Take me to the Moon", weil die Leuchte an einen Orbiter oder ein Raumschiff denken lässt. Die ALIZZ COOPER ist nach dem Musiker Alice Cooper benannt, weil es ein Bild gibt, auf dem er eine Boa Constrictor um den Hals hat und irre guckt.

RCR – AN WELCHES PROJEKT ERINNERT IHR EUCH BESONDERS?

SH Die Dinge, die einen am stärksten herausgefordert haben, sind die, über die man am Schluss am meisten lacht. Mit Michel Sempels hatte ich in Mailand eine Wassersäule für die Eröffnung unserer Show aufgebaut. Das war sehr aufwendig mit Motor, Gabelstapler, Straßensperrung etc. Die Säule stand und wir hatten einen Tag Zeit, um sie mit Wasser zu befüllen. Wir mussten 3.000 Liter sauberes Wasser in die Säule bekommen, das Wasser war allerdings braun. Am Ende haben wird das Problem gelöst, aber wir sind wirklich kurz vor knapp fertig geworden.

T. T. MOON comes from "Take me to the Moon," because the luminaire makes you think of an orbiter or spaceship. ALIZZ COOPER is named after the musician Alice Cooper because of the picture where he has a boa constrictor around his neck and has this crazy look on his face.

RCR – WHICH PROJECT DO YOU ESPECIALLY REMEMBER?

SH The things that challenged you most are the ones you ultimately laughed about in the end. With Michel Sempels I set up a water column in Milan for the opening of our show. It was very complicated and involved a motor, a forklift truck, roadblocks etc. The column was ready and we had a whole day to fill it with water. We had to get 3,000 liters of clean water into the column, but the water was brown. We solved the problem in the end but we were really only ready at the last minute.

AS For Tsinandali in Georgia everything was at the last minute. The building was already full of people while we were installing the luminaires. There was hardly any space to spread out our stuff and when I disappeared for ten minutes to help out in the next room the luminaires had also disappeared when I came back. I speak next to no Georgian and tried in vain to make myself understood. Anyway, to cut a long story short, I met the hotel manager and when I started to explain he suddenly ran off with me hot on his heels. We arrived at the place where rubbish

XENIA RIEMANN-TYROLLER (GEB. 1973, MÜNCHEN) ist seit 2012 Konservatorin an der Neuen Sammlung – The Design Museum. Die Kunsthistorikerin studierte an der Universität zu Köln und wurde an der FU Berlin über den Designer Wilhelm Braun-Feldweg promoviert. Sie war u. a. tätig für Glasmuseum Hentrich in Düsseldorf, Bröhan-Museum in Berlin und Glass and Ceramics Department des Victoria & Albert Museum in London.

XENIA RIEMANN-TYROLLER (BORN 1973, MUNICH) has been a curator at Die Neue Sammlung – The Design Museum since 2012. An art historian, she studied at Cologne University and later gained a doctorate at FU Berlin with a thesis about designer Wilhelm Braun-Feldweg. Among other things, she was involved with the Glasmuseum Hentrich in Düsseldorf, the Bröhan Museum in Berlin, and the Glass and Ceramics Department at the Victoria & Albert Museum in London.

AS Für Tsinandali in Georgien war alles auf dem letzten Drücker. Während wir
die Leuchten installiert haben, war das Gebäude voller Leute. Es gab kaum
Platz, Werkzeuge auszubreiten, und als ich für zehn Minuten weg war, um
im Nebenraum zu helfen, waren meine Teile weg. Ich kann kein Georgisch
und habe vergeblich versucht, mich zu verständigen. Lange Rede – kurzer
Sinn, ich habe einen der Hotelmanager getroffen, und als ich anfing, das zu
erklären, rannte er plötzlich los und ich hinterher. Wir kamen an eine Stelle,
wo der Müllabladeplatz war, von dort fuhr gerade ein riesiger Kipplaster los.
Er hielt den Fahrer an und fünf Leute sprangen in den Kipplaster. Unter
all dem Müll lagen meine sieben Reflektoren und Leuchten unbeschädigt.
Da denke ich immer an unseren alten Mitarbeiter Robert Martin, der im
Verkauf gearbeitet hat, und in solchen Situationen zu sagen pflegte:
„Leute, das sind doch bloß Lampen!"

was dumped and a huge dump truck was just driving off.
He stopped the driver and five people jumped into the truck.
Beneath all the rubbish lay my seven reflectors and luminaires –
undamaged.
And that always makes me think of our old employee Robert
Martin, who worked in sales and used to say in such situations:
"Hey, they're just lamps!"

ROSA CAROLE RODECK
(GEB. 1992, KÖLN)
studierte Produkt-Design an der Bau-
haus-Universität Weimar und Design
Studies an der Kunsthochschule Burg
Giebichenstein Halle. Seit 2016 ist sie
freie Design- und Kunstvermittlerin u. a.
in der Kunsthalle der Hypo-Kulturstiftung
München. Während ihres Volontariats an
der PLATFORM München hospitierte sie
als kuratorische Assistentin in der Neuen
Sammlung – The Design Museum.

ROSA CAROLE RODECK
(BORN 1992, COLOGNE)
studied Product Design at Bauhaus
University in Weimar and Design Studies
at the Kunsthochschule Burg Giebichenstein Halle. Since 2016 she has been a
freelance design and art educationalist,
including at the Kunsthalle der Hypo-
Kulturstiftung in Munich. During her
traineeship at PLATFORM Munich, she
worked as a curatorial assistant at Die
Neue Sammlung – The Design Museum.

Kunst im öffentlichen Raum / Art in Public Space

Seit 1985 entwickelt Ingo Maurer Installationen im öffentlichen Raum. Sie schaffen Lichträume, integrieren Objekte an städtischen oder ländlichen Orten oder inszenieren Architektur. Er hat zahlreiche Projekte weltweit realisiert: in Asien, Europa, der Karibik, Nord- und Südamerika, Russland und Vorderasien. Für diese Projekte werden entsprechend aufwendige Modelle in verschiedenen Maßstäben gebaut. Für München konnte er seit 1998 Farb- und Lichtkonzepte für U-Bahnhöfe entwickeln wie für die Stationen Marienplatz, Münchner Freiheit, Westfriedhof oder Sendlinger Tor.

Since 1985 Ingo Maurer has been devising installations for public spaces. They create light spaces, integrate objects into urban or rural settings, or stage architecture. He has realized countless projects worldwide: in Asia, Europe, the Caribbean, North and South America, Russia, and the Near East. For the projects, correspondingly elaborate models are made on various scales. On behalf of the City of Munich, he has since 1998 been developing color and lighting concepts for subway stations, such as those at Marienplatz, Münchner Freiheit, Westfriedhof and Sendlinger Tor.

U-Bahnhof Westfriedhof, München / Subway Station Westfriedhof, Munich, DE
1998

Licht- und Farbkonzept
Lighting and color concept

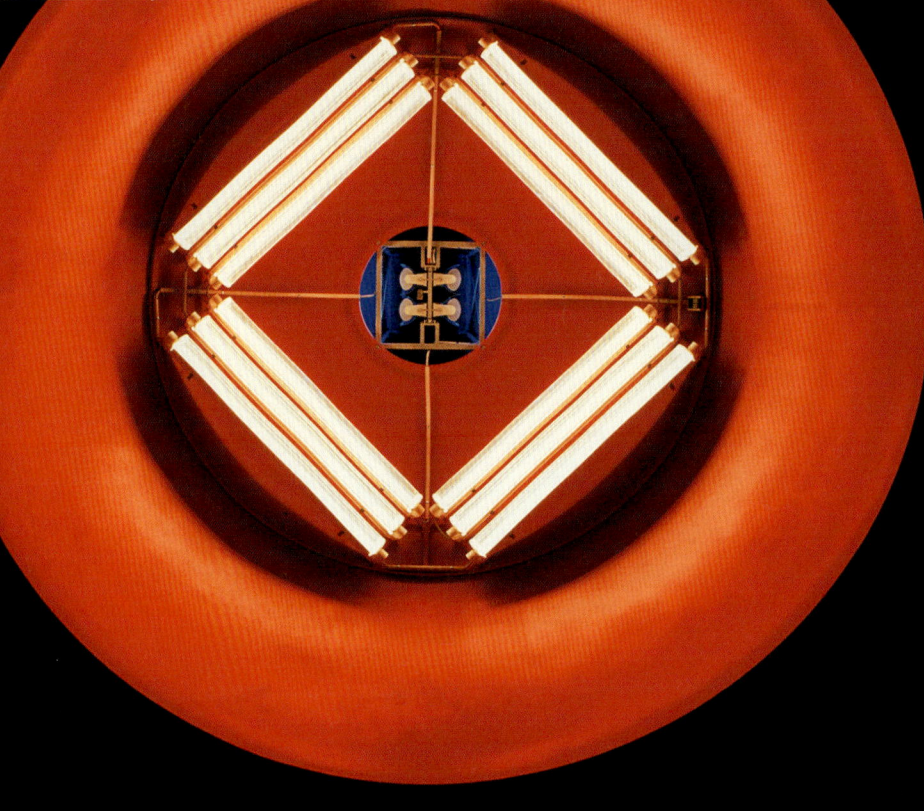

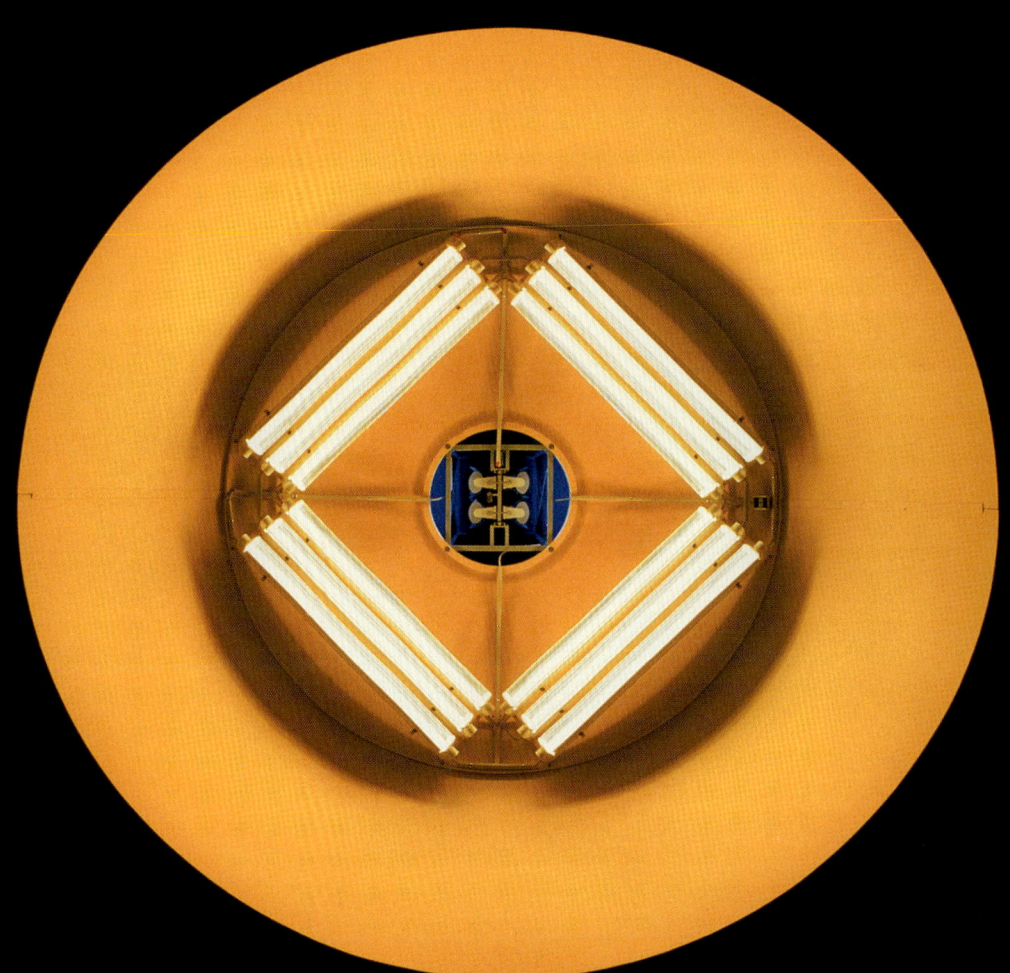

Earthbound – Unbound
Lester B. Pearson Airport, Toronto, CA
2003

Wasserbassin, Kunststoff
Water basin, plastic

Snowflake
U.S. Fund for Unicef, New York, US
2004/2005

Edelstahl, Metall, Glasprismen
Stainless steel, metal, crystal prisms

Friendly Intrusion from Outer Space
Atomium, Brüssel / Brussels, BE
2006

Glasfaser, Kunststoff,
Metall, Aluminium
Fiberglass, plastic,
metal, aluminum

U-Bahnhof Münchner Freiheit, München /
Subway Station Münchner Freiheit, Munich, DE
2009

Licht- und Farbkonzept
Lighting and color concept

Broken Egg
Kunstpark Inhotim / Artpark Inhotim, Belo Horizonte, BR
2013

Konzept
Concept

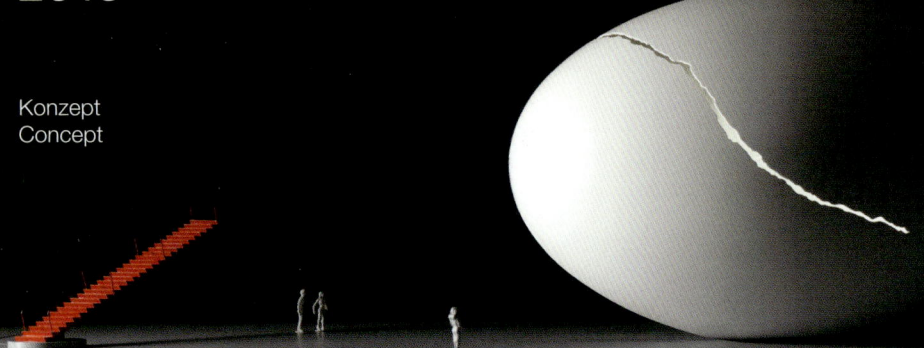

The Tree
Bodega Vega Sicilia, Ribera del Duero, ES
2013

Metall
Metal

Hochöfen Belval / Furnaces Belval, Esch-sur-Alzette, LU
2014

Beleuchtung mit
Lichtobjekten GuddeVol
Illumination with
lighting objects GuddeVol

KUNST IM ÖFFENTLICHEN RAUM / ART IN PUBLIC SPACE

U-Bahnhhof Marienplatz, München / Subway Station Marienplatz, Munich, DE
2015

Licht- und Farbkonzept
Lighting and color concept

Torre Velasca, Mailand / Milan, IT
2016

Beleuchtung
Illumination

Torre Velasca Blue, Mailand / Milan, IT
2019

Beleuchtung
Illumination

Silver Cloud
Residenztheater, München / Munich, DE
2019

Papier, Metall, Ventilatoren
Paper, metal, ventilators

Gare du Nord, Paris, FR
2019

Wettbewerbsbeitrag für Lichtkonzept
Competition entry for lighting concept

U-Bahnhof Sendlinger Tor, München / Subway Station Sendlinger Tor, Munich, DE
2020

Licht- und Farbkonzept
Lighting and color concept

Skizzen / Sketches
1995–2019

Seine ersten Ideen sammelt Ingo Maurer
meistens auf Servietten. Er trägt sie fast immer
bei sich in der Jackentasche, um seine spontanen
Eingebungen unmittelbar zu visualisieren. Neben
der Serviette zeichnet er auf alles, was greifbar ist.
Servietten bieten ihm aber den Vorteil, dass er
sie knittern und rollen kann, ohne dass sie leiden.
Zudem weisen sie durch ihre weiche Oberfläche
eine spezifische Charakteristik auf, die Einfluss
auf das Zeichnen und das Zeichenbild hat.
Die hier gezeigte Auswahl erstreckt sich über
einen Zeitraum von 30 Jahren. Das übliche
Format liegt bei 20 × 20 cm.

Ingo Maurer usually collects his initial ideas on serviettes.
He almost invariably has some in his jacket pocket in order to
visualize immediately whatever occurs to him spontaneously.
In addition to serviettes he draws on anything else that is at
hand. Serviettes have the advantage, he feels, that he can
crumple them or roll them up without them being damaged.
And thanks to their soft surface they influence the drawing
process and product in a specific way. The selection displayed
here covers a period of 30 years. The usual size is 20 × 20 cm.

LED

PROPRIO DAL CUORE

PIAZZA SCALA I.M.

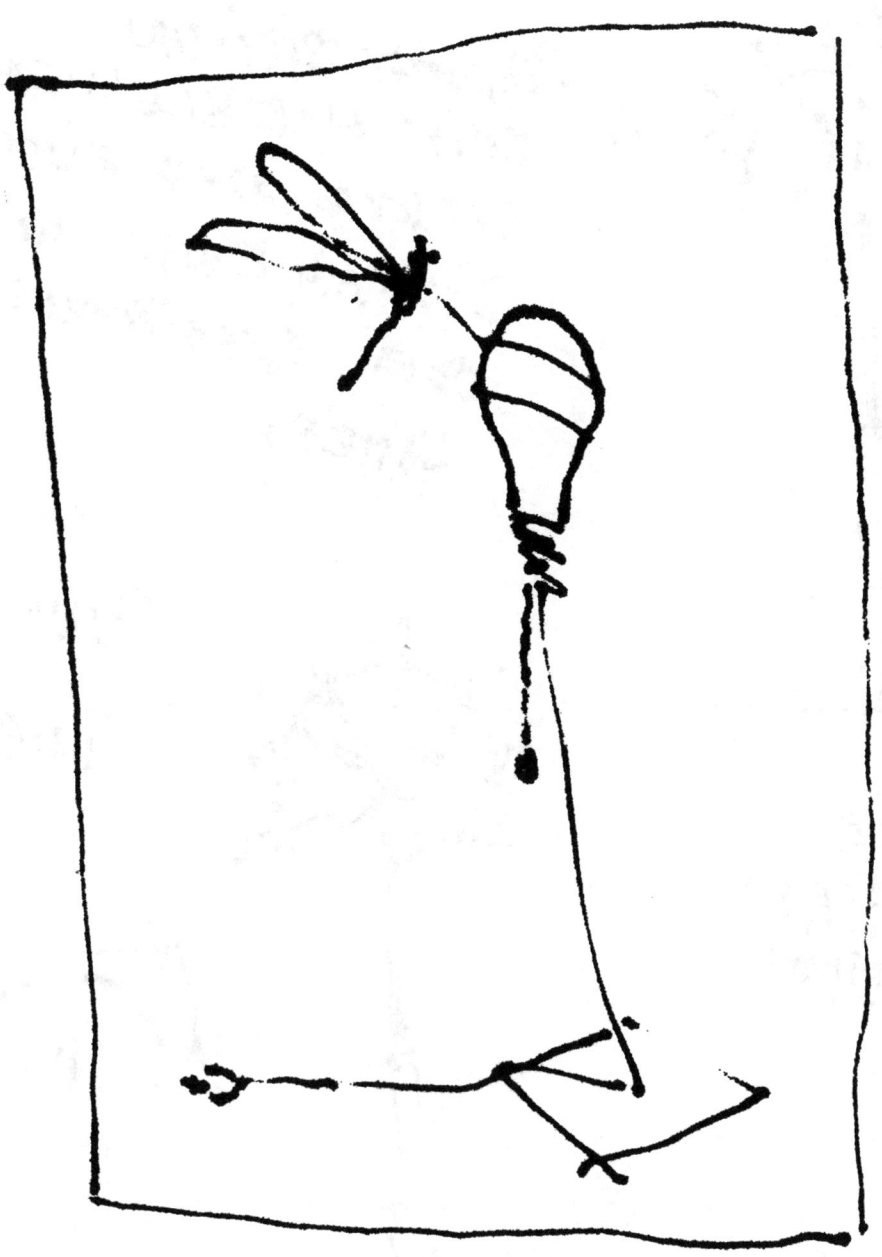

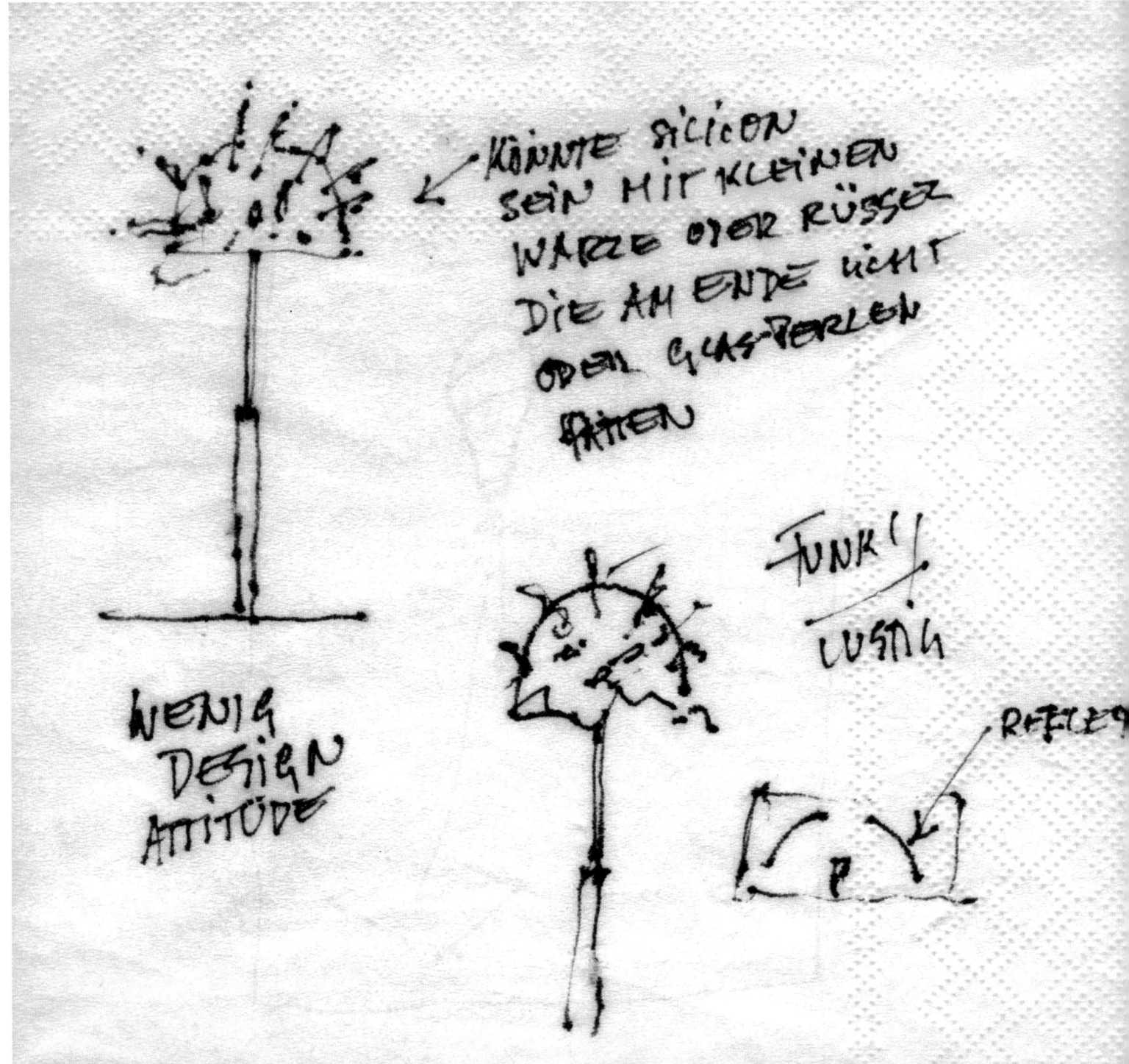

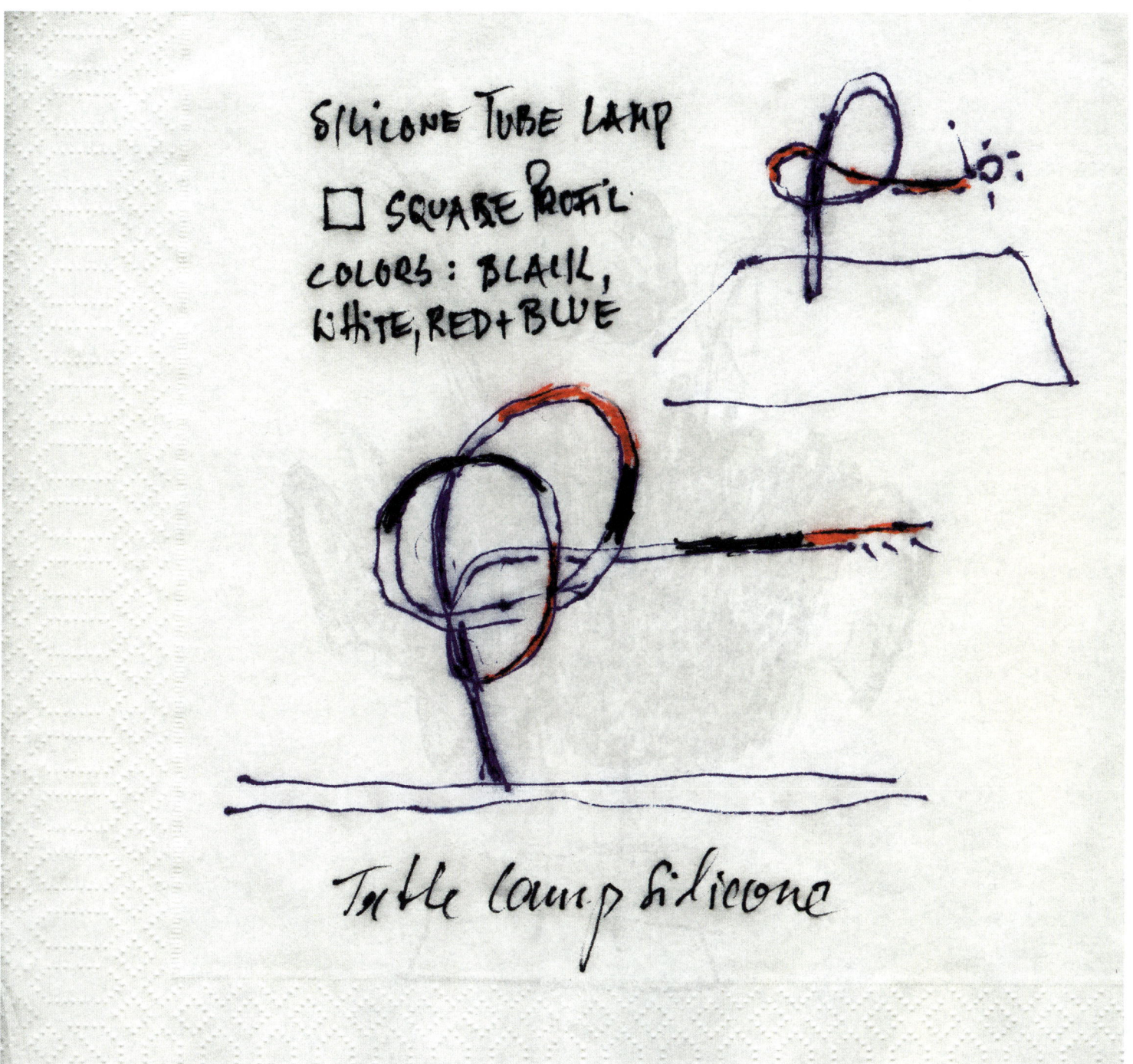

SILICONE TUBE LAMP

☐ SQUARE Profil

COLORS : BLACK,
WHITE, RED + BLUE

Tuble lamp silicone

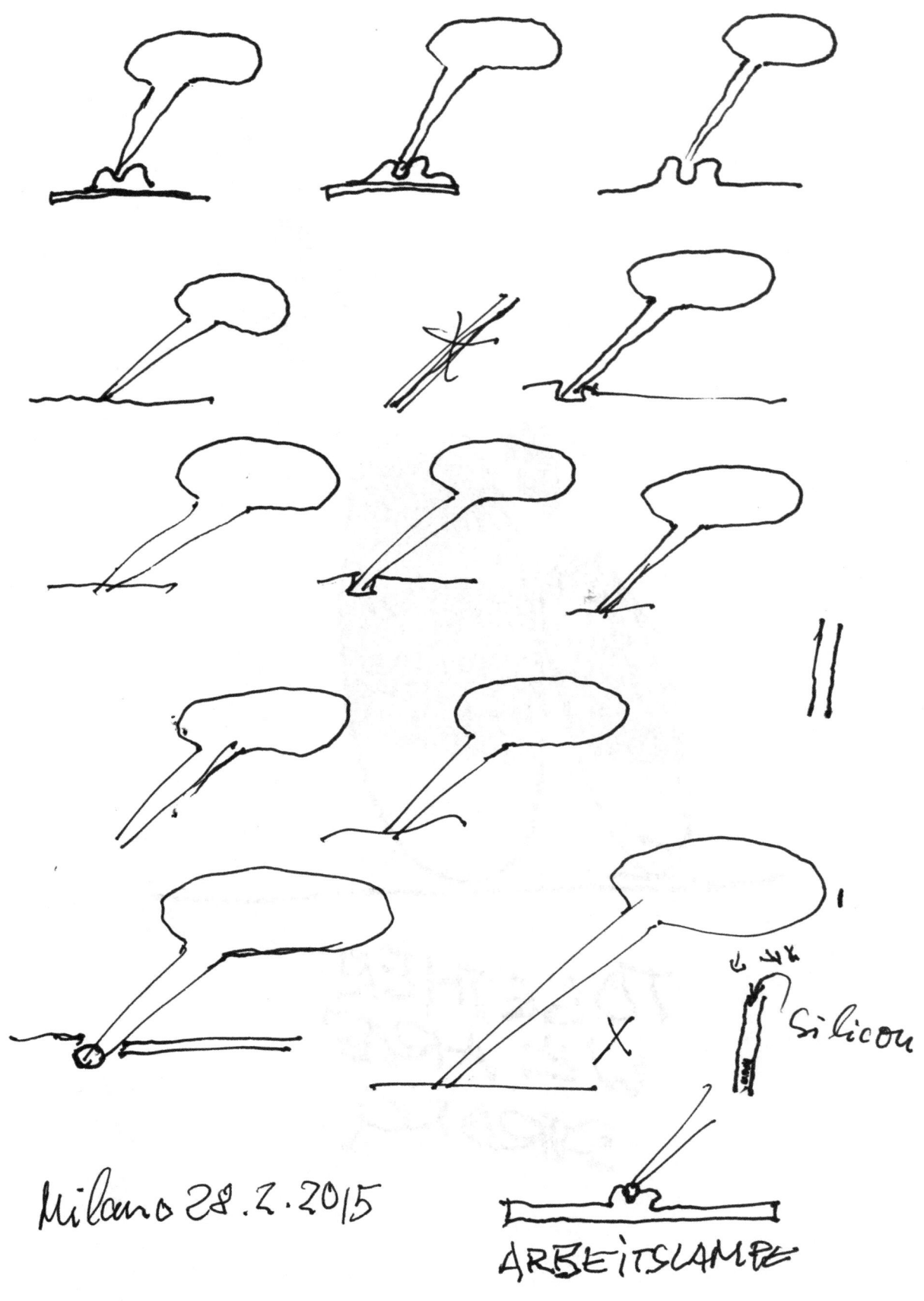

Milano 28.2.2015

ARBEITSLAMPE

Silicon

Anhang / Appendix

Über Ingo Maurer / About Ingo Maurer

Ingo Maurer (1932, Insel Reichenau, Bodensee – 2019, München) machte eine Ausbildung zum Typografen in Deutschland und in der Schweiz. Von 1954 bis 1958 studierte er Grafikdesign in München. 1960 ging er in die USA, wo er als freier Designer in New York und San Francisco arbeitete. 1963 kehrte er nach Europa zurück und machte sich 1966 in München mit seiner Firma Design M selbständig, die seit 1973 unter Ingo Maurer GmbH firmiert.

Ingo Maurer entwirft ungewöhnliche Leuchten und Lichtsysteme, die er in seinem Unternehmen mit über 50 Mitarbeiter*innen in München produziert und weltweit vertreibt.

Zu seinen bekanntesten Entwürfen für die Serienproduktion gehören BULB (1966), das Niedervoltseilsystem YAYAHO (1984), die Flügellampe LUCELLINO (1992) oder der Lüster ZETTEL'Z (1997).

Seit den späten 1980er Jahren entwickelt Ingo Maurer auch Beleuchtungskonzepte und Einzelstücke für private und öffentliche Gebäude. Die Beleuchtung der U-Bahn-Stationen „Westfriedhof" (1998) und „Münchner Freiheit" (2009) in München, der „UNICEF Crystal Snowflake" für New York (2004), die Beleuchtung des Atomium in Brüssel (2006) oder die Lichtinstallation für den Torre Velasca in

Ingo Maurer (1932, Island of Reichenau, Lake Constance – 2019, Munich) trained as a typographer in Germany and Switzerland. From 1954 through 1958 he studied Graphic Design in Munich. In 1960 he moved to the USA where he worked as a freelance designer in New York and San Francisco. In 1963 he returned to Europe, establishing his own company, Design M, in Munich in 1966; as of 1973 the company operated under the name of Ingo Maurer GmbH.

Ingo Maurer designs exceptional lamps and lighting systems, which his company with over 50 employees produces in Munich and distributes worldwide. Among his best-known designs for serial productions are BULB (1966), the low-voltage system YAYAHO (1984), LUCELLINO (1992), the winged bulb, or the chandeliers ZETTEL'Z (1997).

Since the late 1980s, Ingo Maurer has also developed lighting concepts and unique pieces for private clients and public buildings. The lighting for the subway stations "Westfriedhof" (1998) and "Münchner Freiheit" (2009) in Munich, as well as the "UNICEF Crystal Snowflake" for New York (2004), the lighting for the Atomium in Brussels (2006) or the light installation of the Torre Velasca in Milan (2016, 2019) are just a few items on the long list of commission works and spectacular one-offs. From 1999 to 2019, Ingo Maurer ran a showroom in New York. The showroom in Munich was opened in 2009.

He has received numerous awards and accolades, among others, the French order "Chevalier des Arts et des Lettres" in 1986;

Mailand (2016, 2019) sind nur einige Highlights auf der langen Liste der Auftragsarbeiten und spektakulären Einzelstücke.

Von 1999 bis 2019 unterhielt Ingo Maurer einen Showroom in New York. Seit 2009 besteht der Showroom in München.

Er erhielt zahlreiche internationale Auszeichnungen und Ehrungen, u. a. 1986 den französischen Orden „Chevalier des arts et des lettres"; 1999 den Designpreis der Landeshauptstadt München; 2000 den Lucky Strike Designer Award der Raymond Loewy Foundation; 2005 die Ernennung zum Royal Designer of Industry durch die Royal Society of Arts, London; 2006 die Verleihung der Ehrendoktorwürde durch das Royal College of Art, London; 2010 den Designpreis der Bundesrepublik Deutschland für sein Lebenswerk sowie 2011 den Compasso d'Oro des italienischen Verbandes für Industriedesign (ADI); 2015 die Auszeichnung mit dem staatlichen Kulturpreis Bayern. Zuletzt wurde er mit dem Kulturpreis der Bayerischen Landesstiftung in München (2016) geehrt, und in diesem Jahr wurde ihm der Schwabinger Kunstpreis (2019) verliehen.

Design Award of the State Capital of Munich in 1999; the Raymond Loewy Foundation's Lucky Strike Designer Award in 2000; he was appointed Royal Designer of Industry by the Royal Society of Arts, London in 2005; awarded an honorary doctorate by the Royal College of Art, London in 2006; received the Federal Republic of Germany's Design Award for his life's work in 2010 and the Compasso d'Oro from the Italian Association of Industrial Design (ADI) in 2011; he was awarded Bavaria's State Culture Prize in 2015. More recently, he was awarded the Kulturpreis der Bayerischen Landesstiftung in Munich (2016), and this year he was awarded the art prize Schwabinger Kunstpreis (2019).

Ingo Maurer + Team

Ingo Maurer
+
Ralf Altermann
Viktor Antonijevic
Moritz Behrens
Werner Berthold
Albert Brandmair
Reinhold Brandmair
Winfried Brecheler
Silvia Catanese
Sylvie Chevalier
Birget Daenell
Heike Dewald
Fabio Dini
Stella Doerner
Gertraud Eisenreich
David Engelhorn
Petra Fleissner
Thomas Fröhlich
Thomas Happel
Haki Haxhiu
Sebastian Hepting
Elke Herpich
Sandy Hofmann
Xiaoyin Jiang
Marion Kaindl
Manfred Kaiser
Gabriele Kümmerlin
Helmut Lange
Michael Lechner
Vassili Lianos
Dimitra Lionda
Konrad Lohöfener
Marisa Mariscal
Claude Maurer
Eric McNeil
Matthias Mörtlbauer
Ivica Nesic

Hagen Sczech
Michel Sempels
Simone Sinhuber
Dzemal Smajlovic
Bernd Schäfer
Carolin Schlenker-Böhnke
Axel Schmid
Oswald Schneider
Flavia Thumshirn
Evangelia Tsaoussi
Helmut Reitberger
Sebastian Utermöhlen
Isagani Vengco
Jenny Weber
Regina Wilhelm
Eugen Wronek

Diese Publikation erscheint anlässlich der Ausstellung „Ingo Maurer intim. Design or what?", Die Neue Sammlung – The Design Museum, Pinakothek der Moderne, München, 15.11.2019 – 18.10.2020.
This catalog is published on the occasion of the exhibition "Ingo Maurer intim. Design or what?", Die Neue Sammlung – The Design Museum, Pinakothek der Moderne, Munich, November 15, 2019 – October 18, 2020.

HERAUSGEBER / EDITOR
Angelika Nollert, Die Neue Sammlung – The Design Museum
REDAKTION / EDITORIAL
Xenia Riemann-Tyroller
AUTOREN / AUTHORS
Barbara Bloemink, Michele De Lucchi, Bernhard Dessecker, Kim Hastreiter, Nasir Kassamali, Angelika Nollert, Xenia Riemann-Tyroller, Rosa Carole Rodeck, Tom Vack
MITARBEIT / ASSISTANCE
Andrea Czermak, Oliver Krug, Rosa Carole Rodeck
BILDARCHIV / PHOTO ARCHIVE
Michaela Kreuter
Thomas Happel, Michael Lechner, Claude Maurer, Hagen Sczech
LEKTORAT / COPY EDITING
Claire Cahm (Englisch / English)
Andrea Schaller (Deutsch / German)
GESTALTUNG / GRAPHIC DESIGN
wigel, Petra Lüer
ÜBERSETZUNG / TRANSLATION
Jeremy Gaines (Englisch / English), Elvira Vogt (Italienisch / Italian)
FOTOGRAFIE / PHOTOGRAPHY
Kirsten Bucher, Alexander Laurenzo, Anna Seibel
BILDBEARBEITUNG / IMAGE EDITING
Patrizia Hamm
DRUCKEREI / PRINTING
Weber Offset, München

Printed in Germany
ISBN 978-3-96098-704-8

ERSCHIENEN IM / FIRST PUBLISHED BY
Koenig Books Ltd
at the Serpentine Gallery
Kensington Gardens
London W2 3XA
verlag@buchhandlung-walther-koenig.de

Bibliografische Information der Deutschen Nationalbibliothek
Die Deutsche Nationalbibliothek verzeichnet diese Publikation in der Deutschen Nationalbibliografie; detaillierte bibliografische Daten sind über http://dnb.d-nb.de abrufbar.
Bibliographic information published by the Deutsche Nationalbibliothek
The Deutsche Nationalbibliothek lists this publication in the Deutsche Nationalbibliografie; detailed bibliographic data are available in the Internet at http://dnb.d-nb.de.

VERTRIEB / DISTRIBUTION
Buchhandlung Walther König
Ehrenstr. 4
D - 50672 Köln
Tel: +49 (0) 221 / 20 59 6 53
verlag@buchhandlung-walther-koenig.de

Christof Piepenstock, S. / pp. 53, 56
Hagen Sczech, S. / pp. 83, 97, 100, 101, 122/123,
132, 133, 137, 143, 169, 152, 185, 194–197, 205,
210, 246, 247, 280
Anna Seibel, S. / pp. 4–9, 11, 14–15
Ettore Sottsass, S. / p. 91
Deidi von Schaewen, S. / pp. 83 (unten / below),
143 (unten / below), 205 (oben / top)
Axel Schmid, S. / pp. 244/245
Studio Azurro, S. / p. 49
Studio Hinterholzer, S. / p. 39
Markus Tollkopf, S. / pp. 104–108, 234, 235,
Tom Vack, Cover, S. /pp. 34, 42, 43, 46, 50, 51,
54–55, 57, 58), 60–62, 66, 67, 70–72, 98, 99, 102,
103, 105, 108–121, 124–128, 153–166, 167, 168,
170–193, 199, 200, 238, 239, 242/243, 250/251
Hartmut Voigt, S. / p. 86
Die Angaben wurden nach bestem Wissen erstellt.
Sollten dennoch vorhanden sein, bitten wir um
Benachrichtigung. / All Information is given to the
best of our knowledge. Please inform us in the
event of any errors.

Eine Ausstellung der Neuen Sammlung –
The Design Museum in Kooperation mit
Ingo Maurer und seinem Team, München
An exhibition of Die Neue Sammlung –
The Design Museum in cooperation with
Ingo Maurer and his team, Munich

KURATOREN / CURATORS
Angelika Nollert, Xenia Riemann-Tyroller
KURATORISCHE ASSISTENZ /
CURATORIAL ASSISTANT
Rosa Carole Rodeck
AUSSTELLUNGSKONZEPT /
EXHIBITION CONCEPT
Ingo Maurer, Gabriele Kümmerlin,
Hagen Sczech
AUFBAU / SET UP
Ingo Maurer + Team
Albert Brandmair, David Engelhorn,
Gabriele Kümmerlin, Marisa Mariscal,
Hagen Sczech, Michel Sempels,
Sebastian Utermöhlen, Isagani Vengco

REGISTRARIN / REGISTRAR
Waltraud Wiedenbauer
RESTAURATORISCHE BETREUUNG /
CONSERVATION DEPARTMENT
Tim Bechthold, Julia Demeter, Helena Ernst,
Christian Huber
MUSEUMSTECHNIK / TECHNICAL DEPARTMENT
Michel Daume, Cornelius von Heyking,
Florian Westphal
BETEILIGTE FIRMEN / PARTICIPATING FIRMS
Büro für Gestaltung Wangler & Abele
Harald Rüdiger Filmbauten
Folienschriften Martin
Wiese Elektroanlagen
Seeberger Friedl, Marlies Sippl
PRESSE UND ÖFFENTLICHKEITSARBEIT /
PRESS AND PUBLIC RELATIONS
Tine Nehler, Jette Elixmann
hicklvesting, München
ONLINE-REDAKTION / ONLINE EDITORIAL
Andrea Czermak, Jana Walter
ONLINE-VERWALTUNG /
ONLINE ADMINISTRATION
Rainer Schmitzberger

MIT DANK AN / THANKS TO
Ingo Maurer
Claude Maurer
Sarah Utermöhlen
Team Ingo Maurer

FÖRDERER

PIN. FREUNDE DER
PINAKOTHEK DER MODERNE E.V.

KOOPERATIONSPARTNER /
COOPERATION PARTNER

PINAKOTHEK DER MODERNE

Münchner
Volkshochschule